CANDY IS
MAGIC

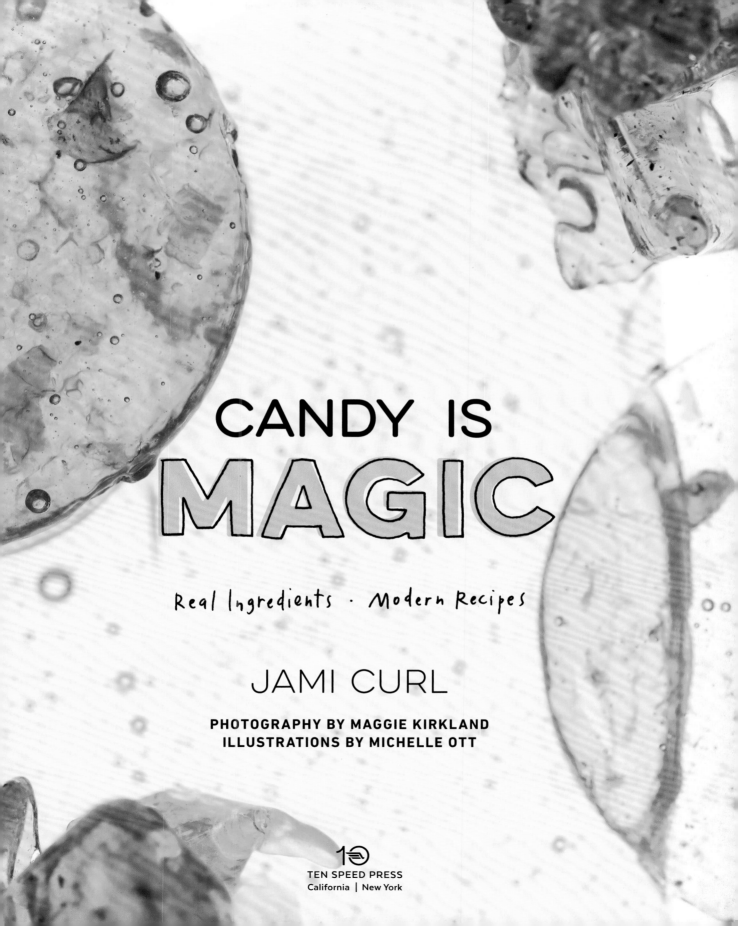

CANDY IS
MAGIC

Real Ingredients · Modern Recipes

JAMI CURL

PHOTOGRAPHY BY MAGGIE KIRKLAND
ILLUSTRATIONS BY MICHELLE OTT

Ten Speed Press
California | New York

FOR THEO
(the real magic)

CONTENTS

RECIPES • VI

INTRODUCTION
A REAL LIFE IN REAL CANDY • 1

CHAPTER ONE
INGREDIENTS, TOOLS, AND FLAVOR • 9

CHAPTER TWO
CRAFTING CORE INGREDIENTS • 33

CHAPTER THREE
LOLLIPOPS • 109

CHAPTER FOUR
CARAMELS • 157

CHAPTER FIVE
DREAMS COME CHEW • 217

CHAPTER SIX
MARSHMALLOWS • 239

CHAPTER SEVEN
GUMDROPS • 269

RESOURCES GUIDE • 291

BECAUSE OF YOU • 297

INDEX • 298

RECIPES

ROASTED FRUIT PURÉES

Roasted Strawberries with Lemon 37

Roasted Blackberries with Lime and Nutmeg 42

Roasted Raspberries with Two Sugars 43

Roasted Cherries with Almond 44

Roasted Blueberries with Vanilla and Orange 46

Roasted Apricots with Coconut and Brown Sugar 47

Roasted Peaches with Ginger 49

INFUSED CREAMS

Popcorn Cream 52

Coffee Cream 55

Chocolate Cream 57

Malted Milk Cream 58

Orange Cream 60

Vanilla Bean Cream 61

Earl Grey Tea Cream 63

   Peppermint Tea Cream 63

   Chai Tea Cream 63

Pepper Cream 64

SYRUPS AND REDUCTIONS

Coffee Syrup 68

Tea Syrup 69

Praline Syrup 70

Wine Reduction (Pinot Noir, Pinot Gris, or Rosé) 71

MAGIC DUSTS

Chocolate Magic Dust 74

Malted Chocolate Magic Dust 88

Five-Spice Magic Dust 89

Doughnut Magic Dust 91

Sweet + Sour Magic Dust 93

Magic Sugar Crystals: Flavored Variety 94

Magic Sugar Crystals: Tinted Variety 95

EASY ICE CREAMS

Easy Vanilla Bean Ice Cream 100

   Coffee or Butter Pecan Ice Cream 100

   Doughnut Magic Dust Ice Cream 101

   Five-Spice Magic Dust Ice Cream 101

Strawberry Ice Cream 102

Chocolate Swirl Ice Cream 103

Chocolate Magic Dust Ice Cream 104

   Chocolate + Ancho Chile Ice Cream 105

   Chocolate + Orange Ice Cream 105

   Chocolate + Malted Milk Ice Cream 105

   Chocolate + Peppermint Ice Cream 105

   Chocolate + Coffee Ice Cream 105

Chai Tea Ice Cream 106

Popcorn Ice Cream 107

LOLLIPOPS

Strawberry Lollipops 118

   Apricot Lollipops 119

   Blueberry Lollipops 119

   Peach Lollipops 119

   Cherry Lollipops 119

   Raspberry Lollipops 119

   Blackberry Lollipops 119

   Blackberry + Tangerine Lollipops 119

Orange Lollipops 122

   Lemon Lollipops 123

   Lime Lollipops 123

Sour Cherry Lollipops 126

   Sour Orange Lollipops 127

   Sour Apple Lollipops 127

   Sour Lemon Lollipops 127

   Sour Raspberry Lollipops 127

Coffee Lollipops 130

Sweet Tea with Lemon Lollipops 131

Pinot Gris Lollipops 133

Pinot Noir Lollipops 134

Rosé Lollipops 135

Pecan Praline Lollipops 136

Honey Vanilla Lollipops 144

Cherry Honey Vanilla Lollipops 145

Sniffle Slayer Lollipops 148

   Throat Soothers 148

Chai Tea Lollipops 149

Mint Lollipops 150

Chocolate Lollipops 151

Chocolate + Olive Oil + Sea Salt Lollipops 152

Caramel Lollipops 153

BEYOND THE LOLLIPOP: HARD CANDY

   Butterscotch Hard Candy 155

   Champagne Hard Candy 155

   Cinnamon Hard Candy 155

   Fruit Punch Hard Candy 155

   Root Beer Hard Candy 155

CARAMELS

Sea Salt Caramels 168

Popcorn Caramels 171

Chocolate Caramels 174

Vanilla Bean Caramels 176

Vanilla Bean + Roasted Fruit Caramels 182

   Apricot + White Chocolate + Coconut Caramels 183

Honey + Hazelnut Caramels 184

Sea Salt + Roasted Pumpkin Seed Caramels 186

Coconut + Toasted Pecan + Chocolate Caramels 188

Apple Caramels 191

Aleppo Pepper + Raisin Caramels 194

Chocolate Malt + Sugar Cone Caramels 196

Smoked Chai Tea Caramels 198

Earl Grey Caramels 200

Coffee + Orange + Smoked Salt Caramels 202

Coffee Caramels 203

Ahoy, Matey! Caramels 206

Chocolate Pretzel Caramels 208

Turtle Caramels 210

Maple + Cracked Black Pepper Caramels 212

DREAMS COME CHEW

Cherry Dreams Come Chew 222

Strawberry Dreams 223

Tangerine Dreams 223

Lemon Dreams 223

Pineapple + Coconut Dreams 223

Watermelon + Lime Dreams 223

Fruit Punch Dreams 223

Blackberry + Tangerine Dreams 228

Vanilla Mint Dreams 229

Chocolate Mint Dreams 230

Cinnamon Dreams 231

Vanilla Cake Dreams 234

Vanilla Cake with Sprinkles 234

MARSHMALLOWS

Vanilla Bean Marshmallows 244

Mint Marshmallows 248

Toasted Coconut Marshmallows 248

Cinnamon Marshmallows 248

Chocolate Marshmallows 254

Strawberry Marshmallows 258

Caramel Marshmallows 260

Chocolate Caramel Coconut Marshmallows 263

Honey + Sea Salt Marshmallows 264

Coffee Marshmallows 266

GUMDROPS

Blackberry Gumdrops 276

Blackberry + Orange Gumdrops 279

Strawberry Gumdrops 279

Strawberry + Lemon Gumdrops 279

Blueberry Gumdrops 279

Blueberry + Cinnamon Gumdrops 279

Apricot Gumdrops 279

Apricot + Almond + Nutmeg Gumdrops 279

Raspberry Gumdrops 279

Raspberry + Vanilla Gumdrops 279

Peach Gumdrops 279

Peach + Ginger + Black Pepper Gumdrops 279

Cherry Gumdrops 279

Cherry Cola Gumdrops 279

Vanilla Gumdrops 280

Black Pepper Gumdrops 282

Cinnamon Gumdrops 282

Cola or Root Beer Gumdrops 282

Citrus Gumdrops 282

Coffee Gumdrops 284

Iced Tea + Lemonade Gumdrops 286

Rosé Gumdrops 288

BEYOND CANDY

Roasted Strawberry Simple Syrup 40

Strawberry Cream Soda 40

Strawberry Bubbly 41

Roasted Fruit Whipped Cream 45

Every Day, Popcorn 54

Vanilla Bean Whipped Cream 56

Earl Grey Tea Whipped Cream 56

Orange Whipped Cream 56

Coffee Whipped Cream 56

Infused-Cream Buttercream 59

Hot or Cold Chocolate 76

Chocolate For Breakfast 78

Hot Chocolate with Vanilla Bean Marshmallows and Mint Crystal Sugar 78

Chocolate Magic Dust Whipped Cream 80

Chocolate Sauce 81

Dark Chocolate Bunny Cake 82

Hot Fudge 86

Peanut Butter Hot Fudge 86

Doughnut Magic Dust Butter 91

Doughnut Magic Dust Glazed Apples 91

Doughnut Magic Dust Cookies 92

Easy Caramel Sauce 179

Chèvre Caramel Sauce 180

Marshmallow Sauce (Or Best Ever Ice Cream Sauce) 251

Marshmallow Brownies 251

Skillet S'mores 252

CANDY KITS AND CELEBRATIONS

Grown Your Own Sugar Crystals! 17

Hot Chocolate and Marshmallow Kit 77

Hot Chocolate Bar! 79

The Gift of Sprinkles 97

Lollipop Bouquet 132

Suprise Inside—Lollipops with Chewy Centers 138

Clouds of Candy 140

Candy Garland & Countdown 146

Caramel Apple Kit 204

Candy Pow Wow 214

Instabration 224

Tiny Piñata 232

Super Sweet Ornament Orbs 236

S'mores Bar 249

A REAL LIFE IN REAL CANDY

My job is made of dreams. I'm a candy maker, and the tools of my trade are imagination and sugar. I believe in magic. Especially the type of magic brought about by spinning my wildest dreams into something sweet to eat. There's no way to argue it, magic is responsible for getting me to where I am today. It's squeezed its way into every facet of my being, and it's given me the ability to approach daily life with a specific sense of wonder and enchantment—two of the required qualities of a candy maker, I'm certain. There's very little that I do that I don't approach with a bright-eyed sense of enthusiasm. And if you've heard me speak, have met me at a candy demonstration, or have taken one of my classes, you know that everything I'm saying here is the exact truth: I'm completely wild about making candy.

I don't remember a time when I wasn't speaking the language of sweets. I don't remember a time when I wasn't analyzing bites of cookies or spoonfuls of ice cream. Chocolate and frozen treats, cakes and biscuits, candy and cookies, hot fudge and caramel sauce—these are my constants. They are my rewards, my gifts, my consolation prizes, my companions, and my coworkers.

In 2005, armed with a family of recipes and a tireless spirit, I opened my first retail bakery. I had just entered my thirties, I was not yet a mom, and I had just ended a successful career as a marketer for engineers and lawyers. Baking as a job was something I could visualize but never thought of as possible, until I made it possible.

Right from the beginning, the days were long. I opened the business in November, and, leading up to that first Thanksgiving, I was easily spending twenty-two-hour days in the bakery turning out pumpkin pies and nutmeg ice cream. I was so happy to be baking that I wouldn't even realize when twenty-two hours had ticked by. Elbow deep in sugar, butter, and flour was exactly where I wanted to be.

Fast-forward eight years and the bakery was more than thirty employees strong. We were featured on television shows and blogs. We were in magazines, books, and newspapers. We were booked weekend after weekend with special orders and wedding cakes. Our café space was always buzzing with early-morning treat seekers, lunch-break cookie grabbers, and after-school snackers. It was all exactly as I had planned, only better. And everything was wonderful. That is, until it wasn't.

What happens when the exact thing you want is no longer what you want? That sounds like a trick question, I know. But it really isn't. For years I had envisioned myself working as a baker, creating treats for people who love them, making birthday-cake dreams come true, celebrating love with the perfect wedding dessert. And here I was, doing it! But after years of the work, I started to feel limited by the concept of a bakery. Cookies and cakes and buns were fantastic, but even with my seasonally inspired approach to the menu, I felt restricted. And worst of all, with each passing day, I felt as if I was losing my creative edge. Balancing the expectations of customers who wanted the same scones and cookies day after day with my own desires to be fulfilled creatively became more and more difficult.

One day, when I could stand the tedium no longer, I put a pot of sugar on a cooktop and began coaxing it into a dark amber liquid—I was making caramel! It was an exercise that I thought was just a distraction. And it was a mere distraction . . . until I felt the wiggling feather of excitement in my creative soul. The feeling that I had been missing and craving was suddenly reappearing. That single pot of caramel brought back the sense of wonder I so badly needed in order to feel fulfilled at work. That was it. I was hooked.

The first batch of candy I prepared for sale ended up being a caramel inspired by that same pot of beautiful dark amber sugar. It was the tiniest batch of sea salt caramel, and I cut it into 1-inch squares. I wrapped the squares in cellophane and dropped them into clear bags, attaching handwritten tags reading "Oregon Sea Salt Caramels." I placed the bags of caramels at our bakery counter and—to my amazement—watched them sell. I was truly inspired by this new breath of sugary life, and couldn't wait to make more. And that's how QUIN was born.

After I mastered caramel—and the art of infusing the candy with flavor so it tasted of something more than straight sugar—I worked on hard candy.

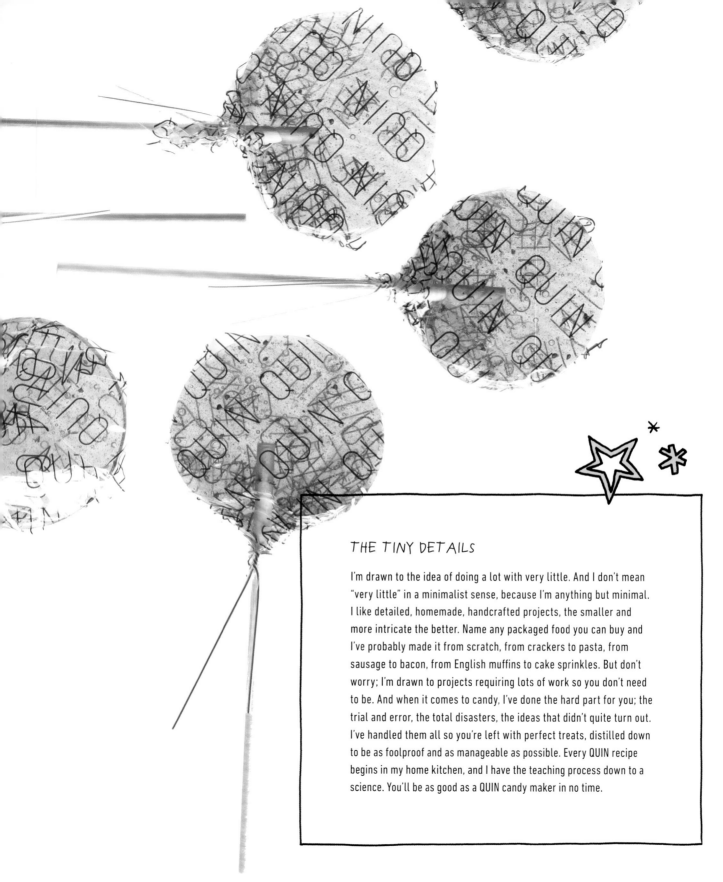

THE TINY DETAILS

I'm drawn to the idea of doing a lot with very little. And I don't mean "very little" in a minimalist sense, because I'm anything but minimal. I like detailed, homemade, handcrafted projects, the smaller and more intricate the better. Name any packaged food you can buy and I've probably made it from scratch, from crackers to pasta, from sausage to bacon, from English muffins to cake sprinkles. But don't worry; I'm drawn to projects requiring lots of work so you don't need to be. And when it comes to candy, I've done the hard part for you; the trial and error, the total disasters, the ideas that didn't quite turn out. I've handled them all so you're left with perfect treats, distilled down to be as foolproof and as manageable as possible. Every QUIN recipe begins in my home kitchen, and I have the teaching process down to a science. You'll be as good as a QUIN candy maker in no time.

I was inspired by the amazing fruit grown in Oregon and wanted to somehow incorporate that bounty into candy. I started with strawberries and made the most beautiful lollipops filled with tiny strawberry seeds and just the slightest shade of pink with no artificial junk inside. From there I tackled all kinds of fruit, from cherries to Oregon marionberries. The pure science and alchemy involved in turning actual fruit into hard candy solidified for me this next chapter in sweets. Candy was my calling.

This calling has led to some amazing, momentous, and mind-shattering events in my career. I've been on television and in all of my favorite magazines, my story and my approach to business have been chronicled in books, my recipes have been featured in cookbooks and newspapers, I've had the honor of speaking to groups across the country, and QUIN has partnered with some of the most respected artisan brands around. To say that I'm thankful for all that I've experienced would be an understatement of monumental proportions.

Of course, all of this special recognition is amazing, but it's not what keeps me going. For me to be working as hard as I do simply to get QUIN or myself in the right magazine or newspaper would be nuts. Not to mention completely inauthentic to who I am. I live and work by a simple rule that says I must pay equal attention to the good *and* the bad. This is the system I've developed to help me stay focused—the positive and the negative have to mean the same. Otherwise, it's too easy to do what I'm doing to gain press or to try to win over nonfans. And at the end of it all, neither the accolades nor the criticisms should guide my business or my life. The good and the bad both teach, inspire, and keep me focused on my ultimate goal: to bring a bit of magic to the lives of others by creating a product of which I'm proud—a product influenced by my intuition, by true flavor, by quality ingredients, and perhaps by a bit of nostalgia.

While I don't have any formal training in baking or candy making, two qualities I've never lacked are a deep-rooted, intense love of treats and zero fear of failure. I'm fairly certain that my sugar obsession started with solid careers in sweets on both sides of my family. My mother's mother had a back-porch doughnut business and sold her sugary creations to construction workers who were building her childhood neighborhood. My father's mother defined *cottage industry* with her array of seasonal candies—from chocolate-dipped nuts to her legendary turtles, she spent the holiday season packing tins of delights for her fans. My own mother would stockpile Christmas and Easter chocolates and then hide them around the house so she could enjoy them almost year-round without my sister and me catching on. Her sweet-toothed shenanigans have become legend in my family. As strange as it may sound, I feel like I'm proof that it's possible to learn to do something as a result of nostalgia and affection for the past. Add in thousands of hours of very hard work and an incurable desire to master the art of sugar, and I know I've gained an invaluable library of knowledge this way.

As for being unafraid to fail? That's a quality I gained when I was a young twenty-something. Both of my parents died just a couple of years apart; my mom died twelve days after telling me about her cancer diagnosis, and my dad just weeks shy of my wedding. I didn't have the opportunity to get to know either of them as an adult, and neither of them had the pleasure of delighting in my little boy. I always think that we all missed out on so much.

The days leading up to and following their deaths were my most difficult, to be certain, but I emerged on the other side with a fearless approach to life—because, really, after living through the deaths of both of your parents, after looking them in the eyes knowing for certain it's the last time, what's left to be afraid of? In the years since, I've thrown myself into my work, and I wake up each day determined to do the things that make me happy. Because happiness, and working to spread it, is the only antidote I've ever found to suffering such profound loss.

When I look at life and start to consider what makes me really happy, it's almost crazy for me to admit that—in addition to my kid, of course—imagining and creating candy is what brings me the most joy. And to be able to share that magic and wonder with others is one of the biggest gifts I've been given. I've invested my life in the act of coaxing sugar into perfect treats and then sharing those treats with others. I've somehow been able to keep it both my greatest passion and my actual job.

And now I'm ready to introduce you to my world of sugar, not just to satisfy your candy cravings but also to provide you with opportunities to use your imagination to create the sweets you want to eat—sweets that you can enjoy on your own or (this is my favorite part) that you can shower on your family, friends, and others. Sharing treats is one sure way to make an ordinary day a lot more magical. It's something that's so simple but is also completely meaningful. In the end, I really just want the people around me to be happy. And if surprising them with treats is one way to do it, I'll be happy making candy forever.

CHAPTER ONE

INGREDIENTS, TOOLS, AND FLAVOR

UNDERSTANDING CANDY

My approach to candy making focuses on three concepts: tested methods, quality ingredients, and developing outstanding flavor.

Skill in candy making comes down to one thing: the successful handling of sugar. Don't worry, you're not getting in over your head with an overload of science. I feel strongly that a person can understand the chemical reactions and hard science of sugar like the greatest laboratory wizard of all time but still never be able to make a perfect lollipop. So instead of scientific facts and figures, I focus on the details you need to know for true success.

1. Forget about your fear of cooking sugar. It's true that melted sugar is hot and sticky. Accept and respect it. Understand it. Take care. Think of it this way: cooking sugar is like any other regular cooking process, from boiling water for noodles to simmering a pot of tomato sauce.

2. Sugar loves water. A scientist would say it's hygroscopic, but I simply say, sugar wants to absorb moisture. Even after it's been cooked into candy, it will continue to look for ways to draw in water, which can result in a candy with a grainy texture (often seen in caramel) or in one that appears to have melted (often seen in hard candy and gumdrops). This means rainy days, hot days, and humid indoor conditions aren't particularly hospitable to candy making. It also means you should never refrigerate or freeze candy to cool it faster; condensation will form and the sugar in the candy will absorb it. Treat your candy kindly. While it can get tricky on especially hot or wet days, candy should be cooled at room temperature.

3. You'll need a few tools. From a thermometer to a kitchen scale, the right tools for cooking sugar are important. I have a few work-arounds if you don't want to commit to specialized candy-making equipment, but some specific tools are necessary.

4. Real candy making takes time. Once you've decided to make your own candy, you must give it all the time it needs. It's not instant. It takes time to develop flavor and texture, to roast fruit and to infuse cream. It takes time to cook just the right amount of moisture out of a recipe so the results are perfect. It takes patience to finish cooking a candy and then allow it to cool for the appropriate amount of time. Time is one of the most important "invisible ingredients" in making real candy.

5. Real candy requires real ingredients. Flavor development is key in making the best candy, and that flavor begins with selecting and preparing top-quality ingredients. From butter to chocolate, flavorings to whole fruit, I use only what I feel is absolutely perfect. If you get the ingredients right, you're already one step closer to real candy.

The plan is for me to teach you a few key skills and then for you to get into your kitchen, grab some sugar, and start cooking. Once you've learned the basic techniques through making my recipes, start dreaming up flavors of your own. Along the way, I'll introduce changes to recipes or ways that you can infuse your own personality into them. I'll also demystify steps like freezing fruit purées, explain ingredient specifics, and share additional techniques.

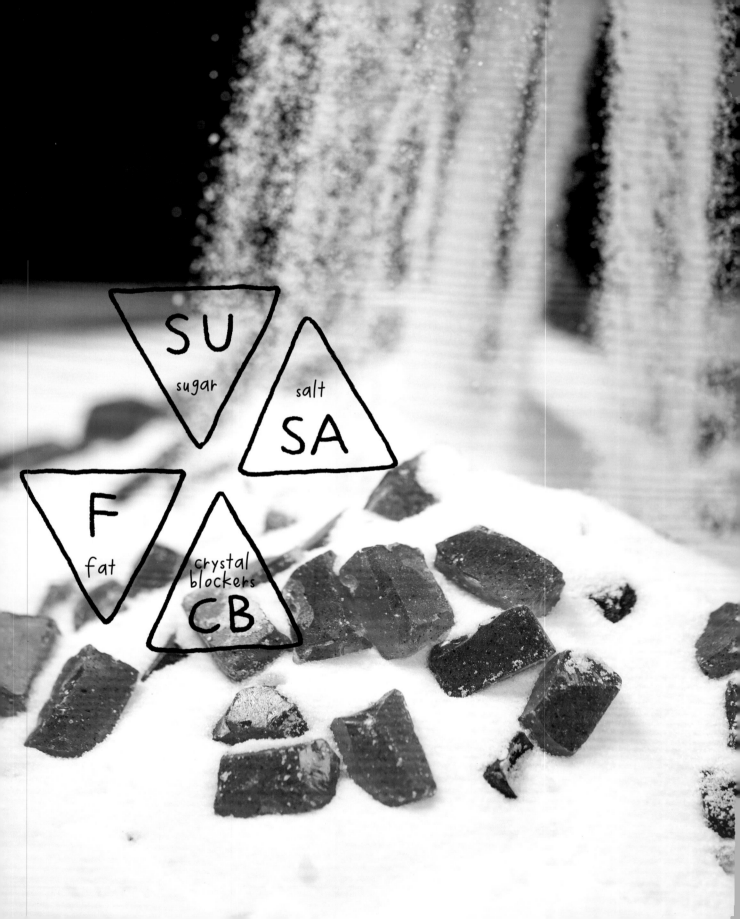

CANDY-MAKING INGREDIENTS

When I started QUIN, I pledged never to use anything that was fake, phony, or less than perfect in our candy. Everything we use, from flavorings to colorings, is real. Crafting candy using real food ingredients is an activity that relies on four main components: **sugar**, the foundation of any candy recipe; **crystal blockers**, the key to preventing crystallization; **fat**, adds flavor and results in a soft, luscious texture; **salt**, enhances flavor, often provides crunch.

SUGAR

My preferred sweetener is pure and natural granulated cane sugar. In addition to cane sugar, I like to enhance recipes with secondary types of sweeteners: honey, molasses, brown sugar, and maple syrup. Remember, these secondary sweeteners are just that—*secondary*. The primary sweetener is always pure granulated cane sugar, which I refer to as simply "granulated" sugar in recipes.

I love sugar. Not just eating it but also the science and mystery behind it. I love the challenge of figuring out reactions, temperatures, and environment and how those factors have a bearing on outcomes. I once was a very controlling person, but three phenomena have taught me to be otherwise: marriage, parenthood, and sugar.

All candy making begins by melting sugar in a pot. That process changes sugar from a lovely granulated crystal into more of a liquid. But the trick is to keep the sugar from turning back into a crystal once it has melted. Recrystallization isn't just a problem when cooking sugar. It's also a problem after the candy has been cooked. Introduce even the smallest disturbance and sugar runs screaming for its most familiar state: the crystal.

In other words, sugar is stubborn. Even if it melts and all the individual granules have disappeared, there's no guarantee it will stay that way. In fact, sugar so badly wants to remain a crystal that seemingly insignificant actions will encourage it to recrystallize. For example, you'll be tempted to stir sugar when it's cooking because it's normal to stir food while it cooks. But if you stir sugar while it's cooking, you're asking for trouble. Stirring a pot of cooking sugar causes unnecessary friction. That friction is all melted sugar needs to start the process of recrystallizing. (I know it sounds like a game of bumper cars, but it's actually chemistry. The bumping and friction allow the correct chemicals to link up so crystals can begin forming.)

Here's another way to look at it: Say you have one or two single granules that stick to the side of an otherwise perfect pot of cooking sugar. One or two tiny crystals—what harm can they cause? In the world of candy making, quite a lot. One tiny crystal can encourage melted sugar to recrystallize. This can lead to a chain reaction of crystal after crystal reforming, and this reaction is exactly what a pot of candy needs to go from good to bad (or from nice and smooth to gritty and grainy). And it's not just renegade sugar crystals that can cause a chain reaction, debris can cause it, too. Even a simple string suspended in a sugar syrup can encourage crystallization. Want to see for yourself? Check out the experiment on the facing page to watch melted sugar regenerate its crystal state right before your very eyes (magic)!

Care must also be taken after the candy is cooked. Allowing perfect hard candy or even caramels to sit around in a damp environment any longer than necessary will allow the sugar to absorb the moisture in the air and use it as permission to begin recrystallizing. On rainy and humid days, after candy has set and cooled, wrap it right away in cellophane or another candy-wrapping substrate. And if you live in a perpetually damp environment and are serious about candy making, it might be a good idea to spend a little money on a small dehumidifier. During all of our shifts at QUIN, we run three massive dehumidifiers that pull any extra moisture out of the air. This helps us to control the outcomes of our candy-making efforts.

CRYSTAL BLOCKERS

Keeping in mind everything you've learned about sugar and its tendency to recrystallize, I'd now like to introduce an ingredient that can help prevent that pesky business from happening in the first place. It's an ingredient I like to call a crystal blocker, or in the world of candy, an ingredient more commonly known as an interfering agent. And my agent of choice? Good-quality glucose syrup. As I've already explained, once sugar is fully melted, it loves to turn itself back into crystals, and unless something is introduced to the mix to prevent that from happening, sooner or later, it will happen. Glucose interferes with that process by standing between individual sugar crystals to prevent them from ganging up and morphing back into a crystallized state. See? It *interferes* in the process, hence, interfering agent.

Other crystal blockers include corn syrup (*not* high fructose), honey, lemon juice, golden syrup, cream of tartar, and brown rice syrup. That said, I prefer the predictable outcome that glucose provides, especially when making candy in a production setting. And although I've listed additional crystal blockers, I strongly recommend that you use glucose syrup to create all of the candy in the recipes that follow.

Glucose syrup for confectionery purposes is made from starches, most commonly corn, potato, or wheat. At QUIN, we use a glucose syrup that's manufactured in France. We chose this particular glucose both because it contains no sulfites (preservatives) and is GMO-free (France has a country-wide ban on the use of GMOs in farming). For information on obtaining glucose syrup (French or not), see the Resources Guide (page 291).

If you'd like to see melted sugar morphing back into a crystallized state, here's a great experiment for you.

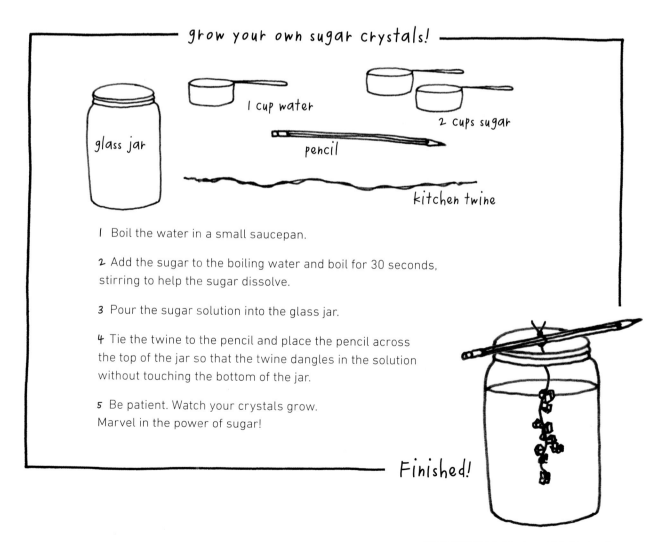

grow your own sugar crystals!

1 cup water

2 cups sugar

pencil

glass jar

kitchen twine

1 Boil the water in a small saucepan.

2 Add the sugar to the boiling water and boil for 30 seconds, stirring to help the sugar dissolve.

3 Pour the sugar solution into the glass jar.

4 Tie the twine to the pencil and place the pencil across the top of the jar so that the twine dangles in the solution without touching the bottom of the jar.

5 Be patient. Watch your crystals grow. Marvel in the power of sugar!

Finished!

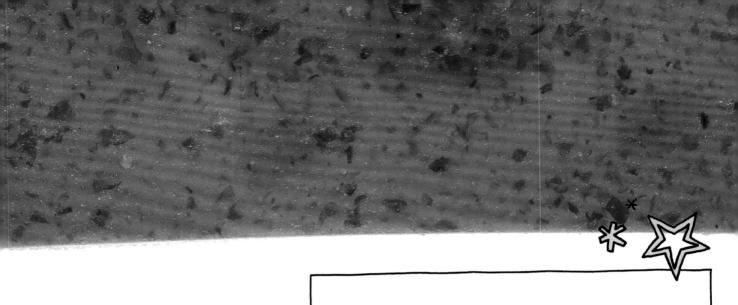

The top image features cherry lollipop candy made WITHOUT glucose. The candy crystalizes nearly instantly and what could be beautiful, translucent candy with pretty bits of cherry peeking out becomes this clouded, gritty, chalky mess. The candy on the bottom is see-through pink with bits of cherry suspended in clear candy. The only difference between the two is the candy on the top was made without a crystal blocker.

GLUCOSE GOES IN FIRST

I always suggest weighing the glucose syrup directly into the pot in which you'll be cooking candy. Glucose syrup is sticky and viscous. If you weigh it into another container and then scrape it out of that container into the pot, the resulting amount will be inaccurate because some of the glucose will cling to the sides of the container. It's just easier, faster, and more accurate to set the pot on the scale, zero out the scale (tare it), and then start plopping in the glucose.

Here's an amazing tip to make that measuring process even easier: Store glucose syrup in your refrigerator. When it comes time to weigh it, put the pot on the scale, wet your hand with cold water, and scoop the glucose out of its container with your wet hand. Do this close to the pot and the glucose will slide right off your hand and into the pot. Don't worry if you end up adding too much, as you can just wet your hand again and scoop out as much as you need to remove.

FAT

Fat is essential in candies that have a soft and luscious, almost melty, texture. You bite into these candies and they may stick to your teeth for a second or two, but as soon as they warm up, you find them melting away. You can cook sugar until it's caramelized, but it's not until you add cream and butter that it takes on some of the best aspects of caramel—soft, smooth, creamy, and rich. My preferred fats for candy making are heavy cream, unsalted butter, coconut milk, olive oil, whole milk, half-and-half, and full-fat yogurt.

You'll never find powdered dairy products in QUIN candy. Of course, there's nothing wrong with shelf-stable, economical ingredients like these, but I prefer the flavor and the overall outcome that fresh dairy products bring to candy. Powdered dairy products are widely used in candy making because they introduce no additional moisture to a recipe. Despite that advantage, as a professional candy maker, I'd rather know what to do about moisture than to shake in a product that science has proven has a shelf life of up to twenty years.

SALT

I wish we could do a candy taste-test together so I could show you in person the difference that the right salt makes in a candy. I know it seems strange that salt could be such an important component of something that's meant to be sweet, but salt brings to life flavors that are otherwise kind of hidden in candy. Butterscotch hard candy is a good example. When I'm trying to explain the hows and whys of candy making, I like to make one batch of butterscotch hard candy without salt and one with the right amount of salt. Here are the results:

Without salt. The candy tastes of flowers and grass (almost like the outdoors), with chamomile and floral scents—it's missing any deep buttery notes and tastes nothing of the toasty, roasty golden flavor that butterscotch is known for. It's quite disappointing if you're expecting mouthwatering butterscotch.

With salt. The butterscotch comes to life! The rich, deep tones of the candy are very present. The floral notes have nearly completely disappeared, and the overall flavor is fully rounded.

The point, of course, isn't just to add salt to candy. Instead, I like to understand what particular flavors salt will make more noticeable within the candy. By completely eliminating salt from one recipe and then making the same recipe with salt, you'll learn more about what salt does and doesn't bring to candy.

You can read all sorts of books on salt, but I like to keep it simple by embracing two main salts for candy making. First, for cooking directly into candy, I reach for kosher salt. Kosher salt is not table salt, so please don't make that mistake. Table salt contains an additive that prevents it from caking. It's also a bit too fine, extremely salty, and not the ideal flavor for perfect candy. Instead, get yourself a box of Diamond Crystal kosher salt, which is reasonably priced, disperses evenly, melts nicely into candy, and isn't harsh.

When it comes to picking a salt to sprinkle directly on candy with flakes that are not only visible but also provide a lovely crunch in the mouth, I turn to flake sea salt. It's delicate and crunchy and can be sprinkled on top of candy (caramels in particular) to add that salty perfection so many people love. I never cook flake sea salt directly into candy because it has a tendency to burn, but it's ideal as a finishing salt. You can find flake salts from around the world on the market today. For information on where to buy flake sea salt, see the Resources Guide on page 291.

I occasionally use a smoked flake sea salt. It's a fantastic addition to the Coffee + Orange + Smoked Salt Caramels (page 202), as it gives them a unique flavor and brings to life aspects of the caramel that would remain hidden without smoked salt.

Here's a quick rundown of my favorite ingredients.

Butter
Always unsalted, period.

Citric Acid
Great for adding a lot or a little pucker to candy.

Chocolate
The best you can afford, from dark milk to bittersweet.

Colorings
Never fake.

Cream
Good-quality heavy cream.

Flavorings
Always natural.

Salt
Kosher salt for cooking into candy and flake sea salt for finishing candy.

Sweetener
Only granulated cane sugar, use substitutions at your own risk.

CANDY-MAKING TOOLS

Generally speaking, the craft of candy is an involved pursuit. While there are a few special tools that will make candy creation easier, you can certainly pull off a batch of caramels or lollipops with basic kitchen implements (except for the sticks for the lollipops and the wrappers for both). That said, there are a few items I insist upon you using.

SCALE

Candy is an art that requires accuracy. I insist that you use a kitchen scale for weighing all of the ingredients that go into the candy recipes that follow. I like to take advantage of every opportunity that can lead to truly successful candy, and a scale provides a ton of opportunity because it's the one way to know that you have the exact right amount of ingredients in a pot or mixing bowl.

Some of the other recipes, such as roasted fruit purées or drinks made with components of candy, don't require the extreme exactness of actual candy; therefore those recipes may rely on pints (as in pints of berries) or on the familiar fluid ounces (as in 8 fluid ounces of milk).

Speaking of scales, I like digital scales that are sensitive, accurate, and capable of weighing as minute as 1 gram. Because we make QUIN candy in small batches, with many additions weighing in at under 1 ounce, we work in grams.

Also be sure to use a scale with a tare feature. This comes in handy because it allows you to weigh ingredients directly into the pot with the pot sitting on the scale and then zero out (tare) the scale before adding the next ingredient. It's the best way to ensure accuracy, save time, and (bonus!) eliminate the number of dishes that need washing.

THE RIGHT POTS

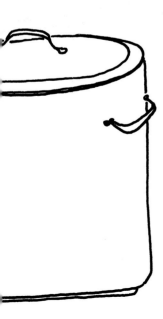

For cooking candy, I recommend two sizes of cooking pot. The first is a 6- to 7-quart heavy-bottomed pot made of nonreactive metal, such as stainless steel. It's okay if the walls of the pot are a bit on the thin side, as long as the bottom itself is thicker. You'll make almost every candy in a pot like this, and while the candy won't fill the entire pot, the tall sides help avoid mishaps when a hot mixture bubbles up or creates a lot of steam, like caramels. Whichever pot you choose, remember that it must always be perfectly clean when you use it or you risk the chance of the sugar recrystallizing. For the second pot, I suggest a heavy 2-quart saucepan, which is ideal for warming creams and for cooking ingredients listed in specific steps in recipes (such as gumdrops).

SPATULA, SPOON, AND WHISK

When candy is cooking, you'll need either a high-heat spatula or a wooden spoon. Remember, sugar shouldn't be stirred when it's cooking (see page 15), so the spatula or spoon will help you poke at it a bit as it's melting (you'll learn all about this process in the individual recipes).

If you opt for a wooden spoon, here's something you should know: Wooden spoons soak up flavors. That soup you made last night that started with onion and garlic and that you stirred with a wooden spoon? Use that same wooden spoon to stir your cooking candy and you run the risk of adding those savory flavors to a candy that's anything but.

I suggest that you buy one or two wooden spoons and reserve them for making sweets. Use a permanent marker to write a little *S* somewhere on the handle. That way they won't get mixed up with the other wooden spoons in your arsenal and you can protect your sweet recipes from tasting like garlic.

Once candy has finished cooking and you're adding additional ingredients off the heat or mixing the candy to emulsify fat into sugar (as you do in caramels), you'll want a whisk for the job. The type of whisk doesn't much matter, as long as the handle is long enough to keep your hands safe from the steam and hot sugar in the pot.

CANDY THERMOMETER

An accurate, instant-read thermometer is essential to successful candy. Sure there are times when a thermometer isn't needed (I'll actually teach you to make fear-free caramels using a color chart instead of a thermometer). But when it comes to lollipops and gumdrops (and other candies that don't take on color in the cooking process), you'll need a thermometer. I like the instant-read thermometers made by ThermoWorks. The Thermapen is my favorite because it gives a very fast read-out, but the ThermoPop is a great (and more affordable) alternative.

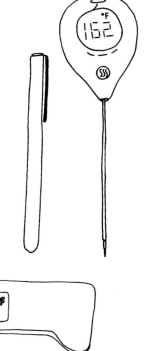

SPOUTED CUP OR CANDY FUNNEL

To get the hot candy syrup for lollipops and gumdrops onto sticks or into molds, you need a vessel that allows you to pour. A glass measuring cup or any other heat-proof vessel with a spout will work well.

If you're going to get serious about candy, I suggest investing in a candy funnel (a good one is about $20). This tool is specific to candy making, and you can purchase it online easily. I prefer one that holds 2 cups and is made of heavy-duty plastic. A candy funnel features a stick-like plunger that blocks the hole at the bottom of the funnel. To use, you lift up gently on the stick and allow hot candy to ooze out until you've filled a mold cavity, then push the plunger back into place to block the flow of candy. This action is repeated until you've used all of the candy in the funnel.

CANDY MOLDS OR NONSTICK MATS

Once a batch of candy has been cooked, you need a place to funnel or pour it. I have detailed information on what's possible on pages 113 and 162. For now, here is a brief look at what will work.

Candy molds come in a million different shapes and are made from a variety of materials. I like all kinds of molds, but mostly rely on just two types. First, a silicone mold. Silicone molds are handy because they can withstand heat and release candy easily. At QUIN, we use silicone molds for gumdrops. For more information, see page 272.

The second type of mold is a lollipop mold. I prefer the kind specifically made for hard candy (made of plastic that can withstand high temperatures), that produce 1½-inch lollipops. For more information on selecting round lollipop molds, see page 112. And for additional mold ideas, see page 154.

Nonstick mats (Silpat is a well-known brand) are incredibly useful for making lollipops, especially if you don't have a mold. You can arrange lollipop sticks on a mat and then pour the candy directly onto one end of the sticks. Even without oiling or buttering the mat, the lollipops will lift off easily once the candy is cool.

12 BY 14–INCH CANDY FRAME OR 9 BY 13–INCH PAN

For candies like caramels that you pour out into a slab, Dreams Come Chew, or marshmallows, you can use either a 12 by 14–inch candy frame or a 9 by 13–inch pan (the kind you'd use for brownies or a cake, but preferably one with straight, rather than gradually sloping, sides). If you use the pan, you will need to very lightly butter it before pouring in the molten candy. Once the candy has cooled and set, you will need to pry it from the pan for cutting.

I prefer a candy frame over a pan for candies that are poured into a slab. The frame is constructed of food-safe acrylic bars, and once the candy has cooled and set, the frame is popped off and you're left with a beautiful slab of candy with perfectly straight edges, ready to be cut. For more on building a candy frame, see the instructions and information on pages 162 to 163.

Still, a 9 by 13–inch pan is great for roasting fruit; so if you have one, you'll be using it. See page 35 for more on that.

ADDITIONAL TOOLS

Here are some other tools that will come in handy in a candy kitchen. You'll see them all again as you work your way through the recipes.

* **Bench scraper** Helpful for moving slabs of candy for cutting.
* **Cellophane wrappers** Natural cellophane is my candy wrapper of choice.
* **Marble tiles** A great alternative to a marble countertop or cutting board to use as a base for a candy frame.
* **Microplane grater** For grating citrus zest and nutmeg.
* **Pastry brush** A little dab with a wet pastry brush on stray grains of sugar in a pot will help fight the recrystallization process.
* **Permanent marker and a roll of masking tape** After you've made any core ingredient or candy, before you store it, label the storage container with the date and what's inside.
* **Twist ties** For securing cellophane wrappers around lollipops.

Now that you're armed with the information on top ingredients and top tools for making candy, let's get to the fun part and start talking about how you can develop flavor. My candy gets a lot of attention for its flavors, and I strive never to create something that's wacky just for the sake of being wacky. Instead I develop flavors that speak to me.

CREATING FLAVOR: CANDY FOR TASTING

Flavor is seasonal, flavor is personal, and flavor is everything when it comes to sweets. One of the single greatest compliments I've received about my candy is that it tastes more than just sweet. It can be deep and complicated, complex yet nuanced, and being able to achieve something within that realm is one of the best reasons to make candy at home.

I never approach candy by dumping a bunch of sugar into a pot and hoping for the best. Instead, I work to create a structure for candy that's rooted in flavor. And when someone eats the candy? Sure, I've seen plenty of people scarf it down, but there are also those who take their time to taste what they have in their mouth, which is an act that's entirely different than merely eating something. I like to think that I make candy for tasting.

I know that creative, alluring flavors (that people want to taste) are seemingly difficult to develop. But I don't necessarily agree. If flavors are based on something you already love to taste, you've at least mostly succeeded in the challenge of flavor creation. For example, you love coffee. And you also love butter and oranges. You like black pepper and maple syrup. At first glance, these may not go together, but coffee and maple syrup are both breakfast stars. And who doesn't love pepper bacon after it's been swiped across a puddle of maple syrup on a breakfast plate? And what about a glass of orange juice with this whole extravaganza? A seemingly unconnected list of foods can come together to make a coffee caramel with a hint of maple plus sparks of orange zest and black pepper. Even if you eliminate one or two ingredients or add in a nut (pecan?) or a touch of coconut, you will still end up with a great piece of candy that's packed with the flavors you love to taste.

My advice when it comes to developing flavors is that limits should not exist, with the exception of one working rule: make candy with flavors and foods you actually want to be tasting. Beyond that, don't let your brain get in the way too much. Candy making with original flavors is a creative endeavor. And we all know what happens when you start to overthink activities that should be purely creative.

But what happens if you are so lacking in flavor inspiration that you can't think of anything at all? Well, you're in luck, because I'm here and I'm ready to show you my approach to flavor development at QUIN.

SEASON AND OCCASION

Of course I love to make candy with seasonal fruits and calendar-inspired ingredients. But I also love to make candy because of a special occasion, often eschewing season and instead focusing on a person or date or important event. In other words, fantastic flavor inspiration can come from the reason you've decided to make candy in the first place. (Pay attention to all of these seemingly tiny details and you'll be more inspired than you thought possible.)

CURRENT EXPERIENCE

The second of my favorite approaches to flavor is paying attention to my current experience. It might be what I'm craving at the moment, or something interesting I've seen at the market. An idea might also come to me when I'm dining—out or in—with friends, or from food I've touched with my hands or put into my mouth and then either loved immediately or needed some time to appreciate.

Where I don't often find inspiration? The Internet. I know, I know! You love the Internet and your daily blog-reading time and your online pinboards and everything else. I'm not saying that the Internet isn't a resource for me. I'm just saying that I don't like being held at a distance from my food experiences. I like *being in* my food, *tasting* my food . . . in real life. I understand and embrace the idea that eating is a visual experience, and that people love seeing gorgeous food photographs online, but I'd rather be eating than looking. Hands-down, any day, experiencing the tastes and aromas of food is what matters to me. I basically want only firsthand accounts of food. Any person who can feel satisfied by looking at photographs of food is a person who completely mystifies me.

INTERNAL VOICE

A third way to develop or think about flavors is by listening to your internal voice. For example, try eating something (it doesn't have to be candy or even sweet) and then think through what you would do differently or what you'd like it to feature instead of a particular flavor that's present. Maybe it's just switching up something, like almonds for peanuts. Or you'd like lemon more than the orange that's in there. It can even be something as subtle as thinking milk chocolate would taste better than dark chocolate. Listen to these thoughts and write them down. What's happening is that your taste and flavor senses are taking over—see the experience through! Remember what the thing you ate tasted and smelled like. Then when you can, get into the kitchen and start experimenting, referring to your notes, your instincts, and your memories of flavors and smells. And use all of this as candy-making inspiration.

TEXTURE AS TASTE

I like to add texture to candy for various reasons, but I never do it without considering the flavor and the texture of the new element, and how both aspects must enhance the candy's taste. For example, waffle-cone bits in a caramel that tastes like chocolate malt ice cream? Delicious, with a pleasing bit of crunch. Popped popcorn embedded in a popcorn caramel? Logical, and fun—and also delicious. That said, because something has a ton of texture doesn't mean it has to bring that texture to the candy. Shards of graham cracker stuck into an otherwise ethereally fluffy marshmallow? I think that would interrupt the experience way too much. Instead, I'd grind the graham crackers into a fine dust and then incorporate the dust into the candy. The result is a marshmallow that tastes like graham crackers without the distracting bits and pieces.

TAKING IT FURTHER: MAKE MORE MAGIC

Now that we're this far into things, you must know that the candy you're about to craft is anything but regular. The reason for this: ingredients! Once you dig in to chapter two, you'll be well on your way to creating a lineup of what I like to call Core Ingredients. And these Core Ingredients can be magicked into all sorts of treats—Doughnut Magic Dust can morph into magic dust butter and glazed apples. Infused creams become cookies and buttercreams. Fruit purées are stirred into drinks and desserts. I could continue babbling on, trying to explain the magic, or you can look for this icon to easily find recipes for sweets that aren't exactly candy but do make use of core candy ingredients. I could say something here about magic, but I won't (I want to, but I won't). Okay, fine: it's magic.

CANDY FLAVOR

① Start with a CORE flavor

Think of this as the underlying flavor of the whole candy. It's something you can build on. It's a starting place that is neither too sharp or too strong or too unfamiliar. I find my most successful candies (even the ones that are a little weird) always have a familiar core. Don't get me wrong, wacky can be fun. But totally wacky is the kind of candy someone tries once. Not over and over. And (for both personal and business reasons) I like to make food that people want to eat over and over.

Fall fruits (apple, pear)

Cola

Cream

Butter

Dark beer

Berries

Vanilla

Wine (red, white rosé, sparkling)

Caramel

Coconut Milk

chocolate (milk, dark)

Stone fruit (peach, nectarine, plum)

white chocolate

② Add a COMPLEMENTARY layer

This layer complements the core flavor but doesn't overpower it. It forms a layer under the guidance of the core flavor and enhances the core flavor— sort of how coffee has the ability to make chocolate taste even more chocolaty.

Cookie

(graham, shortbread, waffle cone)

malt

nuts (hazelnut, pecan, walnut)

Sugar (white, brown)

honey

Salt

(peanut, pretzel, bacon)

Tea (herbal, black, chai)

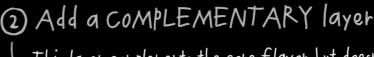

IDEA MACHINE!*

③ Add an optional ACCENT

These options are some of my favorite twists in candy making. From herbs to spices to zingy peppers and zesty citrus. These accents are often very aromatic, and add so much to the flavor of the candy because (of course) the aroma of a food makes a huge impression.

Sea Salt (flake)

Citrus Zest

yogurt

Coconut (toasted, flake, or shredded)

Ginger

cream cheese

sour cream

Cinnamon

Nutmeg

Pepper (black, ancho, Aleppo)

Smoky (salt, sugar, chocolate)

FLAVOR IDEAS IN ACTION

It's easy to see these flavor ideas in action—simply flip to any recipe in the book and you'll see how the candy begins with a CORE flavor that's then enhanced by COMPLEMENTARY flavors and ACCENTS. When you're ready to tackle your own flavor creation, come back to the Candy Flavor Idea Machine for inspiration.

* of course, this isn't an ACTUAL machine

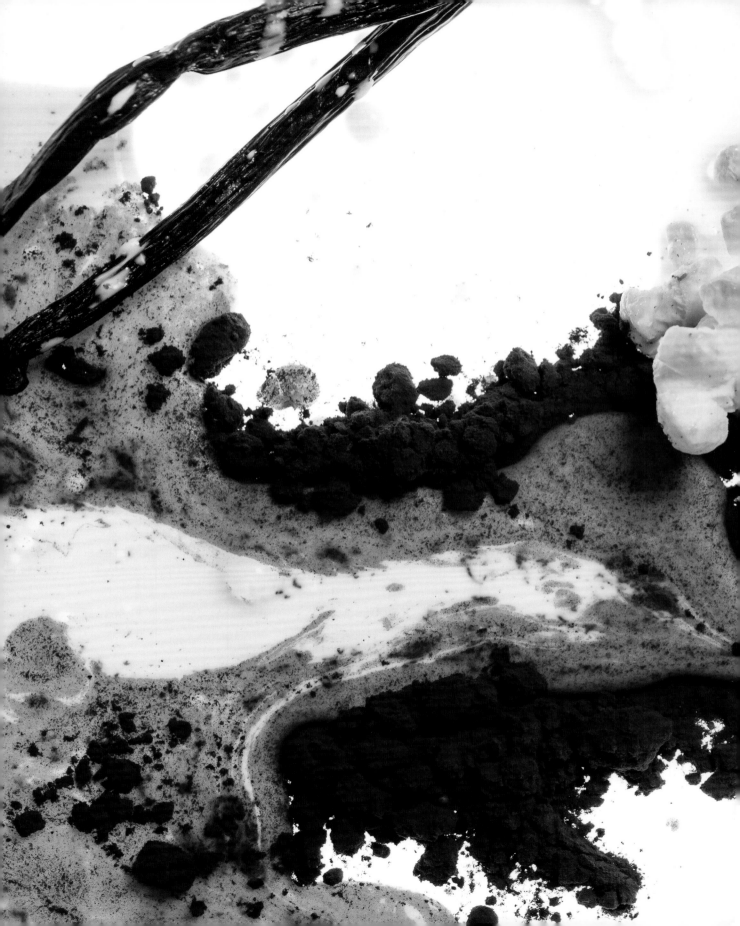

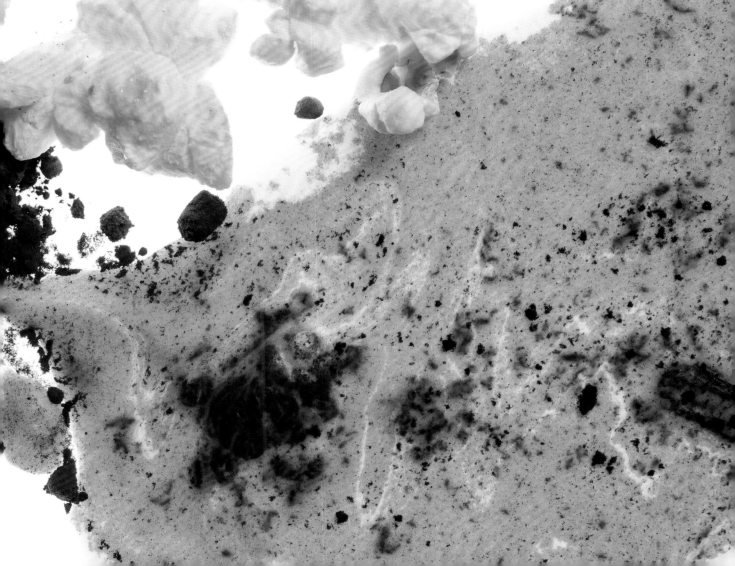

CHAPTER TWO

CRAFTING CORE INGREDIENTS

Now that I've talked a bit about developing flavor, we're going to put that knowledge to work. This chapter features recipes that act as the foundation for countless candies, desserts, drinks, and more. From caramels to cream sodas, the roasted fruit purées, infused creams, syrups, reductions, and magical dusts that follow are the keys to creating sweets with true layers of flavor.

ROASTED FRUIT PURÉES

Roasting fruit intensifies flavor, reduces water content, and results in a silky smooth, intensely flavorful purée good for a multitude of uses. Quality frozen fruit is a great stand-in for fresh fruit, especially if you simply must make cherry lollipops in the middle of winter. Every fruit that follows (fresh or frozen) is roasted at 375°F. This temperature is hot enough for the water in the fruit to evaporate quickly (which intensifies flavor) but no so hot that the fruit takes on too much color or begins to burn. For the roasting vessel, I prefer a 9 by 13–inch pan. The sides must be tall enough to trap the precious juices released by the fruit, and the pan must be large enough to accommodate 3 pints of fruit. Because different batches of fruit vary in juiciness, the roasting times in the recipes are approximate. As long as you hit the minimum time indicated, the fruit will be fine.

Once the fruit is roasted, the next step is to purée it until it's velvety smooth. All of the purées can be used right away, or they can be refrigerated in an airtight container. They also freeze beautifully in freezer-safe jars or ziplock bags. When it comes time to prepare a recipe, simply scoop out or chisel off the amount of purée you need and pop the rest back into the fridge or freezer.

I'm in love with these fruit purées because they can do so much. Once you've got these recipes handled, they can be used to make recipes found in later chapters. There are lollipops and other hard candies, caramels, flavored milks, whipped creams, ice creams, gummy candies, and more—all of them relying on these roasted fruit purées as their foundation.

QUIN is lucky to be nestled in a valley of Oregon known for growing luscious, bright-red strawberries. Around June, the fever hits, the first berries pop up at markets or farm stands and people get a little crazy. And understandably so—strawberries are the first breath of summer we're all longing for, that tiny bit of hope that warmer days are about to emerge from the clouds.

ROASTED STRAWBERRIES
WITH LEMON

**MAKES ABOUT 1 PINT
(OR 2 CUPS)**

3 pints strawberries, hulled

45 grams fresh lemon juice

1 vanilla bean, split and scraped (see page 39)

227 grams granulated sugar

Preheat the oven to 375°F.

Spread out the strawberries in a 9 by 13–inch pan and sprinkle the lemon juice evenly over the top. Nestle the vanilla bean and scrapings in the berries, then shower the sugar over everything.

Slide the pan into the oven and roast the berries for 55 to 65 minutes, rotating the pan if you start to notice one side of the berries getting darker than the other. As the berries roast, they will release a great deal of moisture, so take care when opening the oven, as the steam will be hot. The berries are ready when the tops that are peeking out of the juices are visibly darker than the rest of the berry. There will be a good deal of juice in the pan, and that's perfectly fine.

Remove the pan from the oven and allow the contents to cool slightly. Once cool enough to handle, pluck out the vanilla bean (see page 39). Pour the contents of the pan into a strainer placed over a bowl. Spoon the strawberries into a blender. Next, use a scale to weigh out 100 grams of the reserved juice and add it to the blender with the berries. Whirl the berries and juice on high speed for about 1 minute, until velvety smooth. (See page 39 for my suggestions on what to do with the remaining juice.)

The purée is now ready to use, or it can be refrigerated for up to 1 week or frozen for up to 6 months.

Now that you've strained the berries of their deeply flavored juice, don't pour it down the drain! Here are my top suggestions for what to do with any leftover juice from roasting fruits in this chapter: use it in place of maple syrup on your morning pancakes, waffles, or French toast; stir it into yogurt or hot cereal; spoon it over your favorite ice cream; or drizzle it over ricotta cheese that you've spread on a slice of toast.

And while you're at it, don't throw out that vanilla bean pod. Instead, carefully pull it out of the hot fruit (if your fingers can handle it, squeeze the length of the pod to release any vanilla and clingy fruit back into the pan), carry it to the sink, give it a good rinse inside and out, and set it aside to dry. After a few days, the pod will be ready to stick into your sugar jar, where its sweet, beautiful vanilla scent and flavor will slowly find its way into the sugar.

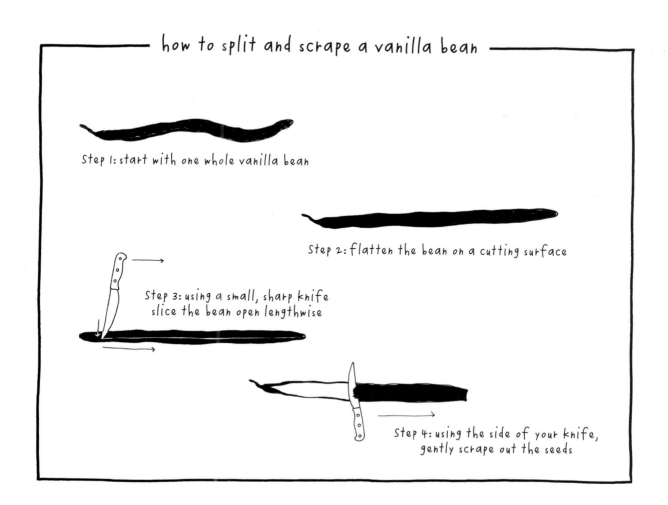

how to split and scrape a vanilla bean

Step 1: start with one whole vanilla bean

Step 2: flatten the bean on a cutting surface

Step 3: using a small, sharp knife slice the bean open lengthwise

Step 4: using the side of your knife, gently scrape out the seeds

ROASTED STRAWBERRY SIMPLE SYRUP

MAKES ABOUT 1 PINT (OR 2 CUPS)

8 fluid ounces water

200 grams granulated sugar

320 grams roasted strawberry purée (see page 37)

This simple recipe produces a fruity syrup that can be used for making sodas, flavored milks, sweet and fruity iced tea, lemonade, mixed drinks, and any other beverage you can imagine. Right now I'm imagining a milk shake.

In a small saucepan, combine the water and sugar and set it over high heat. Bring the mixture to a boil, and boil for exactly 4 minutes, stirring once or twice to help dissolve the sugar. Remove the saucepan from the heat and pour the contents into a large heat-proof measuring cup or pitcher. Set aside to cool completely.

When the sugar syrup has cooled, add the strawberry purée and stir until combined. The fruity syrup is ready to use, or it can be transferred to an airtight container and refrigerated for up to 3 weeks.

STRAWBERRY CREAM SODA

SERVES 2

12 fluid ounces sparkling water

3 fluid ounces Roasted Strawberry Simple Syrup (above)

1 fluid ounce heavy cream

Ice cubes, for serving

This creamy berry-filled soda puts the strawberry simple syrup to great use. And although it may sound over the top, it's delicious with a scoop of vanilla ice cream.

In a pitcher, combine the sparkling water, simple syrup, and cream and mix well. Fill tall glasses with ice, pour in the soda, and serve.

STRAWBERRY BUBBLY

Adding fruit to sparkling wine is rarely frowned upon. Do it and watch the faces of those you're serving light up. They'll think that you're presenting them with a drink that fell from heaven. (I know that's not possible, but I can think of no other way to describe how people respond to this simple, no-work glass of bubbly.) The strawberry simple syrup is perfect here, but peach, blackberry, blueberry, and apricot are super substitutions. And for your nondrinking friends? Substitute sparkling water for the sparkling wine.

Put a heaping 1 tablespoon of Roasted Strawberry Simple Syrup (facing page) into a flute or saucer (coupe), then slowly pour in 3 fluid ounces of chilled Champagne or other sparkling wine. Give it a little stir and serve.

Roasted blackberries are the start of one of the most impressive-looking lollipops you can imagine (see page 119). This purée creates the most beautiful hard candy because the seeds of the berries are still visible if you hold the candy up to the light. This is one of my favorite ways to show how real fruit can be incorporated into candy.

Blackberries are not only visually stunning, they also pair nicely with many other flavors. I find that roasting them with a bit of lime juice, lime zest, and nutmeg adds wonderful zing and a little mystery.

ROASTED BLACKBERRIES
WITH LIME AND NUTMEG

**MAKES ABOUT 1 PINT
(OR 2 CUPS)**

3 pints blackberries

5 grams finely grated
lime zest

30 grams fresh lime juice

227 grams granulated sugar

2 grams freshly grated
nutmeg (see page 92)

Preheat the oven to 375°F.

In a bowl, toss the blackberries with the lime zest, mixing well, then spread out the berries in a 9 by 13–inch pan and sprinkle the lime juice evenly over the top. To save on dish washing, wipe out the bowl you used for tossing the berries with the zest and combine the sugar and nutmeg in it. Give them a little whisk, then pour this sweet stuff evenly over the berries.

Slide the pan into the oven and roast the berries for about 1 hour, rotating the pan if you start to notice one side of the berries getting darker than the other. The berries are ready when they have deflated a bit and have released a good amount of juice.

Remove the pan from the oven and allow the contents to cool slightly. Pour the contents of the pan into a strainer placed over a bowl. Spoon the blackberries into a blender. Next, use a scale to weigh out 100 grams of the reserved juice and add it to the blender with the berries. Whirl the berries and juice on high speed for about 1 minute, until velvety smooth. (See page 39 for my suggestions on what to do with the remaining juice.)

The purée is now ready to use, or it can be refrigerated for up to 1 week or frozen for up to 6 months.

I like to think of raspberries as the finest of fruit. Yielding to gentle pressure, they are delicate and polite little berries. Raspberries never ask for too much; they don't need to be baked into anything to be good, and they make the perfect garnish for a summery salad just as they are—but will fall apart if you try to mix them in. See what I mean? Delicate. One of the truest purposes of the raspberry is to be eaten straight from the vine, or its berry-stained paper box. The best way to approximate that straight-from-the-box experience in a candy is to roast whole raspberries in two kinds of sugar. And that's that.

There's something about the pure taste of a raspberry that screams to be involved in a caramel in some way. I've never been a fan of fruity chocolate, but fruity caramel is a true flavor revelation. Mixing in a bit of fruit elevates the experience to more than just candy. See Vanilla Bean + Roasted Fruit Caramels (see page 182) for the perfect recipe.

ROASTED RASPBERRIES
WITH TWO SUGARS

MAKES ABOUT 1 PINT (OR 2 CUPS)

3 pints raspberries

175 grams granulated sugar

50 grams light or dark brown sugar

Preheat the oven to 375°F.

Spread out the berries in a 9 by 13–inch pan. In a small bowl, combine both sugars and whisk to mix. Shower the sugars evenly over the berries, then give the pan a shake to spread things out a bit.

Slide the pan into the oven and roast the berries for 50 to 55 minutes, rotating the pan if you start to notice one side of the berries getting darker than the other. The berries are ready when they have deflated, have perhaps darkened a bit in places, and are swimming in a pool of bright red juice.

Remove the pan from the oven and allow the contents to cool slightly. Pour the contents of the pan into a strainer placed over a bowl. Spoon the raspberries into a blender. Next, use a scale to weigh out 100 grams of the reserved juice and add it to the blender with the berries. Whirl the berries and juice on high speed for about 1 minute, until velvety smooth. (See page 39 for my suggestions on what to do with the remaining juice.)

The purée is now ready to use, or it can be refrigerated for up to 1 week or frozen for up to 6 months.

I love sweet cherries. I know tart cherries are way up on the culinary pedestal, especially when it comes to filling pies, but I can't help but love the sweet ones—everything from their deep color to their toothsome texture, not to mention the flavor. Sweet cherries make excellent candy, and this purée allows cherry perfection to be used in everything from lollipops to gumdrops.

ROASTED CHERRIES
WITH ALMOND

**MAKES ABOUT 1 PINT
(OR 2 CUPS)**

3 pints sweet cherries, pitted (see facing page)

6 grams almond extract

120 grams granulated sugar

100 grams light brown sugar

Preheat the oven to 375°F.

In a medium bowl, toss the cherries with the almond extract, mixing well. In a small bowl, combine both sugars and whisk to mix. Spread out the cherries in a 9 by 13–inch pan, shower the sugars evenly over the top, and give the pan a little shake to spread things out a bit.

Slide the pan into the oven and roast the cherries for about 1 hour, rotating the pan if you start to notice one side of the cherries getting darker than the other. The cherries are ready when they have broken down a bit, have darkened in spots, and have released the most wonderful-looking juices.

Remove the pan from the oven and allow the contents to cool slightly. Pour the contents of the pan into a strainer placed over a bowl. Spoon the cherries into a blender. Next, use a scale to weigh out 100 grams of the reserved juice and add it to the blender with the cherries. Whirl the cherries and juice on high speed for about 1 minute, until velvety smooth. (See page 39 for my suggestions on what to do with the remaining juice.)

The purée is now ready to use, or it can be refrigerated for up to 1 week or frozen for up to 6 months.

ROASTED FRUIT WHIPPED CREAM

MAKES ABOUT 1 PINT (OR 2 CUPS)

8 fluid ounces heavy cream

Heaping 2 tablespoons roasted cherry purée (see facing page)

1 tablespoon packed light brown sugar

This fruity whipped cream can be used for any dessert in which you'd use whipped cream. It's especially good between layers of vanilla cake that are nestled into some sort of trifle with fresh fruit. But, let's be honest, it'd be just as good heaped on a milk shake or served with a bowl of summer blueberries.

I've used roasted cherry purée here, but any of the roasted fruit purées in this chapter will make an equally splendid whipped cream.

Chill the bowl of your stand mixer and fit the mixer with the whisk attachment, or ready a chilled bowl on a damp kitchen towel and grab your favorite whisk. Pour the cream into the chilled bowl. If using a mixer, start it on low speed and add the cherry purée and brown sugar. Increase the speed to medium and whip the cream until it holds a peak. If using a bowl and whisk, add the cream to the bowl followed by the cherry purée and brown sugar. Using as much stamina as you can muster, whip the cream until it holds a peak. With either method, don't take it too far or you'll be on your way to cherry butter. Use immediately.

THE MESS OF PITTING CHERRIES (AND WHY YOUR HANDS ARE YOUR BEST KITCHEN TOOLS)

Pitting 3 pints of cherries can get messy. There are special cherry pitters on the market and lots of Internet instructions involving a paperclip, but I suggest that you don kitchen gloves and use the most useful of all kitchen tools, your hands. Here's how:

Rinse the cherries in a colander and then place the colander in the sink. Grab a small bowl for stems and pits and place it alongside the colander. Finally, grab an additional bowl for your freshly pitted cherries and place that in your sink with the others.

With your hands deep in the sink, pluck the stem from a cherry, discard it into the pit bowl, and then make a slight tear in the cherry. Use your fingers to ease the pit out of the cherry, discard the pit in the pit bowl, and drop the cherry in the cherry bowl. Now repeat these simple steps over and over. Once you get into a rhythm, this chore flies by. (However, if all else fails, buy frozen cherries that are already stemmed and pitted.)

As a treats enthusiast, I'm constantly looking for innovative ways to reinvent familiar flavors. When I owned a bakery, one of our most popular scone flavors was blueberry enlivened with sparks of orange zest and then rounded out with pure vanilla bean. The berries took on a new life and elevated the humble scone to new heights. I like what the combination of orange and vanilla does for any berry, but there's something special about the way it works with blueberries.

The orange juice and zest called for here can come from juicing and zesting a good-size orange. But I like exactness, so that's what I'm giving you, exactly.

ROASTED BLUEBERRIES
WITH VANILLA AND ORANGE

MAKES ABOUT 1 PINT (OR 2 CUPS)

3 pints blueberries, stemmed

80 grams fresh orange juice

10 grams finely grated orange zest

1 vanilla bean, split and scraped (see page 39)

227 grams granulated sugar

Preheat the oven to 375°F.

In a bowl, toss the berries with the orange juice and zest, mixing well. Spread out the berries in a 9 by 13–inch pan. Nestle the vanilla bean and scrapings in the berries, then shower the sugar over everything. Give the pan a good shake to even everything out.

Slide the pan into the oven and roast the berries for about 45 minutes, rotating the pan if you start to notice one side of the berries getting darker than the other. The berries are ready when they appear to have deflated or popped open and they are awash in their own dark, beautiful juice.

Remove the pan from the oven and allow the contents to cool slightly. Once cool enough to handle, pluck out the vanilla bean (see page 39). Pour the contents of the pan into a strainer placed over a bowl. Spoon the berries into a blender. Next, use a scale to weigh out 100 grams of the reserved juice and add it to the blender with the berries. Whirl the berries and juice on high speed for about 1 minute, until velvety smooth. (See page 39 for my suggestions on what to do with the remaining juice.)

The purée is now ready to use, or it can be refrigerated for up to 1 week or frozen for up to 6 months.

I have to admit that I didn't eat my first fresh apricot until I was an adult enjoying West Coast living. I also have to admit that as soon as I came up with this combination, I was beside myself with excitement. The coconut is a bit unusual, but it really gives this purée an incredible texture and great flavor. The addition of the coconut doesn't change how the fruit is roasted, so just follow the directions and you'll be on your way to terrific confections—including the sublime apricot caramels on page 183—in no time.

ROASTED APRICOTS
WITH COCONUT AND BROWN SUGAR

MAKES ABOUT 1 PINT (OR 2 CUPS)

3 pints apricots, halved and pitted

85 grams unsweetened flake dried coconut

227 grams light brown sugar

3 grams kosher salt

Preheat the oven to 375°F.

In a bowl, toss the apricots with the coconut. Sprinkle the brown sugar and salt on the apricots and toss everything together, mixing well. Spread out the mixture in a 9 by 13–inch pan and give the pan a shake.

Slide the pan into the oven and roast the apricots for 50 to 55 minutes, rotating the pan if you notice any uneven dark spots. The apricots are ready when they appear to be very cooked, have released a small amount of juice, and look slightly caramelized.

Remove the pan from the oven and allow the contents to cool slightly. Spoon the contents of the pan into a blender and whirl on high speed for 1 minute.

The purée is now ready to use, or it can be refrigerated for up to 1 week or frozen for up to 6 months.

My favorite kind of pie is any kind of pie. Stone fruit like peaches, nectarines, and even plums make great pies, especially when a bit of ginger is thrown in. This purée honors that combination and the result is a stupendous mix of flavors perfect for ice cream, whipped cream, and even the most amazing stir-in for morning oatmeal.

I highly recommend using peeled, pitted, and sliced frozen peaches (not what is shown here!) for this recipe. The flavor will be there, and you'll save yourself a lot of work. If you opt for fresh peaches, peel them, pit them, and cut each one into about eight slices.

ROASTED PEACHES
WITH GINGER

MAKES ABOUT 1 PINT (OR 2 CUPS)

3 pints prepared fresh or frozen peaches (see headnote)

1-inch piece fresh ginger, peeled and cut into 10 to 12 slices

150 grams dark brown sugar

75 grams granulated sugar

Preheat the oven to 375°F.

Spread out the peaches in a 9 by 13–inch pan and tuck in the ginger throughout. In a small bowl, combine both sugars and whisk to mix. Shower the sugars evenly over the peaches.

Slide the pan into the oven and roast the peaches for 55 to 60 minutes, rotating the pan if you start to notice one side of the peaches getting darker than the other. The peaches are ready when they are soft and a bit caramelized.

Remove the pan from the oven and allow the contents to cool slightly. Spoon the contents of the pan (don't forget the ginger) into a blender and whirl on high speed for 1 minute.

The purée is now ready to use, or it can be refrigerated for up to 1 week or frozen for up to 6 months.

INFUSED CREAMS

If you can make a cup of tea, you can infuse cream with flavor. It's really that easy. Infused cream is a marvelous way to impart complex layers of flavor to candies, fillings, and custards. At QUIN, we consider infused creams a secret weapon of sorts. All of our best caramels call for them.

Through my work at QUIN, I've found that by infusing cream, we can create any flavor of caramel we want, from banana to popcorn, citrus to coffee. Infused creams also make stellar bases for ice creams (see page 99) and for totally outrageous whipped creams (see page 56). And don't even get me started on the cream soda possibilities (see page 40).

When complementary flavors combine, they take on new life, and that new life is at the center of my approach to candy making. However, how much infused cream to use in a candy varies. For example, caramels call for 220 grams. If some of your cream disappears after the infusion process, don't worry. You can fix the problem by adding a touch of plain cream to make up for what's lacking. And yes, I do weigh my cream. I understand that it's a liquid, but here's the deal: The actual weight of heavy cream varies from one brand to another. Candy making is precise and weighing the cream is the best way I know to aid in a really good—in other words, close to perfect—finished product. That said, I operate on the assumption that heavy cream weighs about 235 grams per 1 cup, with variances in the neighborhood of plus or minus 3 grams.

Probably what I love the most about popcorn cream is the fact that if you drink it, it tastes like buttered popcorn or a night out at the movies. (But who would drink heavy cream? Anyone? Only me? Okay.) You need a food processor for this recipe, and the bowl and the blade of the processor must be completely dry. You want to turn the popcorn into dust, and that won't be possible if there's any moisture around.

One more thing: the popcorn in this recipe is popcorn you'll pop yourself on the stove top. I'm always surprised by the number of people who use a microwave to make popcorn when the stove-top method (especially when popped in coconut oil and a little sugar) produces such superior results. You may be tempted to make this cream with prepopped bagged stuff or even a chemical-laden microwave imposter, but the flavor will never be the same.

POPCORN CREAM

MAKES ABOUT 270 GRAMS

100 grams Every Day, Popcorn (see page 54)

500 grams heavy cream

Place the popcorn in the bowl of a food processor fitted with the blade attachment. Pulse the popcorn until it turns into a fine dust. Empty the popcorn dust into a heat-proof bowl.

Pour the cream into a small saucepan, place over medium heat, and bring to a gentle boil, stirring a couple of times while you're waiting. Once the cream is bubbling, immediately pour it over the popcorn dust, nudging with a spoon to make sure that every speck of dust is saturated with cream. Cover the bowl with plastic wrap and allow the cream to steep for 30 minutes.

Set a fine-mesh strainer over a small bowl and pour the cream-popcorn mixture into the strainer. It will look like some kind of mush, but it will smell like cream and popcorn (and, if you're like me, you'll start to get excited). Press the popcorn mush against the strainer with the back of a large spoon to release as much of the beautiful cream as you can. Discard the mush.

The cream is now ready to use, or transfer it to an airtight container and refrigerate for up to 1 week.

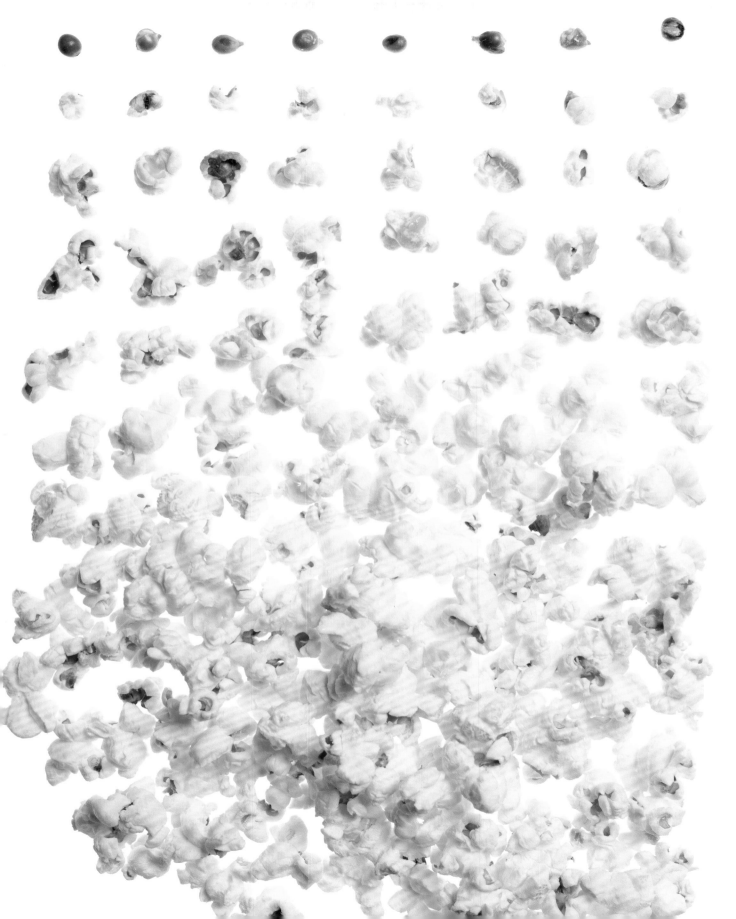

EVERY DAY, POPCORN

MAKES ABOUT 300 GRAMS

114 grams coconut oil

230 grams popcorn kernels
(white or yellow)

75 grams granulated sugar

10 grams kosher salt

The real goal here is popcorn that can be used to make popcorn cream, the key ingredient in Popcorn Caramels (page 171). I pop my corn in refined coconut oil because the oil can stand up to high heat. Beware! Once the aroma of freshly popped popcorn fills your home, a snack attack is inevitable. You are going to need 100 grams of the popcorn for making the cream and another 90 grams or so for topping the caramels. The remaining popcorn? Snack away. And don't be surprised if you're tempted to make this popcorn every day.

Hint: Doughnut Magic Dust (see page 91) makes an especially nice popcorn. Use 90 grams of the dust in place of the 75 grams granulated sugar.

Put the coconut oil in a large pot (with the lid nearby), set it on the stove top, and turn the burner to medium-high. Once the coconut oil has liquefied, sprinkle the popcorn kernels evenly over the oil, then sprinkle the sugar evenly over the kernels. Place the lid on the pot and wait for the kernels to start popping. While you are waiting, get out a sheet pan and put it near the stove. Once the popcorn is off to a start, stand by and listen. You'll want to keep the pot on the heat until there are long pauses between pops. Those pauses should not last more than 10 seconds. As soon as the popping starts to slow, turn off the burner, take the pot off the heat, carefully remove the lid, and pour the popcorn onto the sheet pan. Sprinkle the salt all over the popped corn. The popcorn is ready to use, and (once cool) can be stored in an airtight container for up to 1 week.

I'd put coffee cream in anything. Actually, I'd put plain cream in anything, and I happen to really like coffee, so this coffee-infused cream is high up there on my list of favorites. You basically brew some very strong coffee in hot cream and then strain out the coffee grounds. What's left behind will be a coffee-flavored liquid ideal for making all of the creamy delights we love, from caramels to hot fudge.

I suggest using any coffee here that you like to drink, although my preference leans toward a roast that's rich and robust rather than citrusy or fruity.

COFFEE CREAM

MAKES ABOUT 220 GRAMS

235 grams heavy cream
57 grams ground coffee

Pour the cream into a small saucepan and set the pan over medium heat. Add the ground coffee and allow the cream to come to a boil, stirring frequently while you're waiting. Once the cream has reached a boil, remove the pan from the heat, top it with a lid, and let steep for 10 minutes.

Set a fine-mesh strainer over a small bowl and pour the contents of the saucepan into the strainer. Give the grounds a little nudge to release as much of the flavored cream as possible. Discard the grounds.

The cream is now ready to use, or transfer it to an airtight container and refrigerate for up to 1 week.

INFUSED-CREAM WHIPPED CREAMS

One of the finest uses of heavy cream is, of course, whipped cream. Every infused cream you're learning to make can be whipped into perfect fluffiness—you just pick the cream you'd like, add a little sweetener, and let the magic happen. Some of my very favorites are listed here. For tips on how to whip, see page 45.

VANILLA BEAN WHIPPED CREAM
8 fluid ounces Vanilla Bean Cream (page 61)
30 grams granulated sugar

EARL GREY TEA WHIPPED CREAM
8 fluid ounces Earl Grey Tea Cream (page 63)
35 grams light brown sugar

ORANGE WHIPPED CREAM
8 fluid ounces Orange Cream (page 60)
20 grams granulated sugar
15 grams dark brown sugar

COFFEE WHIPPED CREAM
8 fluid ounces Coffee Cream (page 55)
30 grams granulated sugar

This chocolate cream is the base for a stellar chocolate caramel. The recipe calls for vanilla bean powder, which is made by pulverizing whole vanilla beans. I explain the ins and outs of purchasing your own vanilla bean powder in the Resources Guide (see page 293).

CHOCOLATE CREAM

MAKES ABOUT 235 GRAMS

235 grams heavy cream

24 grams cocoa powder (see page 74)

3 grams vanilla bean powder (see below)

Pour the cream into a small saucepan and set the pan over medium heat. Allow the cream to warm up just a bit and then slowly add the cocoa powder, whisking all the while. Once all the cocoa powder has been stirred in, add the vanilla bean powder and stir to combine. Allow the mixture to get hot enough to steam and barely bubble, stirring it a couple of times as it heats, then remove the pan from the heat.

The cream is now ready to use, or transfer it to an airtight container and refrigerate for up to 1 week.

ABOUT VANILLA BEAN POWDER

The strawberry and blueberry roasted fruit purées (see pages 37 and 46, respectively) rely on whole vanilla beans to impart vanilla flavor to the fruit. Another way to add that wonderful flavor is through one of QUIN's favorite products, vanilla bean powder, which is basically a vanilla bean—pod, seeds, and all—pulverized to a powder. These aren't pods that have been used for another purpose and then ground for adding to recipes for a visual element. You know those specks in big-brand vanilla bean ice cream? They're the result of grinding vanilla beans that have already been stripped of their beautiful flavor. The beans are called "exhausted" vanilla beans, and with good reason. The powder I'm talking about doesn't come from exhausted beans. It's full of potent vanilla flavor, and many of QUIN's recipes would not be the same without it.

From the summer before sixth grade until the summer after my first year of college, I worked on the shores of Lake Erie passing chocolate malts and super-tall soft-serve cones ensconced in rainbow jimmies through a tiny square window into the hands of waiting customers. That job experience undoubtedly paved the way to where I am today. It also certainly didn't hurt that every shift, I got to work with my three best friends and eat unlimited amounts of ice cream.

This malty cream brings me back to those days. It's particularly perfect for Chocolate Malt + Sugar Cone Caramels (see page 196) and makes a delightful whipped cream for milk shakes, hot chocolate, cream pies—don't stop!

MALTED MILK CREAM

MAKES ABOUT 235 GRAMS

235 grams heavy cream

45 grams malted milk powder

Pour the cream into a small saucepan and sprinkle in the malted milk powder. Grab a whisk and get to work; don't stop until the malted milk powder is dissolved and thoroughly mixed in. Set the saucepan over medium heat and warm the cream just until it starts to bubble, giving it a few good stirs while you're waiting for it to get hot enough. Once it bubbles a bit, remove the pan from the heat, give the cream another good stir, and set it aside to cool.

The cream is now ready to use, or transfer it to an airtight container and refrigerate for up to 1 week.

INFUSED-CREAM BUTTERCREAM

MAKES ABOUT 3 CUPS

227 grams unsalted butter, at room temperature

625 grams powdered sugar

45 grams infused cream (see pages 52 to 64)

The more intensely flavored the cream, the greater impact it will deliver in this buttercream. I love any tea-infused cream, but citrus cream (maybe with a bit of chocolate) doesn't sound too bad at all, now, does it?

Any leftover buttercream will keep in the refrigerator for up to 1 week or in the freezer for up to 3 months. Bring refrigerated buttercream to room temperature and stir well before using. If it's frozen, thaw in the refrigerator overnight, then bring to room temperature and stir well before using.

In a stand mixer fitted with the paddle attachment, beat the butter on medium speed until smooth. Add the powdered sugar, a little at a time, beating after each addition until the sugar has disappeared.

With the mixer still on medium speed, add half of the infused cream and beat until smooth. Add the remaining cream, a little at a time, and continue to beat until all of the cream is incorporated and the buttercream is smooth. If you find you need a splash more cream to encourage the buttercream to come together, go slowly. A tiny teaspoon may be all you need.

VARIATION You can mix any of the fruit purées from pages 37 to 49 into these simple buttercreams to make them fresh and fruity. First, follow the recipe using plain cream instead of infused cream. After you've whipped the buttercream together, add in 80 grams of the roasted fruit purée of your choice (I like blackberry and raspberry the most) and stir to combine. Sometimes I leave my buttercreams a bit streaky for added oopmph—this is especially striking when making a blackberry buttercream.

Reminiscent of a vintage frozen novelty, this orange cream can be used to make drinks (everything from cream sodas to milk shakes), ice cream, flavored whipped cream, citrusy vanilla pudding, and custard for French toast, waffles, and more. When you start to think about it, orange makes so many treats taste better than before. Don't deny it.

This recipe works with just about any citrus fruit: lemon, lime, grapefruit, blood orange, or a mix of your favorites. Simply change out the orange zest for the citrus zest of your choice.

ORANGE CREAM

MAKES ABOUT 235 GRAMS

235 grams heavy cream

20 grams finely grated orange zest

Pour the cream into a small saucepan, add the orange zest, and stir well. Set the pan over medium heat and warm the cream just until it starts to bubble, giving it a few good stirs while you're waiting for it to get hot enough. Once it bubbles a bit, remove the pan from the heat, give the cream another good stir, and set it aside to cool.

The cream is now ready to use, or transfer it to an airtight container and refrigerate for up to 1 week.

I bake. A lot. And I always add more vanilla to everything I create. Whether it's a scraped bean, vanilla sugar, or even double-fold (a fancy way of saying "twice as strong") extract, I love that extra kick, especially in cookies. People always (well, sometimes, most of the time, once in a while) praise my cookies, and I swear the only difference between mine and those of the next professional candy maker or baker is a ton of vanilla. It's like the most obvious "secret" ingredient on Earth.

VANILLA BEAN CREAM

MAKES ABOUT 235 GRAMS

235 grams heavy cream

16 grams vanilla extract

5 grams vanilla bean powder (see page 57)

In a small saucepan, combine the cream, vanilla extract, and vanilla bean powder and stir well. Set the saucepan over medium heat and allow the cream to get hot enough to steam but not quite boil, stirring it a few times as it heats. Once it's steaming, remove the pan from the heat and set it aside to cool.

The cream is now ready to use, or transfer it to an airtight container and refrigerate for up to 1 week.

Tea is the ideal ingredient to use for infusing cream. First of all, tea was born to do this steeping thing. And second? Tea already has layers of flavor. That means that infusing tea in cream and then adding that cream to baked goods, turning it into ice cream, or caramelizing it into candy truly results in treats with complex, layered, and sometimes mysterious flavor. One of the most flavorful teas I know is Earl Grey. Is it orange? Are those herbs? It's fresh and fruity but also a little dark—perfect for the caramels on page 200.

EARL GREY TEA CREAM

MAKES ABOUT 220 GRAMS

260 grams heavy cream

6 grams Earl Grey loose leaf tea, or 3 Earl Grey tea bags

Pour the cream into a small saucepan and set the pan over medium heat. Bring the cream to a boil, then promptly remove the pan from the heat. Add the tea to the cream, cover the pan, and let it steep for exactly 12 minutes. Then, use a fine-mesh strainer to strain the loose leaf tea from the cream or remove the tea bags.

The cream is now ready to use, or transfer it to an airtight container and refrigerate for up to 1 week.

PEPPERMINT TEA CREAM Mint-infused cream is extra special and very easy to make. Swap out the Earl Grey tea for peppermint tea. Steep for 12 minutes as directed, and you'll end up with a minty cream that will be screaming to be fashioned into buttercream for cakes and cookies, whipped into cream for topping off hot chocolate, churned into peppermint ice cream, or stirred into the world's best minty chocolate cream soda.

CHAI TEA CREAM Chai tea makes great candy, from caramels to lollipops. Replace the Earl Grey tea with 15 grams of chai and proceed as directed. Then get yourself to page 198 to make Smoked Chai Tea Caramels, a QUIN best seller.

We take seasonal candy seriously at QUIN. These peppery creams are the start of candies that I dreamed up to help get us through a few particularly rough winter months. A little spice to warm up our caramels seemed like the bright spot we needed. And although we use the black pepper cream in a maple caramel (see page 212) and the Aleppo pepper cream in a raisin caramel (see page 194), the pepper possibilities are really up to you. Follow this method with the pepper of your choice and start experimenting. When selecting a pepper for this recipe, here are some tips to keep in mind: Freshly ground black pepper is best, but preground will work just fine. All chile peppers should be dried and then ground. Pepper creams can be used to make a spiced-up version of Chocolate Magic Dust Ice Cream (see page 104), caramels, puddings, whipped creams, and more.

PEPPER CREAM

MAKES ABOUT 220 GRAMS

260 grams heavy cream

20 grams freshly ground black pepper or ground dried chile or chile powder of your choice (ancho or Aleppo would be great)

Pour the cream into a small saucepan, sprinkle in the pepper, and stir well. Set the pan over medium heat. Bring the cream to a boil, then promptly remove it from the heat. Cover the pan and let it steep for exactly 15 minutes. Set a fine-mesh strainer over a small bowl and pour the contents of the pan into the strainer. Discard the pepper in the strainer.

The cream is now ready to use, or transfer it to an airtight container and refrigerate for up to 1 week.

SYRUPS AND REDUCTIONS

Another way to bring great flavor to candy is by using handcrafted syrups and thick reductions. At QUIN, we never fuss with making our own alcohol-based extracts, but we do spend a lot of time cooking concoctions that bring big flavor to candy.

Syrups are made by cooking sugar in a pot and then deglazing the pot with a liquid, such as tea or coffee. Reductions begin with a liquid that contains some naturally occurring sugars, like wine, which is evaporated on the stove top, a process that removes water content and intensifies flavor. None of the syrups and reductions that follow contain dairy and all of them can be used to create wonderful hard candies.

This elixir of true coffee flavor is one of my favorite ingredients. First, it makes a really great sauce on its own—spooned over ice cream, brushed on bacon like a glaze, poured over cake layers, and even stirred into a glass of milk. It's sweet from the sugar but totally balanced with pure coffee. And second, it's the key ingredient in some of my favorite candies (coffee lollipops, anyone?). Get creative with your espresso here. At QUIN, we use various blends from different roasters and are always surprised by the different notes in the resulting syrup. I like to use coffees that are already rich in flavor, going for roasts that have notes of caramel or chocolate. Still, fruitier coffees yield their own special results, so don't rule them out.

If you don't have an espresso maker, you can pick up the brewed espresso when you're out on your daily coffee-shop trip. Refrigerate it in an airtight container until you're ready to use it; it'll keep for a week. When it's time to make this syrup, warm the espresso so it's hot when you add it to the recipe.

COFFEE SYRUP

MAKES ABOUT 730 GRAMS

57 grams glucose syrup

454 grams granulated sugar

8 fluid ounces brewed espresso, hot

Weigh the glucose syrup directly in a heavy-bottomed pot and set over medium heat until it liquefies a bit. Once it has warmed up, it will move more like water than a thick syrup. This is when you add the sugar, sprinkling it evenly over the glucose. When the sugar is in the pot, use a wooden spoon or high-heat spatula to break up the sugar, gently poking it into the glucose. This will help the glucose to saturate the sugar, allowing the two to cook more evenly.

Once the sugar has melted and appears to be melding well with the glucose, increase the heat to medium-high and allow the two ingredients to bubble and cook until the mixture is a rich caramel—or dirty copper penny—color (see the Caramel Color Chart on page 161). When this color has been achieved, remove the pot from the heat and carefully pour in the hot espresso. Allow the steam to billow away and then whisk to combine well. Pour the syrup into a heat-proof bowl and set it aside to cool.

The syrup is now ready to use, or transfer it to an airtight container and refrigerate for up to 6 weeks.

At QUIN, we love to use tea in our candy. Tea, especially when well blended, has many layers of flavor, and they all seem to sing when used to make treats.

QUIN proudly incorporates tea from the late Steven Smith into our sweets. Steven was a supporter of QUIN from the start, and his approach to blending tea was much like our approach to concocting confections. A true artist, artisan, and friend, the teas created by Steven for his company Steven Smith Teamaker are undeniably wonderful elixirs. (See the Resources Guide, page 293, for information on purchasing Smith tea.)

TEA SYRUP

MAKES ABOUT 700 GRAMS

20 grams loose leaf black tea, or 10 black tea bags

8 fluid ounces boiling water

57 grams glucose syrup

454 grams granulated sugar

Place the tea in a glass measuring cup and pour the boiling water over it. Set a timer for 10 minutes. Once the timer dings, strain the tea through a fine-mesh strainer or remove the tea bags.

Weigh the glucose syrup directly in a heavy-bottomed pot and set over medium heat until it liquefies a bit. Once it has warmed up, it will move more like water than a thick syrup. This is when you add the sugar, sprinkling it evenly over the glucose. When the sugar is in the pot, use a wooden spoon or high-heat spatula to break up the sugar, gently poking it into the glucose. This will help the glucose to saturate the sugar, allowing the two to cook more evenly.

Once the sugar has melted and appears to be melding well with the glucose, increase the heat to medium-high and allow the two ingredients to bubble and cook until the mixture is a rich caramel—or dirty copper penny—color (see the Caramel Color Chart on page 161). When this color has been achieved, remove the pot from the heat and carefully pour in the hot tea. Allow the steam to billow away and then whisk to combine well. Pour the syrup into a heat-proof bowl and set it aside to cool.

The syrup is now ready to use, or transfer it to an airtight container and refrigerate for up to 6 weeks.

This syrup makes a very lovely swirl in ice cream—coffee, chocolate, vanilla. Even if you drizzle it over the top rather than swirl it in, it's wonderful. It also makes a good glaze for baked goods, stands in nicely as a topping for waffles or pancakes, and can be turned into a praline lollipop (see page 136). I've also been known to blend it into a milk shake, even though I know I probably shouldn't.

PRALINE SYRUP

MAKES ABOUT 525 GRAMS

208 grams glucose syrup

200 grams light brown sugar

120 grams water

6 grams vanilla extract

4 grams kosher salt

Weigh the glucose syrup, brown sugar, and water directly into a small saucepan. Set the pan on the stove top, turn the heat to medium, and heat until the mixture is boiling. Allow the syrup to boil for about 3 minutes, until it reaches a temperature of 230°F and has reduced and thickened. Remove the pan from the heat, allow the boiling to subside, and then stir in the vanilla and salt.

The syrup is now ready to use, or transfer it to an airtight container and refrigerate for up to 6 weeks.

The spirit of collaboration is very strong in QUIN's hometown of Portland, Oregon. At QUIN, we like to work with artisans who echo our spirit of creativity and results-driven working relationships. One of my favorite collaborations to date has been with Union Wine Company. Ryan Harms and Heather Wallberg of Union have been huge supporters of QUIN from the beginning, and I was happy to work with them to create a line of candy using their wines. We had to start by crafting a very thick, very concentrated version of their vintages. And that's how our wine reductions were born.

I recommend starting with wines that are a little on the sweet side. But you can pick any reasonably priced drinkable red, white, or rosé you like. Just be sure that you like to drink it.

WINE REDUCTION
(PINOT NOIR, PINOT GRIS, OR ROSÉ)

MAKES ABOUT 375 ML (12 FLUID OUNCES)

1 (750-ml) bottle very drinkable red, white, or rosé wine

Pour the wine into a nonreactive saucepan set over medium heat. Bring the wine to a simmer and allow it to bubble nicely (without boiling over) until it has reduced to a thickish syrup of about 1½ cups. In other words, reduce the wine by half. This should take 15 to 20 minutes. Remove the pan from the heat and let cool.

The reduction is now ready to use, or transfer it to an airtight container and refrigerate. It will keep almost indefinitely, but try to use it up within 6 weeks.

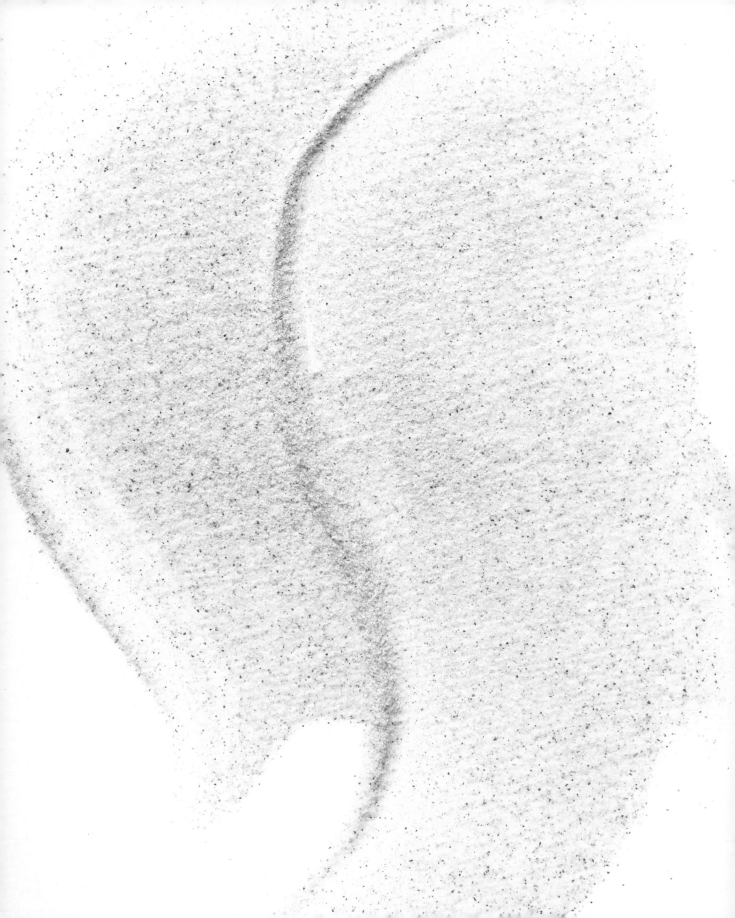

MAGIC DUSTS

Welcome to my favorite ingredient of all time: Magic Dust. This stuff really is magic. All you need to do is grab a whisk and whirl together some sugar and a few other ingredients to create a flavorful powder that you can then put to work in a multitude of ways. Chocolate Magic Dust (page 74) is a revelation; it can be used to make chocolate sauce, hot fudge, chocolate ice cream, chocolate milk, hot chocolate, chocolate lollipops, chocolate caramels, and more. Doughnut Magic Dust (page 91) goes way beyond doughnuts, and Sweet + Sour Magic Dust (page 93) is as lip puckering as it is addictive.

This dust is the foundation of countless recipes, comes together in a flash, and stores beautifully in your pantry. Because the dust is over-the-top usable, I like to make large batches of it. I promise you, if you have the dust at the ready, you will be more likely to use it. Think of it as a pantry staple, and when you want to make a cup of hot chocolate, a glass of chocolate milk, a batch of chocolate ice cream, or any other chocolaty treat, the main component of the recipe is there in the pantry all ready to go.

CHOCOLATE MAGIC DUST

MAKES ABOUT 600 GRAMS

460 grams granulated sugar

116 grams cocoa powder (see below)

2 grams kosher salt

3 grams vanilla bean powder (see page 57)

2 grams ground cinnamon

Pour the sugar into a large bowl. Sift together the cocoa powder, salt, vanilla bean powder, and cinnamon into a small bowl to break up any clumps. Add the sifted mixture to the sugar, grab a whisk, and whisk, whisk, whisk everything together until it looks like a big bowl of sparkly chocolate powder (again, *magic*).

The magic dust is now ready to use. Store in an airtight container or ziplock bags. As long as the container is airtight and moisture-free, the dust will last for up to 12 months.

THE ULTIMATE COCOA POWDER

I've searched high and low for the perfect cocoa powder, and Felchlin cocoa powder is it. There's nothing like it. Touch it and it melts between your fingers. It's nearly black and makes everything replete with chocolate. Made in Switzerland, Felchlin cocoa powder is available online and is sold in 1-kilogram (roughly 2-pound) bags. I promise you it's worth the investment and it keeps well in an airtight container in a dry, cool pantry. Head to the Resources Guide (see page 292) for information on how to find it.

HOT OR COLD CHOCOLATE

Chocolate Magic Dust makes the best hot chocolate. Time after time, QUIN customers have told us that our hot chocolate is the best they have ever had and that they cannot imagine a better version anywhere. I tend to agree, as even I've never had anything like it.

Pour 8 fluid ounces of whole milk into a small saucepan and set it over low to medium heat. (Low heat is good if you are the type to wander away from the stove and get distracted. If you plan on sticking around, medium heat will do just fine.) Heat the milk until it's very steamy but isn't boiling.

Remove the pan from the heat, grab a whisk, and add a rounded 2 tablespoons of Chocolate Magic Dust (see page 74) to the hot milk. Now whisk like crazy until all of the dust has been mixed in and no lumps remain.

If you're drinking hot chocolate, immediately pour the chocolate into your favorite mug and enjoy. If you're craving cold chocolate, once you've whisked the chocolate dust into the milk, transfer the mixture to a covered container and refrigerate until very cold. To serve, give the milk a good shake, then pour it into a glass and drink. (I'm really, really excited for you to try this.)

HOT CHOCOLATE AND MARSHMALLOW KIT

As I've said before, one sure way to make someone feel truly happy (or appreciated or understood or loved) is to give him or her something that you made with your hands and heart.

Pairing a jar or bag of Chocolate Magic Dust (see page 74) with a bundle of homemade marshmallows (see pages 244 to 266) is a nice wintertime gift for so many—teachers, coaches, mentors, babysitters (I mean, think of the Secret Santa possibilities!). The gesture is universally appreciated, and it's so easy.

Scoop some Chocolate Magic Dust into the container of your choice (keeping in mind that 2 tablespoons are used in making one cup of hot chocolate) and put a bunch of marshmallows in a second container (again, keeping in mind that two or three 1-inch marshmallows are perfect for topping a cup of hot chocolate). If you want to get fancy, you can add a special mug, but the chocolate dust and the marshmallows are really all the magic you need. This combination is my holiday season go-to gift, and I like to put the magic dust and the marshmallows in matching containers, say two jars or two coffee bags, and tie them together with a pretty ribbon. Next, I attach a little handwritten instruction card along with a To/From tag. Easy and impressive, but most of all it's a little bit of your heart all wrapped up for someone else.

to:
from:

chocolate
MAGIC
DUST

YOUR
FLUFFY
MARSHMALLOWS

CHOCOLATE FOR BREAKFAST

I certainly hope you took my advice about stocking your pantry with Chocolate Magic Dust (see page 74). Because if you have, then chocolate waffles and chocolate pancakes are just a few steps away. Here's how: For every 1 cup of waffle or pancake batter, add 1½ tablespoons of Chocolate Magic Dust to the dry ingredients in the recipe and then prepare the recipe as usual. If it's a special occasion—or even just a Monday morning—top the pancakes or waffles with one of the flavored whipped creams from page 56. My favorites? Orange or coffee, for sure.

HOT CHOCOLATE WITH VANILLA BEAN MARSHMALLOWS AND MINT CRYSTAL SUGAR

If you have fresh Vanilla Bean Marshmallows (page 244) in your pantry and a container of mint crystal sugar (see page 94) on hand, here's what you do: Make hot chocolate as directed on page 76 and pour it into a mug. Top it with the marshmallows and finish with a sparkly shower of the crystal sugar.

If you're having a party or trying to figure out a fun way to jazz up an event, a hot chocolate bar is the way to go.

Whip up a vat of hot chocolate and pour it into coffee urns, airpots, or insulated pitchers. Then arrange fluffy marshmallows in candy jars or on beautiful platters. Next, get yourself a stack of cups (I recommend to-go paper coffee cups if your event headcount is anything more than the amount of mugs you want to wash) and you're ready. Jars overflowing with marshmallows of different flavors alongside giant, shiny pots filled with hot chocolate are the perfect addition to any wintertime celebration.

Take it from me, you should treat yourself to the culinary delight known as the whipped cream sandwich at least once in your life. My first was prepared by my Grandma Dot. It was Thanksgiving and I was a kid interested in dinner rolls (and butter!) and not much else. Dot (afraid I'd go hungry, bless her heart) saved the day by sandwiching whipped cream between two slices of pumpkin bread and handing it to me on a dinner plate. If ever there was a moment when I thought I wanted to be just like her when I grew up, that was it.

Both Doughnut Magic Dust (see page 91) and Five-Spice Magic Dust (see page 89) make great whipped creams. Simply substitute equal parts of one dust for another. Either version would be so good on pie, sliced fruit, and even (yes, indeed) as the filling in a whipped cream sandwich.

CHOCOLATE MAGIC DUST WHIPPED CREAM

MAKES ABOUT 1 PINT (OR 2 CUPS)

8 fluid ounces heavy cream

35 grams Chocolate Magic Dust (see page 74)

Chill the bowl of your stand mixer and fit the mixer with the whisk attachment, or ready a chilled bowl on a damp kitchen towel and grab your favorite whisk. Pour the cream into the chilled bowl. If using a mixer, start it on low speed and slowly pour in the chocolate dust. Increase the speed to medium and whip the cream until it holds a peak. If using a bowl and whisk, add the cream to the bowl followed by the chocolate dust. Using all the strength in your forearms, whip the cream until it holds a peak. With either method, don't take it too far or you'll be on your way to chocolate butter. Use immediately.

I keep a squeeze bottle of this sauce in my refrigerator so a glass of chocolate milk is never far away. For every cup of milk, I squeeze in about 3 tablespoons of the sauce and then I shake it up (or stir it really well with a fork).

Beyond that, I like to squirt this sauce on ice cream, on spoonfuls of peanut butter (that's kind of a secret, so please don't tell my kid), and on fresh strawberries. I use the sauce to make chocolate milk shakes (I load up my blender with ice cream, add a splash of milk, and squeeze in as much sauce as seems right—which isn't a small amount), and I've even been known to squeeze it into the bottom of my coffee cup, pour in hot coffee, stir, and then add a little half-and-half for a quick-and-easy faux mocha.

CHOCOLATE SAUCE

**MAKES ABOUT
8 FLUID OUNCES**

150 grams Chocolate Magic Dust (see page 74)

95 grams glucose syrup

2 fluid ounces water

2 fluid ounces brewed coffee

In a small saucepan, combine the chocolate dust, glucose syrup, water, and coffee, set the pan over medium heat, and bring the mixture to a boil. Turn down the heat so the pan doesn't boil over but the boil is maintained and cook for 2 minutes (set a timer!). Remove the pan from the heat, pour the contents into a bowl, and let cool to room temperature.

The sauce is now ready to use, or transfer it to an airtight container and refrigerate for up to 1 month (though I have a feeling it'll go much faster than that).

SAVE THAT COFFEE

Don't dump your leftover morning coffee. Designate a jar in your refrigerator, label it, and start saving. I like to add coffee to chocolate cake batter (see page 82), chocolate sauce (above), and even chocolate lollipops (see page 151). With a jar of coffee waiting in the refrigerator, you'll never need to brew small amounts of coffee specifically for a recipe.

I was eight when I gave my mom a Mother's Day card that read, "I love you so much I won't know what to do without a mother like you. I will bring you flowers and everything else—Candy, cookies, and cake." It's as if my eight-year-old self could see the future because I still don't know what to do without her, and I've managed to spend more than half of my adult life creating the "everything else."

My mom was good at cakes. Every year she'd make me a birthday cake in the shape of a bunny. She'd decorate it with candy—licorice, gumdrops, and pieces of chocolate—as the features of the bunny. For a lady who loved candy as much as she did, I'm sure it made her the happiest to bake and decorate a bunny cake for me, especially when it came to sneaking leftover candy. I've carried on the tradition, building bunny cakes for my own kid and delighting in his reaction to them year after year. The cake itself is as easy to make as it is chocolaty, and I think it's best topped with peanut butter buttercream. (If peanut butter won't work for you, feel free to use one of the infused-cream buttercreams on page 59.)

DARK CHOCOLATE BUNNY CAKE

MAKES TWO 8- OR 9-INCH ROUND CAKES AND ABOUT 6 CUPS BUTTERCREAM OR 1 BUNNY CAKE

MAKE THE CAKE Preheat the oven to 350°F. Grease two 8-inch round cake pans (or 9-inch pans if you don't have 8-inch pans) with a thin patina of unsalted butter, covering the bottoms and sides of the pans. Pour 1 tablespoon or so of granulated sugar into each pan and shake and tilt the pans so the sugar creates a uniform shimmer on the bottom and sides. Shake out the excess sugar, then line the bottom of each pan with a circle of parchment paper cut to fit. Your pans are ready for baking.

Sift together the flour, baking soda, baking powder, and salt into a bowl. Set aside. (Now would also be a good time to start thinking about the boiling coffee you'll need at the end of mixing the batter.)

Using a mixer fitted with the whisk attachment, combine the sugar and chocolate dust on low speed. Once the two are combined, you can begin adding the canola oil. With the mixer on medium speed, slowly yet steadily add the oil in a thin stream. Allow the mixer to spin until all

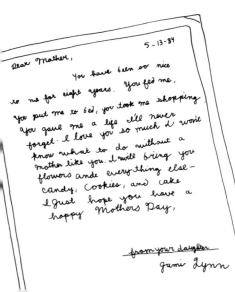

5-13-84

Dear Mother,

You have been so nice to me for eight years. You fed me, you put me to bed, you took me shopping. You gave me a life I'll never forget. I love you so much I won't know what to do without a mother like you. I will bring you flowers and everything else—candy, cookies, and cake. I just hope you have a happy Mothers Day,

from your daughter
Jami Lynn

FOR THE CAKE

Unsalted butter and granulated sugar, for preparing pans

210 grams all-purpose flour

8 grams baking soda

6 grams baking powder

5 grams kosher salt

254 grams granulated sugar

242 grams Chocolate Magic Dust (see page 74)

4 fluid ounces canola oil

2 large eggs, at room temperature, beaten until blended

8 fluid ounces whole milk

16 grams vanilla extract

8 fluid ounces brewed coffee, heated until boiling

FOR THE PEANUT BUTTER BUTTERCREAM

404 grams all-natural peanut butter (contains just peanuts and salt), at room temperature

340 grams unsalted butter, cut into 1-inch cubes, at room temperature

57 grams chèvre, at room temperature

156 grams powdered sugar, sifted

5 grams kosher salt

5 grams vanilla extract

Candies and other treats for decorating (see page 85)

of the oil is incorporated into the chocolate dust and sugar. At this point, the batter will resemble a thick brownie batter. Now add the beaten eggs, keeping the mixer running. Once the eggs are in, continue mixing until the contents of the mixer bowl are uniformly mixed and smoothed out a bit—it could take a full minute.

Next, add the milk, a bit at a time, allowing each addition to mix in fully before adding more. Add the vanilla and mix thoroughly. Now, stop the mixer, detach the whisk, and hold the whisk to manually whisk the contents of the bowl, paying special attention to anything at the bottom of the bowl that hasn't been mixed in yet.

Reattach the whisk and add the dry ingredients. Turn on the mixer speed to low and mix until the dry ingredients have disappeared.

With the mixer still on low speed, carefully add the hot coffee in a steady stream, then let the mixer run for about 30 seconds. Stop the mixer, detach the whisk, and again use it to whisk everything together manually. Carefully divide the cake batter evenly between the prepared pans.

Slide the pans into the oven and bake for about 35 minutes, until a tester inserted into the center of each cake comes out with only a few soft crumbs attached. Take care not to overbake the cakes.

Set the pans in their pans on cooling racks to cool for 20 minutes, then run a knife around the inside edge of each pan to loosen the cakes. Ease each cake out of its pan and onto a cooling rack. Allow the cakes to cool completely.

MIX THE BUTTERCREAM In a stand mixer fitted with the paddle attachment, beat together the peanut butter, butter, and chèvre on medium speed until smooth, creamy, and evenly mixed. (Room temperature ingredients are key and guarantee a lump-free, beautifully whipped buttercream.) Turn the mixer speed to low and add the powdered sugar, a little at a time, and continue to mix until all of the sugar is completely incorporated. Return the speed to medium, add the salt and vanilla, and mix until all of the ingredients are fully combined and the buttercream is light and fluffy, about 2 minutes. (The buttercream is now ready to use or it can be refrigerated for up to 3 days. Just be sure to cover it tightly before refrigerating and allow it to come to room temperature before using.)

CONTINUED

Use one cake to create ears and a bow tie.

Cut ear-shaped wedges in the cake—the wedges are the ears, the center part becomes the bow tie.

Place the ears at the top of the remaining whole cake, and the bow tie at the neck.

CUT THE CAKE AND ASSEMBLE THE BUNNY Cover a large cutting board or platter with a piece of parchment paper. Set the first cake on the prepared surface.

Now, take a look at the illustration. See how the ears are actually two wedges that are cut from the bottom and top of the second cake? Also notice that after the ears are cut away what's left is a hunk of cake that's the shape of a bow tie. Using a knife (and the illustration as a guide) make the cuts to transform the second cake into two ears and one bow tie. Set the ears atop the first cake like a bunny, then settle the "bow tie" section at the "neck" of the first cake.

DECORATE AND CREATE A BUNNY FACE Use an offset spatula to cover the entire cake in a very thin layer of buttercream. There will certainly be areas of cake peeking through, and that's perfectly fine. Keep going, taking care not to tear the cake while you seal in any renegade crumbs with this very light "crumb coat." Once the entire bunny is covered, slide the platter into the refrigerator to chill. When the crumb coat feels firm, take the platter from the refrigerator and slather the bunny with the remaining buttercream, taking care to seal in all the areas around the ears and the bow tie.

Now that your bunny is covered in a nice coat of buttercream, you'll add facial features using candy and other treats! **Let's start with ears:** Fill them in with bits of chopped-up marshmallow or wisps of cotton candy. **On to eyes:** With lots of care and a sharp kitchen knife, you can cut the stick off a lollipop right at the base of the candy. Use these as the eyes, placing a disc of chocolate or a slice of gumdrop on top to hide the stick and create cute pupils. **Nose:** A bit of gumdrop or a Dreams Come Chew cut into a triangle really works. **Cheeks and whiskers:** Dreams Come Chew are perfect—use just a bit of candy and shape it into flat rounds for cheeks. Use a complementary color for whiskers—roll a little candy into thin whiskers and give them a little twist prior to placing them on. **Mouth:** Caramel works perfectly! Just roll a bit of it into thin lines, then form the lines into two connecting curves. **Bow tie:** I like to get real crazy with the bow tie! Gumdrops, hard candies, bits of chocolate—anything goes! Just remember, it's your cake! Get as wacky as you want and make the best bunny you can imagine.

DECORATE WITH CANDY!

Marshmallows
Fluffy marshmallows create fun and fluffy ears.

Hard candy and gumdrops
Round candy can be arranged into polka dots for a very jazzy bow tie.

Dreams Come Chew or Caramels
Soft and stretchy candy can be magicked into cheeks, whiskers, and a mouth.

I like hot fudge warmed up and ladled onto ice cream, I like it cold as a cake filling, and I like to dip different treats, like cupcakes or strawberries or halves of cookies, into it. I rarely, rarely make hot fudge (unless I have a cake in the works), because if it's just sitting in my refrigerator, I will eat it as if it's yogurt, and no one needs to be doing that.

HOT FUDGE

MAKES ABOUT 1 PINT (OR 2 CUPS)

236 grams heavy cream

216 grams Chocolate Magic Dust (see page 74)

200 grams light brown sugar

114 grams unsalted butter

3 grams kosher salt

10 grams vanilla extract

In a medium saucepan, combine the cream, chocolate dust, brown sugar, butter, and salt. Set the pan over medium heat and stir the contents as the butter melts.

Bring the mixture to a simmer, now stirring only occasionally to encourage the chocolate dust to melt into the mixture. Once it's simmering, turn down the heat to medium-low and continue at a low simmer, stirring occasionally, for 2 minutes (set a timer!). When the 2 minutes are up, give the mixture a good whisking while still on the heat, then remove the pan from the heat and pour the contents into a heat-proof bowl. Add the vanilla and whisk until combined.

The hot fudge is now ready to use, or transfer it to an airtight container and refrigerate for up to 3 weeks. To reheat, use either a double boiler and reheat gently or (gasp!) a microwave and short bursts of power just until the fudge is molten. Don't allow it to boil or the fats will separate from the sugars, and you don't want that.

PEANUT BUTTER HOT FUDGE Once you've made the basic hot fudge, you can turn it into peanut butter hot fudge with the help of some room-temperature, well-stirred natural peanut butter (look for a brand that contains only peanuts and salt, no extra oils or sugar). After you've poured the cooked fudge into a bowl, allow it to cool for about 30 minutes, then stir in 3 tablespoons room-temperature peanut butter. (Room temperature is important here, or the peanut butter will not mix well with the fudge.) Peanut butter hot fudge makes a nice cake frosting and a hilarious (but so good) alternative to chips and dip at a party! Put it, cold or warm, in a small bowl and surround it with banana chips. It's like a party trick and a party snack all in one.

This dust makes everything you can make with Chocolate Magic Dust creamy, malty, and perfect. It's fantastic as ice cream, makes a great hot fudge (see page 86) for sundaes, and also produces the creamiest mug of hot chocolate you can imagine.

MALTED CHOCOLATE MAGIC DUST

MAKES ABOUT 290 GRAMS

215 grams Chocolate Magic Dust (see page 74)

75 grams malted milk powder

In a bowl, combine the chocolate dust and malted milk powder and whisk until the malted milk powder is completely incorporated.

The magic dust is now ready to use. Store in an airtight container or ziplock bags and keep in a cool, dry place for up to 6 months.

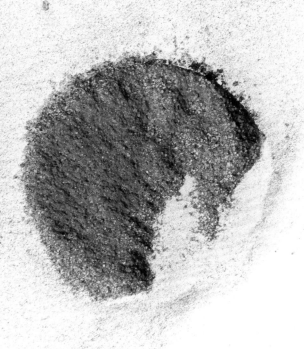

Chinese five-spice powder is a warming mix of spices that are familiar and unexpected at the same time. The sweetness of cinnamon is paired with astringent fennel and licorice-like anise, then combined with the sharpness of pepper; the final mix is balanced with the deep headiness of clove. I love this magic dust sprinkled on buttered toast or baked into just about everything. Plus, warm milk mixed with Five-Spice Magic Dust is a really nice way to say good-night.

FIVE-SPICE MAGIC DUST

MAKES ABOUT 520 GRAMS

500 grams granulated sugar

20 grams Chinese five-spice powder

Pour the sugar into a large bowl, add the five-spice powder, and whisk together until completely blended.

The magic dust is now ready to use. Store in an airtight container or ziplock bag and keep in a cool, dry place for up to 6 months.

ABOUT CINNAMON

From Ceylon to Vietnamese (Saigon), korintje to cassia, the variations of cinnamon are a delight to the (my) senses. I like to bake with Vietnamese cinnamon because of its intense aroma. You know how cinnamon gum and cinnamon candy smell so bold that it's clear the "cinnamon" in them is fake? That's how Vietnamese cinnamon smells—and it's completely real! Vibrant, rich, and spicy sweet, it's exactly what you think of when you think *cinnamon*.

At QUIN, we rely on Ceylon cinnamon for candy making because of its even, mellow cinnamon flavor with a blush of citrus notes. Its color is not as deep as that of Vietnamese cinnamon, and it's more palate-friendly, delivering absolutely zero bite—which makes it ideal for melding with other flavors in candy. Check the Resources Guide (see page 291) for tips on where to buy.

Yes, it's called Doughnut Magic Dust, but is it only for doughnuts? No. This cinnamony-sugary concoction is great stirred into oatmeal, makes the most perfect mug of warm milk, is terrific on toast, and renders softly scented yet hugely flavored popcorn.

DOUGHNUT MAGIC DUST

MAKES ABOUT 520 GRAMS

500 grams granulated sugar

10 grams ground cinnamon

5 grams vanilla bean powder (see page 57)

3 grams kosher salt

2 grams freshly grated nutmeg (see page 92)

Pour the sugar into a large bowl. Sift the cinnamon, vanilla bean powder, salt, and nutmeg directly over the sugar, and then whisk to combine.

The magic dust is now ready to use. Store in an airtight container or ziplock bags and keep in a cool, dry place for up to 6 months.

DOUGHNUT MAGIC DUST BUTTER

Soften 113 grams unsalted butter. In a bowl, cream together the butter and 3 tablespoons Doughnut Magic Dust. Scoop the butter out of the bowl and onto a piece of plastic wrap. Use the plastic wrap to shape the butter into a small log or disk, then wrap fully and refrigerate.

DOUGHNUT MAGIC DUST GLAZED APPLES

Peel, core, and dice 2 apples. Melt 2 tablespoons Doughnut Magic Dust Butter (above) in a skillet over medium heat. Add the apples and cook until slightly softened. Once the apples are soft and the sugar has caramelized a bit, remove the pan from the heat. Serve the warm apples over waffles, French toast, pancakes, or oatmeal. Or, chill the apples and stir into yogurt or cold cereal. The chilled apples are also good mixed into ice cream; Easy Vanilla Bean Ice Cream (see page 100) would be great, and Butter Pecan Ice Cream (see page 100) would be divine. (And yes, pears work quite nicely prepared this way, too.) Store in an airtight container in the refrigerator for up to 1 week.

CONTINUED

DOUGHNUT MAGIC DUST COOKIES

Replace a portion of the granulated sugar in your favorite ginger-molasses cookie recipe with Doughnut Magic Dust (see page 91). Even replacing ½ cup of plain granulated sugar with magic dust will add a ton of flavor to your cookies.

One of my very favorite scents on Earth is that of nutmeg. If I could have it my way, nutmeg would be my daily perfume—woodsy but sweet, with a bit of mystery. When used in something like Doughnut Magic Dust, I highly recommend freshly grated. The flavor is much more powerful than that of the preground stuff. Buy a little jar of whole nutmeg and get your hands on a Microplane; you really should have one anyway: citrus, cheese, nutmeg, chocolate—it will grate them all.

To grate a whole nutmeg, using medium pressure, scrape it in an up-and-down motion on a roughly 5-inch section of a Microplane for about 30 seconds. This will yield approximately 2 grams grated nutmeg. Repeat the action to arrive at the amount you need and then sprinkle it into your recipe. Don't forget to delight in the gorgeous nutmeg scent that will surround you.

I see it all the time. People are either really into sour candy or they are completely against it. For those who love sour, it's an addiction. They cannot get enough. Once they have it, they want more of it. This Sweet + Sour Magic Dust can cause that reaction, so watch out. It is the ideal accompaniment to lickable planks of hard candy reminiscent of the candy sticks with sugary dip from your childhood. (See page 154 to re-create this sweet dream for yourself.)

Candy dredged in sour stuff has such wide appeal that it's best just to go ahead and dip lollipops (see pages 118 to 154) and roll gumdrops (see pages 276 to 288) in this sweet-and-sour dust to add some lip-puckering fun to the mix. Citric acid has a tendency to break down moisture in candy and cause it to get sticky, so dip the candies in the dust when you know you'll be enjoying them that day.

SWEET + SOUR MAGIC DUST

MAKES ABOUT 250 GRAMS

200 grams granulated sugar

50 grams citric acid

In a medium bowl, combine the sugar and citric acid and whisk well to combine.

Transfer to an airtight container or ziplock bag and store in a cool, dry spot for up to 6 months.

Crystal sugar is a secret weapon. Easy to buy online or in cake-decorating stores, it can be flavored or colored and then sprinkled on cupcakes for decoration and on the tops of sweet buns for crunch. Use mint crystal sugar to finish a cup of hot chocolate; lemon crystal sugar is the perfect pucker atop strawberry shortcake. And vanilla crystal sugar? I'd go ahead and put it on everything. Check the Resources Guide (see page 292) for tips on purchasing crystal sugar and natural flavorings.

MAGIC SUGAR CRYSTALS
FLAVORED VARIETY

MAKES ABOUT 680 GRAMS

680 grams crystal sugar

6 grams natural flavoring (I like lemon, orange, or mint)

Line a sheet pan with a piece of parchment paper and set aside.

Weigh the sugar and flavoring directly into a bowl. Don some kitchen gloves or food-service gloves and use your fingers to blend the flavoring into the sugar. Pretend that you're almost polishing the sugar, rubbing handfuls of it with your fingers to disperse the flavoring evenly throughout.

Once the flavoring has been rubbed all through the sugar, pour the sugar onto the sheet pan and smooth it out in a flat layer. Allow the sugar to dry. This could take an hour or two, depending on how warm it is in your kitchen and what the weather is like. You'll know when the crystals are completely dry because they'll lose their clumpy texture.

When the sugar is dry, it's ready to use. Store in an airtight container in a cool and dry spot, away from direct sunlight, for up to 6 months.

MAGIC SUGAR CRYSTALS
TINTED VARIETY

MAKES ABOUT 680 GRAMS

680 grams crystal sugar

6 grams natural coloring, the shade of your choice

Line a sheet pan with a piece of parchment paper and set aside.

Weigh the sugar and coloring directly into a bowl. Don some kitchen gloves or food-service gloves and use your fingers to blend the coloring into the sugar. Pretend that you're almost polishing the sugar, rubbing handfuls of it with your fingers to disperse the coloring evenly throughout.

Once the coloring has been rubbed all through the sugar, pour the sugar onto the sheet pan and smooth it out in a flat a layer. Allow the sugar to dry. This could take an hour or two, depending on how warm it is in your kitchen and what the weather is like. You'll know when the crystals are completely dry because they'll lose their clumpy texture.

When the sugar is dry, it's ready to use. Store in an airtight container in a cool and dry spot, away from direct sunlight, for up to 6 months.

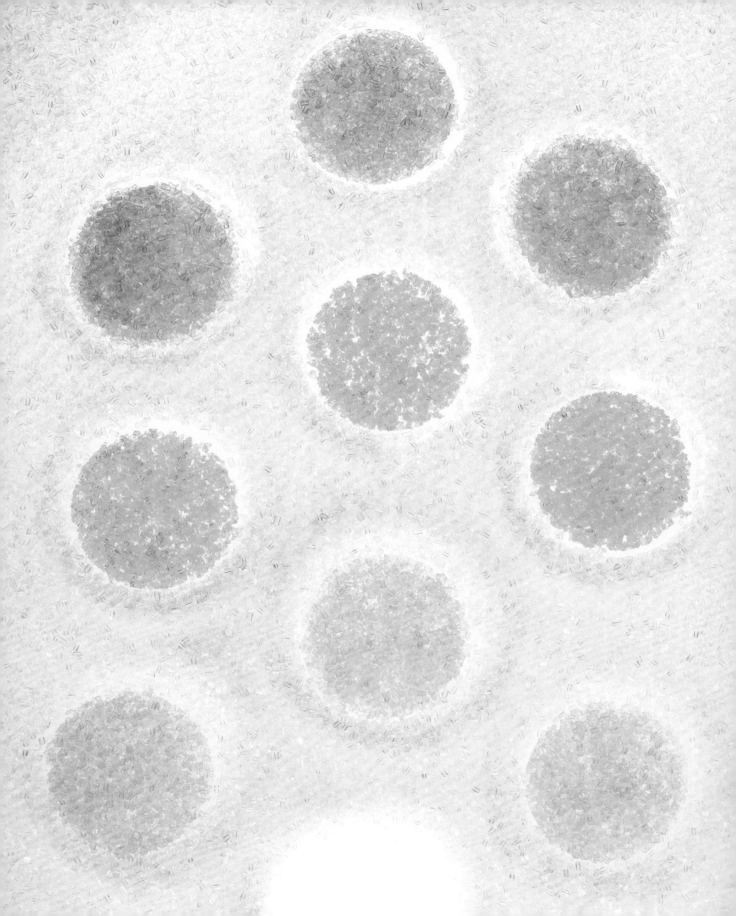

THE GIFT OF SPRINKLES

I often joke that if business goes sour at QUIN, we can always sell flavored and tinted magic sugar crystal sprinkles to pay the bills. I'm not sure what it is about crystal sprinkles, but I'm telling you, people love them and are willing to pay buckets of money for them. Save your bucket of money by learning to make them at home.

For storage and gift giving, I like using glass jars with screw tops. (These same jars work well for all of the magic dusts, especially if you prepare a little idea card explaining how to use the dusts. Get crazy and present a special someone with a trio of jars—Chocolate Magic Dust, mint Magic Sugar Crystals, and Doughnut Magic Dust will make nearly anyone happy.) See the Resources Guide (page 294) for information on obtaining the perfect screw-top jars, then make some sprinkles, fill the jars, and get to giving.

EASY ICE CREAMS

It hardly seems fair to even call these recipes when they're actually more like cheats. Here's the thing, many of the infused creams you've learned to make can be transformed, almost instantly into ice cream. I know it sounds almost like magic, and it sort of is, but there's a method to the magic.

This method of making ice cream produces a result that's best enjoyed within two or three days of churning. There are no emulsifiers or ingredients to extend shelf life, so don't put off enjoying your delights. That said, if there's a particular ice cream recipe you already love, by all means, follow it. But you should also incorporate what you've learned so far—the infused creams, roasted fruit purées, and syrups can be used to make great ice cream bases. And the caramels, marshmallows, and other ideas that are coming up all provide endless inspiration.

Consider this a base recipe. Learn it and you'll possess the key to coffee, strawberry, praline, and other great ice cream flavors in no time. It's the type of "recipe" that impels me to make long lists of possibilities. While not being able to sleep would normally be something I wouldn't be very happy about, if it's ice cream that's keeping me up, how can I possibly complain?

EASY VANILLA BEAN ICE CREAM

MAKES ABOUT 1 PINT; SERVES 4

Double batch (470 grams) Vanilla Bean Cream (page 61)

100 grams granulated sugar

Pour the vanilla cream into a small saucepan and set the pan over medium-low heat. Allow the cream to warm just until it's steamy, stirring occasionally so it doesn't scorch on the bottom of the pan. This will take between 10 and 15 minutes.

Once the cream is steamy, add the sugar and stir to mix. Keep the pan on the heat for 2 to 3 minutes more, stirring with a spoon so the sugar dissolves. Pull up a little of the cream from the bottom of the pan with the spoon and then let it pour off the spoon slowly, looking for undissolved sugar as the cream falls back into the pan. Repeat this test until you no longer see undissolved sugar.

Remove the pan from the heat, pour the contents into a heat-proof bowl, and allow the mixture to cool completely. Cover and refrigerate the ice cream base for at least several hours or up to overnight.

Pour the chilled ice cream base into an ice cream maker and churn according to the manufacturer's instructions. Transfer to a freezer-safe container and store in the freezer for up to 3 days.

COFFEE OR BUTTER PECAN ICE CREAM Proceed as directed, replacing the 100 grams granulated sugar with 125 grams Coffee Syrup (page 68) for coffee ice cream.

I also like to use Praline Syrup (page 70) in place of the sugar, along with a handful of buttered and toasted pecans, to make quick work of butter pecan ice cream. (You can use any of the syrups from chapter two in the vanilla ice cream base the same way you use the coffee or praline syrups.)

DOUGHNUT MAGIC DUST ICE CREAM Proceed as directed, replacing the 100 grams granulated sugar with 125 grams Doughnut Magic Dust (see page 91).

FIVE-SPICE MAGIC DUST ICE CREAM Proceed as directed, replacing the 100 grams granulated sugar with 125 grams of Five-Spice Magic Dust (see page 89).

SWIRL YOUR ICE CREAM

From peanut butter to cookie crumbles, salted nuts to melted marshmallow, you can create swirly, crunchy ice cream that is sure to impress. I usually add ¼ to ½ cup of extras to a pint of ice cream. I wait until the ice cream is just about as frozen as my machine will get it, then I sprinkle or spoon in the good stuff and continue to churn until it's mixed in completely. Next, I scoop the concoction out of my machine and into a container and then I shove that container into the freezer as quickly as possible. This is the only way I know how to keep myself from eating it all. Good luck.

I love all ice cream, but I particularly love this pretty pink strawberry ice cream. It's simple to make because it starts with my Easy Vanilla Bean Ice Cream and adds strawberry purée to it.

To create other fruit-flavored ice creams, swap out the strawberry purée for any of the other roasted fruit purée recipes starting on page 42.

STRAWBERRY ICE CREAM

MAKES ABOUT 1 PINT; SERVES 4

470 grams Easy Vanilla Bean Ice Cream base (see page 100), prepared but not churned

125 grams roasted strawberry purée (see page 37)

After the ice cream base has cooled for 10 minutes, stir in the strawberry purée and let cool completely. Cover and refrigerate for at least several hours or up to overnight.

Pour the chilled ice cream base into an ice cream maker and churn according to the manufacturer's instructions. Transfer to a freezer-safe container and store in the freezer for up to 3 days.

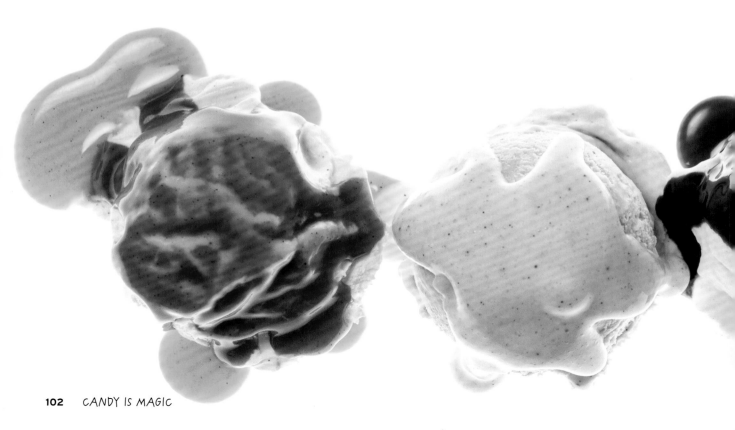

This is an excellent spin on Easy Vanilla Bean Ice Cream because chocolate sauce is brought into play. When you're scooping this ice cream into bowls for dessert (or for breakfast or lunch—that's fine, too), top it with some salty roasted peanuts. And if it's a party? Don't forget the sprinkles.

CHOCOLATE SWIRL ICE CREAM

**MAKES ABOUT 1 PINT;
SERVES 4**

1 pint Easy Vanilla Bean
Ice Cream (see page 100),
freshly churned

120 grams Chocolate Sauce
(see page 81)

Scoop one-fourth of the ice cream into a freezer-safe container, and then spoon about one-fourth of the chocolate sauce on top of it. Repeat this ice cream–sauce layering until all of the ice cream has been removed from the ice cream maker and is nestled between nice layers of the sauce. Take a clean spoon and swirl the ice cream with the sauce a bit, then cover the container and place in the freezer until firm, or up to 3 days. If you just can't wait until it's firm, you really can eat it any time you like—just know it will be more like soft serve than hard scoop.

Why magic? Mainly because this ice cream recipe calls for just two simple ingredients. Just two! And the method couldn't be easier. Warm the cream, whisk in the dust, chill, and then churn in your ice cream maker. But the real reason I call this magic? Because it's so good; so rich, so chocolatey, so perfect.

CHOCOLATE MAGIC DUST ICE CREAM

MAKES ABOUT 1 PINT; SERVES 4

16 fluid ounces heavy cream

135 grams Chocolate Magic Dust (see page 74)

Pour the cream into a small saucepan and set it over low heat to warm gently. When the cream is warm, add the chocolate dust and whisk until it melts. If you're having trouble getting the dust to melt completely into the cream, just continue to whisk while the pan is still over low heat.

Pour the ice cream base into a container, cover tightly, and refrigerate for at least a few hours or up to overnight.

Give the chilled chocolaty cream a good shake (or a good whisking if it's not in a shakable container), pour it into an ice cream maker, and churn according to the manufacturer's instructions.

Scoop the ice cream into a freezer-safe container and freeze for a few hours or until hard (if you can wait that long) before serving.

FLAVOR GUIDE

Chocolate Magic Dust Ice Cream can shift
and change into a million different flavors.
Okay, I might be exaggerating a bit, but it
really is virtually limitless in possibility.
Here are some of my favorites:

CHOCOLATE + ANCHO CHILE ICE CREAM
Substitute Pepper Cream (see page 64) made with ancho chile
powder for the plain cream and proceed as directed.

CHOCOLATE + ORANGE ICE CREAM
Substitute Orange Cream (see page 60) for the plain
cream and proceed as directed.

CHOCOLATE + MALTED MILK ICE CREAM
Substitute Malted Milk Cream (see page 58) for the
plain cream and proceed as directed.

CHOCOLATE + PEPPERMINT ICE CREAM
Substitute Peppermint Tea Cream (see page 63)
for the plain cream and proceed as directed.

CHOCOLATE + COFFEE ICE CREAM
Substitute Coffee Cream (see page 55) for the plain
cream and proceed as directed.

Do you like pie? How about pie with ice cream? Yes. (Yes to both, I hope.) This ice cream is truly at home alongside a slice of pie. Everything from apple to pumpkin (and especially pecan); nestle a scoop onto a plate and serve it with pie. (Note: Chai Tea Ice Cream's deliciousness factor is in no way compromised when not served with pie. It's just that pie is so good. Especially when served with this ice cream.)

CHAI TEA ICE CREAM

MAKES ABOUT 1 PINT; SERVES 4

Double batch (440 grams) Chai Tea Cream (see page 63)

100 grams light brown sugar

Pour the chai cream into a small saucepan and set the pan over medium-low heat. Allow the cream to warm just until it's steamy, stirring occasionally so it doesn't scorch on the bottom of the pan. This will take between 10 and 15 minutes.

Once the cream is steamy, add the brown sugar and stir to mix. Keep the pan on the heat for 2 to 3 minutes more, stirring with a spoon so the sugar dissolves. Pull up a little of the cream from the bottom of the pan with the spoon and then let it pour off the spoon slowly, looking for undissolved sugar as the cream falls back into the pan. Repeat this test until you no longer see undissolved sugar.

Remove the pan from the heat, pour the contents into a heat-proof bowl, and allow the mixture to cool completely. Cover and refrigerate the ice cream base for at least several hours or up to overnight.

Pour the chilled ice cream base into an ice cream maker and churn according to the manufacturer's instructions. Transfer to a freezer-safe container and store in the freezer for up to 3 days.

Popcorn Ice Cream is something you should delight in at least a few times in your life. It makes an excellent sundae with a drizzle of warm caramel sauce and a topping of Every Day, Popcorn (see page 54).

POPCORN ICE CREAM

MAKES ABOUT 1 PINT; SERVES 4

Double Batch (540 grams) Popcorn Cream (see page 52)

125 grams light brown sugar

Pour the popcorn cream into a small saucepan and set the pan over medium-low heat. Allow the cream to warm just until it's steamy, stirring occasionally so it doesn't scorch on the bottom of the pan. This will take between 10 and 15 minutes.

Once the cream is steamy, add the brown sugar and stir to mix. Keep the pan on the heat for 2 to 3 minutes more, stirring with a spoon so the sugar dissolves. Pull up a little of the cream from the bottom of the pan with the spoon and then let it pour off the spoon slowly, looking for undissolved sugar as the cream falls back into the pan. Repeat this test until you no longer see undissolved sugar.

Remove the pan from the heat, pour the contents into a heat-proof bowl, and allow the mixture to cool completely. Cover and refrigerate the ice cream base for at least several hours or up to overnight.

Pour the chilled ice cream base into an ice cream maker and churn according to the manufacturer's instructions. Transfer to a freezer-safe container and store in the freezer for up to 3 days.

CHAPTER THREE

LOLLIPOPS

MAGIC ON A STICK

It wasn't until I made my first fruity lollipop (with Oregon strawberries) that I fell under the spell of hard candy. To see that beautiful, transparent pink candy on a stick, to hold it up to the light and see it full of tiny strawberry seeds, and to know that I made it with my hands? It's as close to wizardry as I'll ever get in my life.

I've made hard candy in every shape I could dream of—lollipops, three-dimensional rectangles, round drops, lozenges, jewels, flat sticks, mustaches, bunnies, and even the state of Ohio. Hard candy is magic because it can be made into any shape you want. That said, I find it's easiest to begin with the most famous hard candy of all, the lollipop.

Just as the shapes of hard candy are vast and varied, so are the methods for adding flavor. In this chapter, I focus on my five favorite lollipop methods.

* Lollipops made with roasted fruit purée and natural flavoring
* Lollipops made with citrus zest
* Sour lollipops
* Lollipops made with reductions and syrups
* Lollipops made with butter, chocolate, and other bakery-inspired flavors

Hard candy has to cook to a specific temperature to achieve that "hard crack" status. Because the candy takes on no color as it cooks, it's difficult to tell what's going on in the pot. A thermometer takes the guesswork out, and you'll be able to achieve that hard crack every time.

LOLLIPOP TECHNIQUE

Like I said, I've made lots of hard candy in my time, in all shapes and sizes, but my favorite remains the lollipop. There's something about candy on a stick that I just adore, and I know I'm not alone. At QUIN, we sell an awful lot of lollipops around Mother's Day, when we gather a mix of flavors and colors and tie them together to make beautiful candy bouquets (see how you can do the same on page 132). Before we get to the recipes, let's examine the lollipop process from start to finish.

PREPARE A LOLLIPOP STATION

Before you make a batch of candy for lollipops, it's best to think through your end result. Let's start with a discussion of using lollipop molds or doing without. A mold produces a perfectly round lollipop. The recipes in this chapter were written with a 1½-inch round lollipop mold in mind. If you'd rather not use a mold, you can always make beautiful lollipops by arranging lollipop sticks on a nonstick mat and pouring the hot candy over one end of them.

MOLD

If you're using a lollipop mold, you'll need to prepare enough cavities to hold about 60 lollipops. To do this, you'll want to brush each cavity with just the slightest shimmer of vegetable oil. The best way to do this is to tip a bit of oil onto a paper towel and dab the mold cavities with the towel. Take special care to wipe only the smallest amount of oil in each cavity—you're not looking to taste it; you're just looking for help in getting a clean release from the molds. After some experimenting, you may find that your candy releases just fine from the mold with no oiling at all. If that's the case, lucky you! You can skip this step. Once the mold has been prepped with oil (or not), place a lollipop stick in each of the openings.

NONSTICK MAT

If you're pouring your lollipops onto nonstick mats, I have some good advice for you: create a lollipop template. It's what we do at QUIN, and it's very helpful when trying to produce uniform lollipops without a mold. Most nonstick mats are nearly see-through, which means you can slide the template under the mat and use it as a visual target for exactly how big to make your lollipops. Using a marker and pieces of butcher paper or parchment paper, draw 1½-inch circles all over the paper, spacing them about 2 inches apart. Place the template under the nonstick mat and then place the lollipop sticks partway into each lollipop target on the template. Now you have a place to aim the hot candy that's coming out of the funnel or cup.

THERMOMETER

Accurate temperatures are key in getting hard candy just right. Here's how to temp candy: Give the pot a single swirl, then stick the thermometer in the center of the pot, without touching the bottom. In a few seconds the thermometer will give you a temperature reading. Repeat this action as the candy is cooking—eventually arriving at the correct temperature. Between temp tests, give the sensor a wipe with a damp towel to remove any hardened candy that could interfere with accurate readings.

FUNNEL OR SPOUTED CUP

You'll need a candy funnel or spouted cup (see page 24) to pour the hot candy into a mold or onto a stick. Neither vessel needs any preparation other than to be clean and dry.

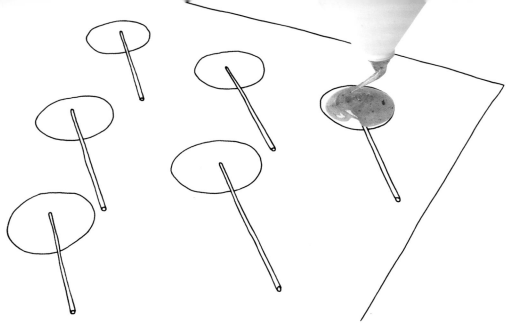

COOKING AND POURING THE CANDY

The cooking is easy—follow the recipes, use a thermometer, and you'll have lollipop candy ready for sticks in no time.

Once the candy is ready, you'll pour it into a candy funnel or spouted cup, then you'll pour a little candy into each prepared mold cavity or on top of sticks that you've placed on a nonstick mat. Whether you're using a funnel or a cup with a spout, always pour a little less candy than you think you should, as the candy will expand as it settles. (If you've ever made pancakes, you kind of know how this goes.) Another tip for both methods: Work quickly, because the candy begins to cool as soon as you take it off the heat; and the colder it gets, the thicker it becomes, and the more difficult it is to pour. Another disadvantage of cold candy? Waste! You can't reheat the candy to make it pourable again, so you really want to get as much out of the funnel or cup as you can. Sounds like a lot of pressure, but it's not. Once you get the hang of it, you won't think twice about timing because you'll be pouring lollipops like you were born to do it.

To pour with a funnel: First, check to make sure the stopper is blocking the hole in the bottom of the funnel. Then carefully fill the funnel with hot candy. With the opening of the funnel very close to the mold cavity or mat target, slowly lift the stopper to allow the hot candy to flow through. Start slowly and maintain a slow and steady hand, closing the stopper before you think you should (remember, the candy will expand) and moving on to the next target or mold cavity. If you've made a lollipop that's too small, you can always add a little more candy. But making a huge lollipop smaller? Downright impossible. Repeat this process until you've used all of the candy.

To pour with a spouted cup: Carefully fill the cup with hot candy. Tip the spout toward the mold cavity or mat target to fill it, tipping the cup back before the cavity or target is completely full. Repeat this process until you've used all of the candy.

SOAK THE EQUIPMENT

Immediately after you've poured your last lollipop (and while your lollipops are cooling), plop the funnel (or spouted cup) and the whisk into your cooking pot, carry the pot over to your sink, and fill the pot with hot water. The water will start the loosening process, releasing the sugary candy from the sides of the pot—and making cleanup so much easier. I'm rarely as frustrated with myself as I am when I realize I've forgotten to soak my pot. This soaking rule applies to every candy recipe, not just hard candies. If you're on dish duty, you'll thank me, I promise.

WRAP THE CANDY

Always allow lollipops to cool completely before wrapping them. My favorite test is to remove a lollipop from the mold or mat and hold it to the back of my wrist. When I can feel no warmth at all, I know the lollipops are ready to wrap. The lollipops on the mat are easy to pick up. For lollipops in molds, you'll need to press your fingers gently across the back of the mold until the candy loosens and eventually pops out.

To wrap each lollipop, place a 5-inch square cellophane wrapper on your work surface and set the lollipop on the center of the cellophane, positioning the top of the lollipop just below the center line of the cellophane (yes, you have to imagine the center line). Fold the wrapper down onto the lollipop; the top of the wrapper should now pretty much align with the bottom of the wrapper, enclosing the candy. Fold each side to the back of the lollipop, then gather all of the cellophane at the bottom of the lollipop with the stick at the center and give the cellophane a good twist. I suggest you secure the cellophane with a twist tie.

Lollipops should be stored in a cool and dry place. After about 6 months, you may start to notice what looks like a white coating growing from the lollipops (and it is!). That's the sugar doing its best to recrystallize. They're still fine to eat (if you have them around that long).

LOLLIPOPS MADE WITH ROASTED FRUIT PURÉE AND NATURAL FLAVORING

Creating beautiful hard candies with blackberry seeds or bits of cherry skin suspended in translucent sweetness is one of my favorite ways to work with sugar. Alone, the fruit in a lollipop adds color, texture, and those gorgeous seed and skin attributes. But where the fruit needs a little help is in the flavor department. Because hard candy is cooked to such a high temperature, a lot of the flavor of the fruit disappears. To make up for that, I like to add a bit of natural flavoring. The real fruit combined with the natural flavoring results in hard candy that looks and tastes exactly like the fruit from which it is derived.

I have a couple of companies that I rely on for natural flavorings (see page 292). When buying flavorings, there are two important details to consider: suitability for high-heat applications and strength of flavor. Many flavorings and extracts made with alcohol evaporate quickly when added to hot liquid candy. In contrast, emulsions and oils specifically made for use with high heat are ideal for flavoring hard candies because the flavor compounds don't evaporate. In terms of strength, all of the recipes you'll find in this book were tested (and are made regularly at QUIN) with concentrated flavorings. Don't worry too much, of course, if you choose a flavoring brand and realize it doesn't produce the flavor or strength you want; you'll know to make adjustments next time.

Lollipops made with roasted fruit purée and natural flavoring all begin pretty much the same way: cooking sugar, glucose syrup, and water in a pot to a specific temperature. Once that temperature is met, the fruit purée and flavoring are added.

Here's a recipe for fruit lollipops made with roasted strawberry purée and natural flavoring, followed by a flavor guide for creating jewel-like lollipops using other fruit purées from chapter two. Wrap the finished lollipops as directed on page 115.

STRAWBERRY LOLLIPOPS

**MAKES ABOUT SIXTY
1½-INCH LOLLIPOPS**

267 grams glucose syrup

400 grams granulated sugar

150 grams water

20 grams roasted strawberry purée (see page 37)

18 grams natural strawberry flavoring

Set up the lollipop station as directed on page 112.

Weigh the glucose syrup, sugar, and water directly into a heavy-bottomed pot, then set the pot over medium-high heat and bring the lollipop syrup to a boil. Once the syrup is boiling, swirl the pot often to make sure the sugar is cooking evenly. At first the syrup will bubble fast and light. Then it starts to slow down and the bubbles get a bit slower and thicker. This means the syrup is nearly ready.

Test the temperature of the syrup; as soon as it reaches 315°F, remove the pot from the heat. Give the candy syrup a good stir, then add the strawberry purée and the strawberry flavoring. (If you are making one of the variations, add any substitutions at this point.) Whisk together the contents of the pot until the candy no longer looks foamy and any active bubbling has stopped.

Using great care, immediately pour the syrup into a candy funnel or spouted cup and pour the lollipops as directed on page 114. Let the lollipops sit for about 30 minutes, until completely cool and hard. They are now ready for wrapping.

FLAVOR GUIDE

Use the following guide to create new lollipop flavors by substituting the suggestions for the roasted strawberry purée and natural strawberry flavoring used to create Strawberry Lollipops. Now's the perfect time to use those roasted fruit purées you mastered in chapter two.

APRICOT LOLLIPOPS

32 grams roasted apricot purée (see page 47)

6 grams natural apricot flavoring

BLUEBERRY LOLLIPOPS

32 grams roasted blueberry purée (see page 46)

6 grams natural blueberry flavoring

PEACH LOLLIPOPS

32 grams roasted peach purée (see page 49)

6 grams natural peach flavoring

CHERRY LOLLIPOPS

15 grams roasted cherry purée (see page 44)

6 grams natural cherry flavoring

RASPBERRY LOLLIPOPS

32 grams roasted raspberry purée (see page 43)

6 grams natural raspberry flavoring

3 grams vanilla bean powder (see page 57)

BLACKBERRY LOLLIPOPS

32 grams roasted blackberry purée (see page 42)

6 grams natural blackberry flavoring

5 grams citric acid

BLACKBERRY + TANGERINE LOLLIPOPS

15 grams roasted blackberry purée (see page 42)

12 grams natural tangerine or orange flavoring

3 grams natural blackberry flavoring

2 grams citric acid

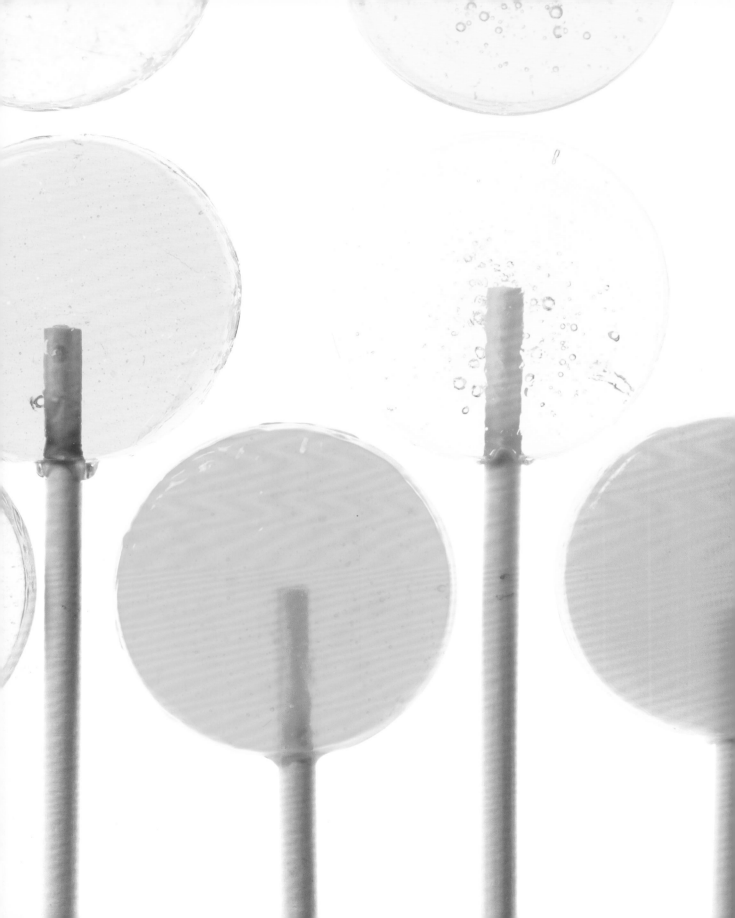

LOLLIPOPS MADE WITH CITRUS ZEST

Just as roasted fruit purées can make beautiful lollipops, so do citrus fruit zests. The following recipes come together the same way as lollipops made with roasted fruit purée, but zest replaces the purée.

We use natural coloring in our zest-flavored recipes, and they react in high-heat applications in the same way natural flavorings do. When selecting a natural coloring, be sure to pick one that can withstand high heat.

A ray of candy sunshine, these zippy orange lollipops are bright and tangy. My favorite way to enjoy them is with a Surprise Inside (see page 138)—I prepare the candy for the lollipops, then add a chewy chocolate center. The orange candy wraps itself around the chocolate chew and the result is beautiful—bright orange candy with that visible chocolate center. (Highly recommend.)

ORANGE LOLLIPOPS

MAKES ABOUT SIXTY 1½-INCH LOLLIPOPS

267 grams glucose syrup

400 grams granulated sugar

150 grams water

12 grams natural orange flavoring

2 grams finely grated orange zest

2 grams citric acid

2 grams natural orange coloring

Set up the lollipop station as directed on page 112.

Weigh the glucose syrup, sugar, and water directly into a heavy-bottomed pot, then set the pot over medium-high heat and bring the lollipop syrup to a boil. Once the syrup is boiling, swirl the pot often to make sure the sugar is cooking evenly. At first the syrup will bubble fast and light. Then it starts to slow down and the bubbles get a bit slower and thicker. This means the syrup is nearly ready.

Test the temperature of the syrup; as soon as it reaches 315°F, remove the pot from the heat. Give the candy syrup a good stir, then add the orange flavoring, orange zest, citric acid, and orange coloring. (If you are making one of the variations, add the substitutions at this point.) Whisk together the contents of the pot until the candy no longer looks foamy and any active bubbling has stopped.

Using great care, immediately pour the syrup into a candy funnel or spouted cup and pour the lollipops as directed on page 114. Let the lollipops sit for about 30 minutes, until completely cool and hard. They are now ready for wrapping.

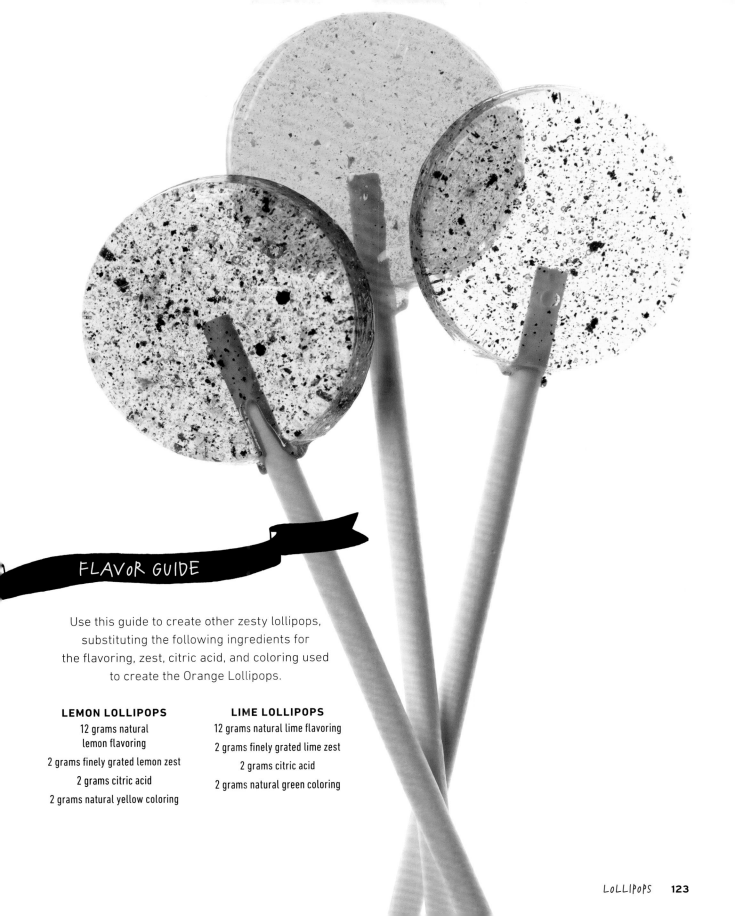

Use this guide to create other zesty lollipops,
substituting the following ingredients for
the flavoring, zest, citric acid, and coloring used
to create the Orange Lollipops.

LEMON LOLLIPOPS
12 grams natural
lemon flavoring

2 grams finely grated lemon zest

2 grams citric acid

2 grams natural yellow coloring

LIME LOLLIPOPS
12 grams natural lime flavoring

2 grams finely grated lime zest

2 grams citric acid

2 grams natural green coloring

SOUR LOLLIPOPS

These lip-puckering lollipops are perfectly tart. Any fruit flavoring, from cherry to orange to apple to lemon to raspberry, can be made sour. Use the cherry recipe as a template and incorporate any flavoring you'd like from the flavor guide that follows. Color is also up to you. At QUIN, we color our sour cherry lollipops red and our sour orange lollipops orange, but we add no color to our sour apple lollipops and they turn out a lovely russet.

I know you know this person—the person who loves sour stuff so much that even the most sour candy isn't lip-puckering enough? My favorite sour-loving friend buys citric acid powder in bulk and then actually dips sour candy into the powder to make it even more sour. It's really one of my favorite things to watch (while cringing). These sour lollipops are just the right amount of tart—nothing over the top, but certainly not tame.

SOUR CHERRY LOLLIPOPS

MAKES ABOUT SIXTY 1½-INCH LOLLIPOPS

267 grams glucose syrup

400 grams granulated sugar

120 grams water

12 grams natural cherry flavoring

24 grams citric acid

3 grams natural coloring (red, orange, green, or yellow)

Set up the lollipop station as directed on page 112.

Weigh the glucose syrup, sugar, and water directly into a heavy-bottomed pot, then set the pot over medium-high heat and bring the lollipop syrup to a boil. Once the syrup is boiling, swirl the pot often to make sure the sugar is cooking evenly. At first the syrup will bubble fast and light. Then it starts to slow down and the bubbles get a bit slower and thicker. This means the syrup is nearly ready.

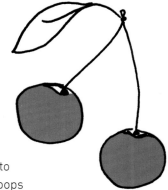

Test the temperature of the syrup; as soon as it reaches 315°F, remove the pot from the heat. Give the candy syrup a good stir, then add the cherry flavoring, citric acid, and coloring. (If you are making one of the variations, add the substitutions at this point.) Whisk together the contents of the pot until the candy no longer looks foamy and any active bubbling has stopped.

Using great care, immediately pour the syrup into a candy funnel or spouted cup and pour the lollipops as directed on page 114. Let the lollipops sit for about 30 minutes, until completely cool and hard. They are now ready for wrapping.

FLAVOR GUIDE

Use the following guide to create other lip-puckering lollipop flavors by substituting the suggestions for the cherry flavoring, citric acid, and coloring used to create the Sour Cherry Lollipops.

SOUR ORANGE LOLLIPOPS
12 grams natural orange flavoring
24 grams citric acid
3 grams natural orange coloring

SOUR APPLE LOLLIPOPS
12 grams natural apple flavoring
24 grams citric acid

SOUR LEMON LOLLIPOPS
12 grams natural lemon flavoring
24 grams citric acid
3 grams natural yellow coloring

SOUR RASPBERRY LOLLIPOPS
12 grams natural raspberry flavoring
24 grams citric acid
2 grams natural red coloring

LOLLIPOPS MADE WITH REDUCTIONS AND SYRUPS

One great way to use the syrups and reductions in chapter two is to make lollipops. I'm partial to coffee-flavored lollipops because I can't resist anything with coffee, but we find that wine-flavored lollipops are a big hit at QUIN with just about anyone who likes drinking wine.

I'm more than happy to put my sugary thinking cap on to come up with unique ways to highlight artisanal products. At QUIN, I've been able to work out some of the best, strongest partnerships with coffee roasters and coffee shops who want to add something extra to their customer experience by offering candy made with their coffees. This recipe calls for the Coffee Syrup from chapter two and for a tiny amount of salt. It's a great combination, as you'll see.

COFFEE LOLLIPOPS

MAKES ABOUT SIXTY 1½-INCH LOLLIPOPS

267 grams glucose syrup

400 grams granulated sugar

150 grams water

85 grams Coffee Syrup (see page 68)

3 grams vanilla extract

2 grams kosher salt

Set up the lollipop station as directed on page 112.

Weigh the glucose syrup, sugar, and water directly into a heavy-bottomed pot, then set the pot over medium-high heat and bring the lollipop syrup to a boil. Once the syrup is boiling, swirl the pot often to make sure the sugar is cooking evenly. At first the syrup will bubble fast and light. Then it starts to slow down and the bubbles get a bit slower and thicker. This means the syrup is nearly ready.

Test the temperature of the syrup; as soon as it reaches 315°F, remove the pot from the heat. Give the candy syrup a good stir, then add the coffee syrup, vanilla, and salt. Whisk together the contents of the pot until the candy no longer looks foamy and any active bubbling has stopped.

Using great care, immediately pour the syrup into a candy funnel or spouted cup and pour the lollipops as directed on page 114. Let the lollipops sit for about 30 minutes, until completely cool and hard. They are now ready for wrapping.

I'm not ashamed to admit that I've enjoyed many a glass of sweet tea in my life—likely from a mason jar and even more likely while sitting on a screened porch in the summertime. These lollipops remind me of those days. Just like sweet tea with a slice of lemon squeezed in, the first taste that hits you is the refreshing citrus—sweet, not sour—followed by the complex flavor of the tea. One of my favorite attributes of this candy is that the first lick always tastes different from the last.

SWEET TEA WITH LEMON LOLLIPOPS

MAKES ABOUT SIXTY 1½-INCH LOLLIPOPS

267 grams glucose syrup

400 grams granulated sugar

150 grams water

85 grams Tea Syrup (see page 69)

1 gram natural lemon flavoring

Set up the lollipop station as directed on page 112.

Weigh the glucose syrup, sugar, and water directly into a heavy-bottomed pot, then set the pot over medium-high heat and bring the lollipop syrup to a boil. Once the syrup is boiling, swirl the pot often to make sure the sugar is cooking evenly. At first the syrup will bubble fast and light. Then it starts to slow down and the bubbles get a bit slower and thicker. This means the syrup is nearly ready.

Test the temperature of the syrup; as soon as it reaches 315°F, remove the pot from the heat. Give the candy syrup a good stir, then add the tea syrup and lemon flavoring. Whisk together the contents of the pot until the candy no longer looks foamy and any active bubbling has stopped.

Using great care, immediately pour the syrup into a candy funnel or spouted cup and pour the lollipops as directed on page 114. Let the lollipops sit for about 30 minutes, until completely cool and hard. They are now ready for wrapping.

LOLLIPOP BOUQUET

I love to gather 8 to 12 lollipops together and then secure their sticks with ribbon. It creates a "bouquet" that's perfect for any occasion at which you would give flowers. Lollipop bouquets make inspired teacher gifts, great surprises for Mom or Grandma, and terrific shower (bridal, baby, whatever you shower) favors. Here's what you'll need:

* 8 to 12 lollipops of your choice
* Twine or ribbon
* To/From tag

Gather the lollipops together in a tight bundle. Take a length of twine or ribbon and secure the bundle by wrapping it around the sticks a few times and then tying the ends into a bow. Now you are ready to attach a To/From tag and give the bouquet away.

to: Sharon
love, Jami

Union Wine Company makes wine and QUIN makes candy—and together, we have made some serious magic. What I love about working with Union is that they embrace big ideas. Pinot Noir cotton candy spun on-site at a food festival? Yes. Gumdrops made with rosé? Yes. Pinot Gris caramel-coated popcorn? Yes. Sparkling wine–flavored candy that actually fizzes in your mouth? Another yes. I've had so much fun working with Union wines—every project seems a little crazier than the last, but we always seem to make the crazy work.

While special projects for specific events are fun, I've also worked extensively with Union to create candies that each of us can market and sell. Some of our best sellers are wine-flavored lollipops. While developing the lollipop recipes, I was always solidly satisfied with the fruity overtones of the candy. But, because the alcohol present in the wine is removed in the cooking process, I was continually disappointed that the candy never tasted of booze. So I went through every ingredient I could think of that might impart the boozy flavor that was lost and finally landed on a combination of apple cider vinegar and instant yeast. Stirred into the sugar syrup after it has come to temperature, this was all the candy needed to taste exactly like fruity wine.

PINOT GRIS LOLLIPOPS

MAKES ABOUT SIXTY 1½-INCH LOLLIPOPS

267 grams glucose syrup

400 grams granulated sugar

130 grams Pinot Gris reduction (see page 71)

16 grams apple cider vinegar

2 grams finely grated lemon zest

2 grams instant yeast

2 grams natural raspberry flavoring

1 gram citric acid

Set up the lollipop station as directed on page 112.

Weigh the glucose syrup, sugar, and wine reduction directly into a heavy-bottomed pot, then set the pot over medium-high heat and bring the lollipop syrup to a boil. Once the syrup is boiling, swirl the pot often to make sure the sugar is cooking evenly. At first the syrup will bubble fast and light. Then it starts to slow down and the bubbles get a bit slower and thicker. This means the syrup is nearly ready.

Test the temperature of the syrup; as soon as it reaches 315°F, remove the pot from the heat. Give the candy syrup a good stir, then add the vinegar, lemon zest, yeast, raspberry flavoring, and citric acid. Whisk together the contents of the pot until the candy no longer looks foamy and any active bubbling has stopped.

Using great care, immediately pour the syrup into a candy funnel or spouted cup and pour the lollipops as directed on page 114. Let the lollipops sit for about 30 minutes, until completely cool and hard. They are now ready for wrapping.

Another fun project with Union Wine Company was bringing these red wine lollipops to life. Union does such a nice job of turning Oregon grapes into wine, and their efforts with Pinot Noir are unmistakably good. The wine reduction recipe calls for any Pinot Noir that you like to drink, and that's true. But if you find one with notes of cherry and maybe blackberry or chocolate or cola, you've got yourself the ideal wine for making the reduction for this candy.

PINOT NOIR LOLLIPOPS

**MAKES ABOUT SIXTY
1½-INCH LOLLIPOPS**

267 grams glucose syrup

400 grams granulated sugar

130 grams Pinot Noir reduction (see page 71)

16 grams apple cider vinegar

4 grams roasted blackberry purée (see page 42)

2 grams instant yeast

2 grams cocoa powder (see page 74)

1 gram natural cherry flavoring

Set up the lollipop station as directed on page 112.

Weigh the glucose syrup, sugar, and wine reduction directly into a heavy-bottomed pot, then set the pot over medium-high heat and bring the lollipop syrup to a boil. Once the syrup is boiling, swirl the pot often to make sure the sugar is cooking evenly. At first the syrup will bubble fast and light. Then it starts to slow down and the bubbles get a bit slower and thicker. This means the syrup is nearly ready.

Test the temperature of the syrup; as soon as it reaches 315°F, remove the pot from the heat. Give the candy syrup a good stir, then add the vinegar, blackberry purée, yeast, cocoa powder, and cherry flavoring. Whisk together the contents of the pot until the candy no longer looks foamy and any active bubbling has stopped.

Using great care, immediately pour the syrup into a candy funnel or spouted cup and pour the lollipops as directed on page 114. Let the lollipops sit for about 30 minutes, until completely cool and hard. They are now ready for wrapping.

Finally! A lollipop made with everyone's favorite summer party girl: rosé. QUIN's rosé candies all start with Union Wine Company's rosé, which is very lively and quite fruity. Because the wine has notes of strawberry and watermelon in it, I wanted to create a candy that highlighted those flavors while also tasting of pure summer. When making the wine reduction, select a rosé that's sweet, with major fruit notes, and everything else will fall in line.

ROSÉ LOLLIPOPS

MAKES ABOUT SIXTY 1½-INCH LOLLIPOPS

267 grams glucose syrup

400 grams granulated sugar

100 grams rosé reduction (see page 71)

15 grams apple cider vinegar

4 grams instant yeast

3 grams natural strawberry flavoring

2 grams natural pineapple flavoring

1 gram citric acid

Set up the lollipop station as directed on page 112.

Weigh the glucose syrup, sugar, and wine reduction directly into a heavy-bottomed pot, then set the pot over medium-high heat and bring the lollipop syrup to a boil. Once the syrup is boiling, swirl the pot often to make sure the sugar is cooking evenly. At first the syrup will bubble fast and light. Then it starts to slow down and the bubbles get a bit slower and thicker. This means the syrup is nearly ready.

Test the temperature of the syrup; as soon as it reaches 315°F, remove the pot from the heat. Give the candy syrup a good stir, then add the vinegar, yeast, both flavorings, and citric acid. Whisk together the contents of the pot until the candy no longer looks foamy and any active bubbling has stopped.

Using great care, immediately pour the syrup into a candy funnel or spouted cup and pour the lollipops as directed on page 114. Let the lollipops sit for about 30 minutes, until completely cool and hard. They are now ready for wrapping.

You'll need to ready some pecan halves for this recipe, as you will be placing one in the middle of each lollipop just after you pour the candy. As the candy cools, the pecan becomes almost one with it. But be sure to toast your nuts! Nuts that haven't been toasted always taste like an attic to me (old and musty), and that's the last flavor you'd want in candy. You can toast nuts either in the oven or in a pan on the stove top. I prefer the stove-top method because that way I don't forget that I'm toasting nuts. Place the nuts halves in a single layer in a dry skillet, set it over medium-high heat, and allow the nuts to toast until they are fragrant and taking on color. Stir the nuts a bit to flip them over and continue to toast (shaking the pan occasionally) until your kitchen smells wonderful and the nuts have darkened but haven't burned.

PECAN PRALINE LOLLIPOPS

MAKES ABOUT SIXTY 1½-INCH LOLLIPOPS

267 grams glucose syrup

400 grams granulated sugar

135 grams water

100 grams Praline Syrup (see page 70)

2 grams vanilla bean powder (see page 57)

60 pecan halves, toasted (see headnote)

Set up the lollipop station as directed on page 112.

Weigh the glucose syrup, sugar, and water directly into a heavy-bottomed pot, then set the pot over medium-high heat and bring the lollipop syrup to a boil. Once the syrup is boiling, swirl the pot often to make sure the sugar is cooking evenly. At first the syrup will bubble fast and light. Then it starts to slow down and the bubbles get a bit slower and thicker. This means the syrup is nearly ready.

Test the temperature of the syrup; as soon as it reaches 315°F, remove the pot from the heat. Give the candy syrup a good stir, then add the praline syrup and vanilla bean powder. Whisk together the contents of the pot until the candy no longer looks foamy and any active bubbling has stopped.

Using great care, immediately pour the syrup into a candy funnel or spouted cup and pour the lollipops as directed on page 114. As soon as they have been poured, place a toasted pecan half in the center of each lollipop. Let the lollipops sit for about 30 minutes, until completely cool and hard. They are now ready for wrapping.

SURPRISE INSIDE
LOLLIPOPS WITH CHEWY CENTERS

Chewy candy at the center of a lollipop? It might sound impossible, but it's not!

READY THE MOLDS

To begin, prepare enough 1½-inch round molds for a batch of 60 lollipops.

CHOOSE A CENTER

Next, choose a chewy center. I like to mix and match fruit lollipops (see pages 118 to 127) with fruity Dreams Come Chew (see pages 222 to 228). I like chocolate lollipops (see page 151) with mint centers (see page 229) and caramel lollipops (see page 153) with chocolate centers (see page 230). But you can surprise yourself with creations like a chocolate-centered (see page 230) cherry lollipop (see page 119). Or a lemon-centered (see page 223) Sniffle Slayer (see page 148).

I say this a lot: The options are really only limited by your own flavor imagination.

Now that you know what kind of lollipop you're making (and the chewy center you'll put inside it), you're really ready to make magic.

1

Grab a length of chewy candy and roll it into a rope about ½ inch thick and 7½ inches long.

Next, slice the rope into pieces that are ⅛ inch wide.

Take these discs (which are now ½ inch wide and ⅛ inch thick) and press them onto the top of each of the 60 lollipop sticks. Set the sticks aside (but not inside the molds).

2 Cook the candy for the lollipop following the recipe for the flavor of your choosing. As soon as the candy has finished cooking, pour it into a candy funnel or spouted cup and then, working quickly, pour just a dime-size amount of candy into each of the 60 mold cavities.

3 Set the funnel or cup aside and quickly place all of the prepared sticks inside the molds, with the chewy candy end of the stick resting atop the lollipop candy you've just poured into the mold.

4 Continue to pour the hot candy over each stick, covering the chewy candy, and filling each mold cavity completely.

Allow the Surprise Inside lollipops to cool completely before popping them out of the molds and wrapping them.

Clouds of Candy

If you think you've seen it all when it comes to candy, wait 'til you get a load of this! It will turn any party into a special event.

If you break hard candy into pieces and place the pieces inside a cotton candy machine, they will spin themselves into cotton candy. It's super easy—just plop any hard candy you'd like (handmade or not!) into the machine.

My personal favorite hard-candy-to-cotton-candy transformation occurs when I drop the butterscotch candy from page 155 into the machine. It spins into a cloud that's rich and buttery and a little salty— basically the exact opposite of what you'd expect (which really adds to the magic!). You really must try it.

Here's how:

Obtain a cotton candy machine (party-rental companies and libraries are great places to start).

Turn on the machine (following the instructions, of course) and drop the candy pieces into the well of the machine. A few minutes later the flossy, sugary delight will start flying around the inside of the machine. Use a stick or a cone and spin the candy around it until you've made a nice cloud (alternatively, grab the candy with your hands and shape it into a cloud, then nestle that cloud into a paper cone). Delight and amaze your friends with this most magic of candy tricks.

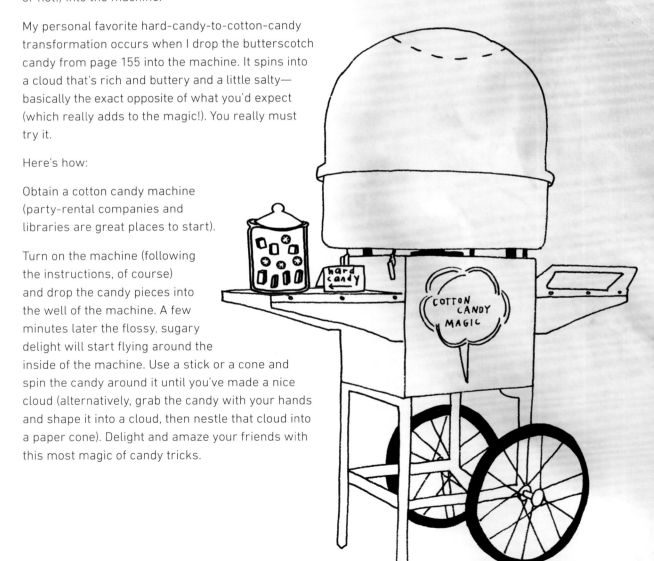

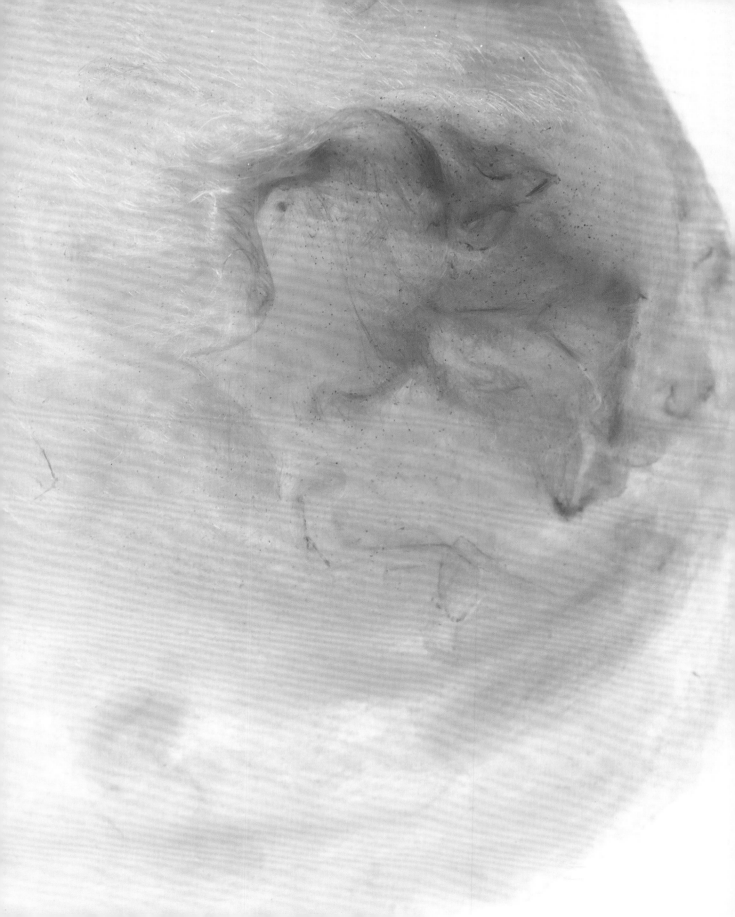

LOLLIPOPS MADE WITH BUTTER, CHOCOLATE, AND OTHER BAKERY-INSPIRED FLAVORS

When people announce that a dessert they're eating is "too rich," I can honestly say I have no idea what on Earth they are talking about. "Too rich" is a phrase that has never passed my lips. In fact, when I'm eating most desserts, I'm secretly wishing they could somehow be richer.

Many hard candy flavors are light and bright and fruity, and although I like them a lot, my heart belongs to deeper flavors. I love the vanilla, brown sugar, chocolate, nut, and caramel flavors you find in a bakery case. Here are some of the hard candies that take me back to my days as a baker.

I like people who keep bees because I've found that they react to bees the same way I react to sugar—as an obsession that never seems to bottom out. Grab a beekeeper and get him or her chatting, and you'll hear about a deep-rooted, totally connected, and laser-like obsession. And I love it. This lollipop honors that obsession by turning the fruit of the labor of thousands of bees into candy. See? Totally connected.

HONEY VANILLA LOLLIPOPS

**MAKES ABOUT SIXTY
1½-INCH LOLLIPOPS**

200 grams glucose syrup

400 grams granulated sugar

60 grams honey

150 grams water

2 grams vanilla bean powder (see page 57)

1 gram kosher salt

Set up the lollipop station as directed on page 112.

Weigh the glucose syrup, sugar, honey, and water directly into a heavy-bottomed pot, then set the pot over medium-high heat and bring the lollipop syrup to a boil. Once the syrup is boiling, swirl the pot often to make sure the sugar is cooking evenly. At first the syrup will bubble fast and light. Then it starts to slow down and the bubbles get a bit slower and thicker. This means the syrup is nearly ready.

Test the temperature of the syrup; as soon as it reaches 315°F, remove the pot from the heat. Give the candy syrup a good stir, then add the vanilla bean powder and salt. Whisk together the contents of the pot until the candy no longer looks foamy and any active bubbling has stopped.

Using great care, immediately pour the syrup into a candy funnel or spouted cup and pour the lollipops as directed on page 114. Let the lollipops sit for about 30 minutes, until completely cool and hard. They are now ready for wrapping.

Cherries lend themselves to more robust flavors. Something about that deep, dark flavor works with ingredients like honey, brown sugar, vanilla, and, of course, chocolate. The addition of cherry in this recipe really (and perhaps surprisingly) boosts the richness of the candy.

CHERRY HONEY VANILLA LOLLIPOPS

MAKES ABOUT SIXTY 1½-INCH LOLLIPOPS

200 grams glucose syrup

400 grams granulated sugar

60 grams honey

130 grams water

20 grams roasted cherry purée (see page 44)

2 grams natural cherry flavoring

1 gram vanilla bean powder (see page 57)

Set up the lollipop station as directed on page 112.

Weigh the glucose syrup, sugar, honey, and water directly into a heavy-bottomed pot, then set the pot over medium-high heat and bring the lollipop syrup to a boil. Once the syrup is boiling, swirl the pot often to make sure the sugar is cooking evenly. At first the syrup will bubble fast and light. Then it starts to slow down and the bubbles get a bit slower and thicker. This means the syrup is nearly ready.

Test the temperature of the syrup; as soon as it reaches 315°F, remove the pot from the heat. Give the candy syrup a good stir, then add the cherry purée, cherry flavoring, and vanilla bean powder. Whisk together the contents of the pot until the candy no longer looks foamy and any active bubbling has stopped.

Using great care, immediately pour the syrup into a candy funnel or spouted cup and pour the lollipops as directed on page 114. Let the lollipops sit for about 30 minutes, until completely cool and hard. They are now ready for wrapping.

Candy Garland

stamp numbers on bolt bags and make your own candy countdown!

5   4   3

I have always been just one step below Christmas-elf status during the holiday season. I love (love!) the days leading up to Christmas, mostly because they allow me to turn my house into a wonderland of vintage, glittery holiday decorations. (These are some of my favorite objects in the world, and I'd probably display them year-round if it wouldn't be so weird—and such a glittery mess.) I also love everything else about the season, from the trees to the songs to the good cheer and merriment, in whatever way I can get it. Incorporating candy into my holiday decoration extravaganza was a goal of mine, and it was accomplished when I came up with a truly inspired creation: *The Candy Garland.*

It all starts with a couple of yards of ribbon (I like the sturdiness of grosgrain), a bunch of candies (caramels, Dreams Come Chew, lollipops), some festive bells, a stack of sparkly metallic pipe cleaners, handfuls of colored beads, and whatever else you've got around that can be tied to a ribbon and turned into a festive, candy-laden garland. You can make a lot of them and decorate your entire tree, or you can make a small selection and deck just a few of your halls.

pipe cleaners

To begin, tie a piece of candy to the ribbon, then slide on a bell or twist on a sparkly pipe cleaner, tie on another piece of candy, slide on another bell, string on a wooden bead, and add more candy, repeating until you've filled the entire length of ribbon. When your ribbon is bedazzled with candies and bells and other festive bits, it's ready for hanging.

grosgrain ribbon

& Countdown

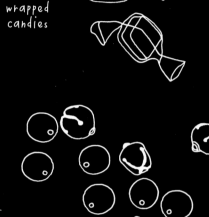

wrapped candies

bells and sequins

If there's a particular event you're looking forward to, a Countdown garland is a great way to watch the days tick by. For this version, gather together the same types of decorative elements as for the Candy Garland, but instead of stringing the candies onto the ribbon, you'll tuck them into tiny drawstring bags (sometimes called bolt bags), each marked with a number. Then, like an Advent calendar that knows no season, one bag will be opened each day of the countdown. This is even more fun if the bags are tied on the ribbon randomly so they have to be hunted down. (Look for tips on where to find bolt bags in the Resources Guide, page 295.)

For a *Countdown*, you'll need plenty of ribbon, candy, bells, beads, tiny drawstring bags, and a numbered rubber-stamp set and stamp pad or a permanent marker, preferably in a festive color.

Begin by figuring out how many bags you'll need on the countdown garland. Once you know, stamp or draw the corresponding numbers on the bags. For example, if your event is 29 days away, you'll want to stamp or draw numbers 1 through 29 onto individual bags. Fill each bag with a piece of candy and then tie the bags to a piece of ribbon that's long enough to accommodate all the bags plus all the extra decorative flourishes you've assembled. Hang the garland, then start the countdown!

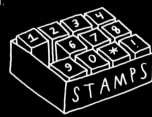

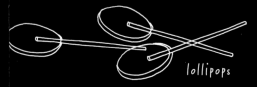

lollipops

I developed this lollipop during a rough cold-and-flu season. Everyone I knew, including QUIN's tiny staff, had been hit by a bug, so I took care of them by making them candy. Later, when QUIN started selling these lollipops to the public, a writer from a local weekly paper picked up on it, bought some, ate them, and then complained that her cold didn't disappear. I didn't get the opportunity to address her issues publicly, so excuse me while I do it now: I never, ever claimed a lollipop could cure the common cold. In fact, last time I checked (and I check a lot because I have an elementary school–aged child), *nothing* can cure the common cold. I'm just a simple candy maker trying to make people happier through sugar, not an actual miracle worker tackling a worldwide affliction.

That said, these spicy, gingery, lemony lollipops have been known to clear congestion and, at the very least, boost morale

SNIFFLE SLAYER LOLLIPOPS

MAKES ABOUT SIXTY 1½-INCH LOLLIPOPS

267 grams glucose syrup

400 grams granulated sugar

150 grams apple cider

20 grams fresh lemon juice

10 grams local honey

4 grams finely grated lemon zest

3 grams ground ginger

2 grams cayenne pepper

1 gram kosher salt

Set up the lollipop station as directed on page 112.

Weigh the glucose syrup, sugar, cider, lemon juice, and honey directly into a heavy-bottomed pot, then set the pot over medium-high heat and bring the lollipop syrup to a boil. Once the syrup is boiling, swirl the pot often to make sure the sugar is cooking evenly. At first the syrup will bubble fast and light. Then it starts to slow down and the bubbles get a bit slower and thicker. This means the syrup is nearly ready.

Test the temperature of the syrup; as soon as it reaches 310°F, remove the pot from the heat. Give the candy syrup a good stir, then add the lemon zest, ginger, cayenne, and salt. Whisk together the contents of the pot until the candy no longer looks foamy, any active bubbling has stopped, and the spices are running evenly throughout the syrup.

Using great care, immediately pour the syrup into a candy funnel or spouted cup and pour the lollipops as directed on page 114. Let the lollipops sit for about 30 minutes, until completely cool and hard. They are now ready for wrapping.

THROAT SOOTHERS Still packed with the alleviating powers of honey, lemon, and ginger, these tone down the heat. Prepare the lollipops as directed but omit the cayenne pepper. Or, if you want only a bit less fire, you can scale back the cayenne to a heat level of your choice.

I find great comfort in a mug filled with something warm to drink. Tea or coffee, I really don't discriminate. But there's something even more comforting about chai. The intoxicating spices and affinity for milk and sugar make chai the ideal candidate for candy making.

CHAI TEA LOLLIPOPS

MAKES ABOUT SIXTY 1½-INCH LOLLIPOPS

156 grams glucose syrup

400 grams granulated sugar

60 grams chai tea concentrate (see page 291)

60 grams unsalted butter, cut into ½-inch cubes

5 grams kosher salt

1 gram ground cardamom

1 gram ground cinnamon

1 gram freshly ground black pepper

16 grams vanilla extract

Set up the lollipop station as directed on page 112.

Weigh the glucose syrup, sugar, and chai concentrate directly into a heavy-bottomed pot, then set the pot over medium-high heat and bring the lollipop syrup to a boil. Once the syrup is boiling, swirl the pot to make sure the boil is strong enough that it won't vanish, then add the butter steadily but gradually, giving the pot a good swirl after all of the butter is added. Allow the candy to continue cooking, swirling the pot occasionally to distribute the heat evenly and avoid hot spots.

Test the temperature of the syrup; as soon as it reaches 305°F, remove the pot from the heat. Give the candy syrup a good stir, then add the salt, cardamom, cinnamon, and pepper and again give the syrup a good stir. Next, stir in the vanilla. Whisk together the contents of the pot until the candy no longer looks foamy and any active bubbling has stopped.

Using great care, immediately pour the syrup into a candy funnel or spouted cup and pour the lollipops as directed on page 114. Let the lollipops sit for about 30 minutes, until completely cool and hard. They are now ready for wrapping.

WHAT'S MEDIUM-HIGH HEAT?

Many of my recipes call for "medium-high heat." But what does that mean? In my world, it means that you turn the stove one or two notches above medium. If your stove knob goes from 1 to 10, with 1 being low and 10 being high, medium-high heat is either a 6 or a 7 on the knob. Now, you'll still need to watch the ingredients in the pan. If the action is looking wild in there, you should turn down the heat a bit. If your stove is sluggish and a bit old (and the majority of the recipes in this book were tested on just such a stove—the one in my house), you need to up the heat a notch. You know your stove best, so make the adjustments you know you'll need to make based on my 1-to-10 description.

These lollipops are cool and refreshing, with a flavor reminiscent of mint buttercream (especially when it's piled on a chocolate cake). Cooking up beautifully and almost crystal clear, they are ideal candidates for projects beyond simply eating a lollipop; break them into pieces to create shards of ice for a gingerbread house, leave them intact and tie them into small bundles with ribbon for party favors, or give them as gifts with the suggestion of using them as hot chocolate swizzle sticks. You can also turn this candy into a round drop or a nice rectangle (see page 154). Do that and they become more of a breath mint than a lollipop.

If you can't find natural mint flavoring, peppermint oil will do just fine. Depending on the type of peppermint oil, you may find that you need to use a bit less than what's called for here. Of course, if you like it very minty, use the full amount.

MINT LOLLIPOPS

**MAKES ABOUT SIXTY
1½-INCH LOLLIPOPS**

267 grams glucose syrup

400 grams granulated sugar

150 grams water

3 grams natural mint flavoring or peppermint oil

Set up the lollipop station as directed on page 112.

Weigh the glucose syrup, sugar, and water directly into a heavy-bottomed pot, then set the pot over medium-high heat and bring the lollipop syrup to a boil. Once the syrup is boiling, swirl the pot often to make sure the sugar is cooking evenly. At first the syrup will bubble fast and light. Then it starts to slow down and the bubbles get a bit slower and thicker. This means the syrup is nearly ready.

Test the temperature of the syrup; as soon as it reaches 315°F, remove the pot from the heat. Give the candy syrup a good stir, then add the mint flavoring. Whisk together the contents of the pot until the candy no longer looks foamy and any active bubbling has stopped.

Using great care, immediately pour the syrup into a candy funnel or spouted cup and pour the lollipops as directed on page 114. Let the lollipops sit for about 30 minutes, until completely cool and hard. They are now ready for wrapping.

These lollipops make one of my favorite foods, chocolate, more portable. This recipe calls for coffee and salt as well, because both add depth to the chocolate flavor. It also calls for lemon juice, which is included because of its ability to keep sugar from crystallizing. But the lemon juice also does something else. As you'll see when you read through the ingredients list, this recipe (and a few others) calls for butter. The lemon juice helps cut the fatty taste brought by the butter, but it also allows the butter to do its job of creating a candy that delivers a delightful shatter when bitten.

CHOCOLATE LOLLIPOPS

**MAKES ABOUT SIXTY
1½-INCH LOLLIPOPS**

156 grams glucose syrup

400 grams granulated sugar

60 grams brewed coffee
(see page 81)

10 grams fresh lemon juice

60 grams unsalted butter,
cut into ½-inch cubes

20 grams cocoa powder
(see page 74)

7 grams kosher salt

Set up the lollipop station as directed on page 112.

Weigh the glucose syrup, sugar, coffee, and lemon juice directly into a heavy-bottomed pot, then set the pot over medium-high heat and bring the lollipop syrup to a boil. Once the syrup is boiling, swirl the pot to make sure the boil is strong enough that it won't vanish, then add the butter steadily but gradually, giving the pot a good swirl after all of the butter is added. Allow the candy to continue cooking, swirling the pot occasionally to distribute the heat evenly and avoid hot spots.

Test the temperature of the syrup; as soon as it reaches 305°F, remove the pot from the heat. Give the candy syrup a good stir, then add the cocoa powder and salt. Whisk together the contents of the pot until the candy no longer looks foamy and any active bubbling has stopped.

Using great care, immediately pour the syrup into a candy funnel or spouted cup and pour the lollipops as directed on page 114. Let the lollipops sit for about 30 minutes, until completely cool and hard. They are now ready for wrapping.

Olive oil in a lollipop? I understand any hesitation you might be having. But I ask you to trust me. If you use quality olive oil, you will be rewarded with a deeply flavored candy that's rich yet grassy, and completely smooth—a candy that shatters into perfect little shards in your mouth. And I can't not talk about the salt. It's prominent here—the perfect ingredient to tie together the olive oil and the chocolate.

CHOCOLATE + OLIVE OIL + SEA SALT LOLLIPOPS

MAKES ABOUT SIXTY 1½-INCH LOLLIPOPS

156 grams glucose syrup

400 grams granulated sugar

60 grams brewed coffee (see page 81)

30 grams good-quality olive oil

20 grams cocoa powder (see page 74)

10 grams kosher salt

Set up the lollipop station as directed on page 112, but instead of using vegetable oil to swipe on your molds, use a bit of olive oil.

Weigh the glucose syrup, sugar, and coffee directly into a heavy-bottomed pot, then set the pot over medium-high heat and bring the lollipop syrup to a boil. Once the syrup is boiling, swirl the pot to make sure the boil is strong enough that it won't vanish, then add the olive oil in a steady stream, giving the pot a good swirl after all of the oil is added. Allow the candy to continue cooking, swirling the pot occasionally to distribute the heat evenly and avoid hot spots.

Test the temperature of the syrup; as soon as it reaches 305°F, remove the pot from the heat. Give the candy syrup a good stir, then add the cocoa powder and salt. Whisk together the contents of the pot until the candy no longer looks foamy and any active bubbling has stopped.

Using great care, immediately pour the syrup into a candy funnel or spouted cup and pour the lollipops as directed on page 114. Let the lollipops sit for about 30 minutes, until completely cool and hard. They are now ready for wrapping.

Crunchy caramel on a stick—now that's my kind of lollipop. I love to grab one of these at the QUIN factory and, ahem, test it for "quality" more often than I should be admitting. But, I can't help it. These lollipops are caramelly and rich with just the right amount of salt.

If you'd like to move beyond the stick with these lollipops, here are a few ideas: Break the candy apart and bake it into cookies (chocolate chip and sugar cookies are my choices). Or break the candy into bits and sprinkle them all over the top of a beautifully frosted cake or cupcakes. That little caramelly crunch is amazing on everything from chocolate buttercream to vanilla cream cheese frosting.

CARAMEL LOLLIPOPS

MAKES ABOUT SIXTY 1½-INCH LOLLIPOPS

156 grams glucose syrup

400 grams granulated sugar

27 grams water

20 grams fresh lemon juice

13 grams vanilla extract

60 grams unsalted butter, cut into ½-inch cubes

7 grams kosher salt

Set up the lollipop station as directed on page 112.

Weigh the glucose syrup, sugar, water, lemon juice, and vanilla directly into a heavy-bottomed pot, then set the pot over medium-high heat and bring the lollipop syrup to a boil. Once the syrup is boiling, swirl the pot to make sure the boil is strong enough that it won't vanish, then add the butter steadily but gradually, giving the pot a good swirl after all of the butter is added. Allow the candy to continue cooking, swirling the pot occasionally to distribute the heat evenly and avoid hot spots.

Test the temperature of the syrup; as soon as it reaches 305°F, remove the pot from the heat. Give the candy syrup a good stir, then add the salt. Whisk together the contents of the pot until the candy no longer looks foamy and any active bubbling has stopped.

Using great care, immediately pour the syrup into a candy funnel or spouted cup and pour the lollipops as directed on page 114. Let the lollipops sit for about 30 minutes, until completely cool and hard. They are now ready for wrapping.

BEYOND THE LOLLIPOP: HARD CANDY

Hard candy doesn't always have to be in the form of a lollipop with a stick. Molds exist for many amazing shapes that don't involve lollipop sticks at all. My favorite is the hard candy rectangle that allows you to turn hot candy syrup into tiny bricks. The molds have removable slats, so after the syrup has cooled and set, the slats lift out to release perfect rectangles. I also like to use a funnel or spouted cup to plop the candy into small rounds (about the size of a nickel) on a nonstick mat. They are the ideal shape for a throat drop, making them well suited to the mint (see page 150), Sniffle Slayer (see page 148), and Throat Soother (see page 148) recipes. Another good idea is to pour the hot candy into a thin layer onto a nonstick mat, allow it to cool, and then break it shards like sea glass. A nice coating of granulated sugar on all of these hard candies will prevent them from sticking together too badly.

Candy planks, which are easy to make, are another good alternative to lollipops. Using a funnel or spouted cup, pour straight lines of candy about 4 inches long onto a nonstick mat. Allow the candies to cool and set, then wrap them individually in the same cellophane wrappers you use for lollipops. These planks are delicious dipped into Sweet + Sour Magic Dust (see page 93). They're an updated version of lickable candy sticks dipped in sour powder and are a QUIN specialty we call Sour Supreme.

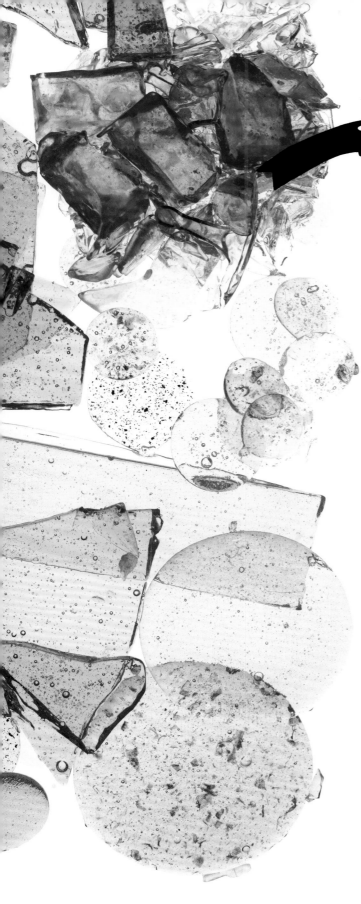

If you combine what you learned about flavor in chapter two and what you just learned about lollipops and other hard candy in this chapter, you're well on your way to dreaming up your own creations. With the whole world of natural flavorings available to you, you'll no doubt produce some sensational candies. Here are some ideas to inspire you—all flavors can be made into any candy you can dream up, from lollipops to drops.

BUTTERSCOTCH HARD CANDY

Don't forget to add vanilla bean powder and some salt to make it special. Follow the directions for Mint Lollipops on page 150, but leave out the mint flavoring and add 18 grams butterscotch flavoring, 3 grams vanilla bean powder (see page 57), and 5 grams salt.

CHAMPAGNE HARD CANDY

Create your own Champagne reduction by following the method for wine reductions on page 71. Use the Rosé Lollipops recipe on page 135 as a guide, but be sure to taste the Champagne (or at least read the label description) first to figure out what kind of fruity flavorings you should add to the candy. Common flavors you can taste in Champagne (depending on the grapes used to make it) are strawberry, almond, lemon, orange, cherry, honey, cream, apple, yeast, toast, and nuts.

CINNAMON HARD CANDY

Add a tiny bit of red coloring for a beautiful candy. Follow the directions for Mint Lollipops on page 150, omitting the mint flavoring and adding 10 grams cinnamon flavoring plus a small splash of natural red coloring.

FRUIT PUNCH HARD CANDY

Dashes of your favorite natural fruit flavorings will create the punch of your dreams. Follow the directions for Orange Lollipops on page 122, adding a few different natural fruit flavorings of your choice. If you need help deciding on flavors, see the recipe for Fruit Punch Dreams on page 223.

ROOT BEER HARD CANDY

I love root beer candy, and I especially love root beer floats. You can replicate those soda fountain flavors by adding a good amount of vanilla bean powder to a root beer–flavored candy. One more time— root beer float. Follow the directions for Mint Lollipops on page 150, omitting the mint flavoring and adding 20 grams root beer flavoring and 3 grams of vanilla bean powder (see page 57).

CHAPTER FOUR

CARAMELS

CARAMEL PERFECTION

Caramel that's barely caramel does not excite me. I like caramel that walks the line between sweet perfection and slight bitterness. A caramel that's been given the cooking time it needs to develop full flavor. A caramel that's genuine in ingredients and relies only on caramelized sugar and pure dairy for realness. I'm not talking about those tiny, pale bricks available in the bulk section of your grocery store. I'm talking about real, true caramelized sugar with heavy cream and butter added.

It's true that my approach to cooking caramel is a bit different than some. Instead of cooking the sugar and the fats together from the start, I caramelize the sugar first and then add heavy cream, butter, and additional flavor-building ingredients. From there, I whisk and whisk to ensure the fat is completely emulsified into the sugar. The result is a perfectly smooth, complexly flavored candy. If I add additional flavor, I prefer to add it by first flavoring the heavy cream and then whisking the cream into the caramelized sugar.

The caramel recipes that follow yield large batches; about 160 pieces if made in a candy-frame setup (don't worry; I'll teach you how to do it) or about 115 pieces if made in a 9 by 13–inch pan. Because caramel has a minimum shelf life of 3 months, and because I've included multiple uses for caramel throughout this book, you should fret not about finding a use for it all. You can give dozens of caramels as gifts and use the remaining candy as a dip for caramel apples (see page 204), as an addition to perfect brownies (see page 251), as the chewy center of a lollipop (see page 138), or any other amazing idea I know you're cooking up.

CARAMEL TECHNIQUE

I talk to a lot of people about caramel, and while nearly everyone seems to love eating it, most of them are terrified to cook it. If you relax a little bit and treat cooking caramel not unlike cooking a pot of tomato sauce, you'll be fine.

So, once you've overcome the initial fear, then what? Well, to start, let's both admit that you'll probably burn a pot or two of caramel somewhere along the way. I've certainly done it. And it's not a big deal. The trick is to realize that the sugar is burned *before* you add the cream and butter, because the dairy products are the most expensive ingredients in the recipe. That said, you really do need to pay visual attention to your caramel nearly every step of the way. Commit to looking in that pot and understanding what's going on. Stop relying on the numbers on a thermometer and instead connect with the cooking process. In fact, I'd like to suggest that you put your thermometer away and rely only on visual cues. The caramel takes a journey from start to finish, and I know what it's supposed to look like every step of the way, with the final step being a very specific color.

Here is how I like to describe that journey: A pot of caramel begins with melting the sugar into the glucose syrup (see page 16 for the story behind glucose and its role in the candy-making process). What you'll see when you look into the pot is the sugar starting to melt. If you notice a couple of sugar crystals clinging to the side of the pot, use a damp pastry brush to swipe them away.

Once the sugar has melted completely, the contents of the pot will be transparent and liquid. A lot of quick bubbling action will be happening. Then, as more and more moisture evaporates, the bubbling will start to slow. Now, instead of boiling like water, the mixture will bubble like thick, sugary lava.

Once the glug-glug lava-like bubbling has started, the contents of the pot will begin to change color, going from clear to a hint of golden brown to a more uniform golden brown to a beautifully bronzed amber (see the following color chart). It's at this point that the pot is removed from the heat and the fat and additional ingredients are added. Then the entire pot is whisked and whisked (for a full 5 minutes) until the fat is completely mixed into the sugar.

Caramel Color Chart

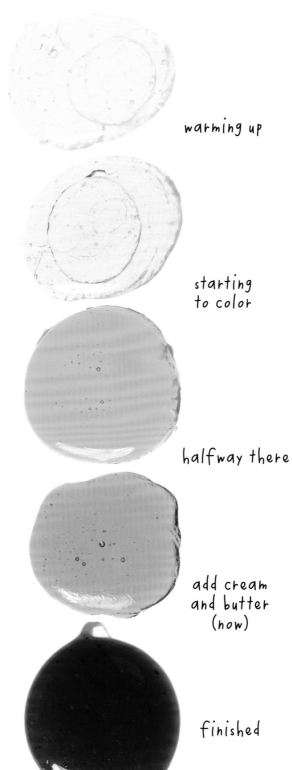

warming up

starting
to color

halfway there

add cream
and butter
(now)

finished

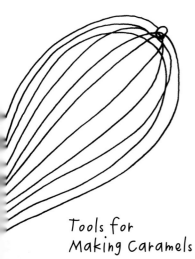

Tools for Making Caramels

* Candy-cooking pot
* High-heat spatula or wooden spoon (to poke)
* Pastry brush and small bowl of cold water
* Small saucepan to warm cream
* Whisk

THE CARAMEL SETUP

At QUIN, we use a candy frame to shape our caramel into manageable slabs. If we didn't contain the oozy, hot candy in some way, it would create a massive candy puddle, and while that sounds amazing, it sure would be a pain to cut.

To create perfect rectangles of candy ready for cutting, I like to use food-safe acrylic bars—four per setup—to create a caramel frame, which I set up on a hard surface to create an interior that measures 12 by 14 inches. What kind of hard surface? I prefer marble boards or even a heat-proof countertop like quartz. I use ordinary masking tape to secure the bars in place, and then I pour the hot candy into the 12 by 14–inch frame. Finally, I use a whisk to coax the caramel into the corners of the frame. Once the caramel has settled in evenly, it cools into a perfect rectangle, ready to be freed from the frame and cut into 1-inch squares.

Marble (or other) solid-surface boards are relatively easy to find at good cookware shops or online. Just make sure the board is large enough to accommodate a 12 by 14–inch slab of candy. Food-safe acrylic bars can be purchased from a local plastics shop or ordered online in any length, width, and height you want. I use four 14 by 1 by 1–inch bars for my candy frame.

If you'd rather skip all the candy-frame business, you can pour the hot caramel into a very lightly buttered 9 by 13–inch pan. The candy will need to be nudged and lifted from the pan for cutting, the yield will be smaller, and the pieces will be slightly thicker than they would be if you used a frame, but the flavor (and what's more important than that?) will be exactly the same.

Once the candy has cooled and set (it takes a minimum of 3 hours for the candy to be cool to the touch and have a slight firmness, but I prefer to let it sit overnight), you can cut it and then wrap it. Following is a breakdown of the process from start to finish.

THE FIRST STEP IS TO SET UP YOUR CANDY FRAME.

You will need:

* Four 14 by 1 by 1–inch
  food-safe acrylic bars
* Marble or other heat-proof solid work surface
* Masking tape
* Unsalted butter

1 Spread the lightest sheen of butter in a 14-inch square on the work surface.

2 Arrange the acrylic bars, placing two bars widthwise across the ends of two bars laid lengthwise to make a rectangular frame with interior dimensions of 12 by 14 inches.

3 Using ordinary masking tape, tape the acrylic bars into place, taking care that the tape is on the tops and outsides of the bars only. Do not put any tape on the insides of the bars. It's best to put one piece of tape in the center of each bar and then to secure all four corner joints.

4 Your frame is now ready for candy. Pour it in! Allow the candy to cool and set.

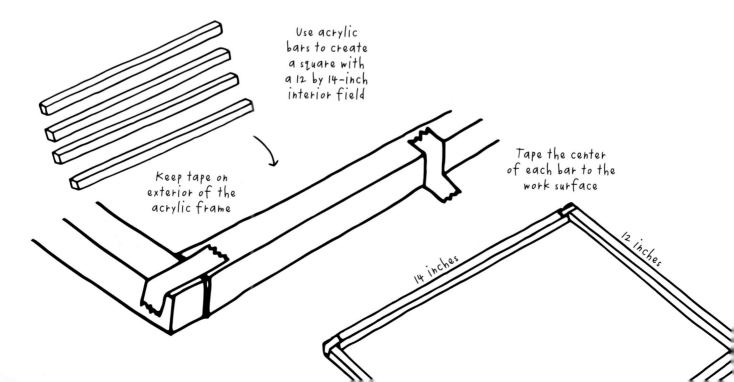

Use acrylic bars to create a square with a 12 by 14-inch interior field

Keep tape on exterior of the acrylic frame

Tape the center of each bar to the work surface

14 inches

12 inches

NEXT, CUT THE CARAMEL.

You will need:

* Paper towel
* Cutting board
* Bench scraper or wide metal spatula
* Ruler
* Sharp knife

Remove acrylic bars and use the bench scraper or metal spatula to convince the caramel to release from the buttered surface

1 Dampen the paper towel with water, lay it flat on a countertop or other work surface, and place the cutting board on top of the towel. Press down on the cutting board to "stick" it into place. This will prevent the board from sliding around as you're cutting. (This is a great general tip that can be put to use every time you're cutting or chopping on a board.)

2 To remove the acrylic bars, peel off the tape and then sharply tap the bars with the handle of the bench scraper or metal spatula. If you do this with enough force, the bars will pop right off. If you've used a 9 by 13–inch pan, start at one corner and pry the candy away from the pan, continuing to lift along one of the 9-inch ends until you've slowly worked the candy out.

3 Use the bench scraper or spatula to convince the caramel to release from the surface on which you poured it. Carefully peel the candy off the surface and then carry it in your hands to the cutting board. The candy will bend and stretch, but once you have it on the cutting board, you can shape it back up or flatten it out as necessary.

4 Starting on the long (14-inch) side of the candy slab, use the ruler and the knife to score it in 1-inch increments on the edge. Next, score the shorter (12-inch) side of the candy slab in 1-inch increments. Now, connect these score marks to create 1-inch-wide lines extending from both the long and short sides of the slab. Finally, cut along these lines to create 1-inch squares of candy.

Score, then cut the candy into 1-inch squares

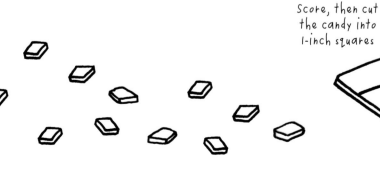

THE CANDY IS NOW READY TO WRAP.

You will need:

* 5-inch-square cellophane wrappers

1 Place a 1-inch square of candy in the center of
a cellophane wrapper.

2 Bring the bottom edge of the wrapper up and over the candy,
then fold the top down, overlapping the bottom.

3 To close, tightly twist the ends of the wrapper in opposite directions.

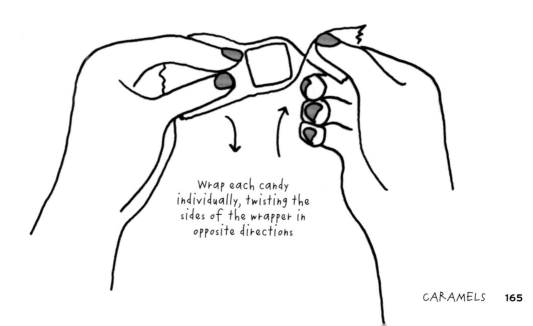

Wrap each candy
individually, twisting the
sides of the wrapper in
opposite directions

ADDITIONAL CARAMEL TIPS

CLEAN POT

Anything less than a perfectly clean pot is not perfect. I like clean, clean kitchen tools, especially when it comes to making caramel. A tiny bit of an abrasive cleaner (I like Bar Keepers Friend) sprinkled onto the bottom of a pot that's less than perfectly shiny will make it sparkle and ensure that you'll have a much easier time determining the color of your expertly cooked caramel.

SWIRL THE POT

One key to cooking candy evenly is what I call *swirling the pot*. Instead of stirring the contents with a spoon or a spatula, which encourages sugar crystallization and a less than desirable texture, I hold on to the sides of the pot (protecting my hands with a kitchen towel) and move it in a few quick (yet gentle) circular swirls. You want what's inside to move around enough to cook evenly, but you don't want to aggravate it too much. When cooking caramel, swirl the pot occasionally to keep the contents cooking evenly. As you're swirling, feel free to gently tip the pot to one side or the other so you can see the color on the sides of the pot compared to the color in the center. Keep things moving until all of the syrup is a uniform color.

Behold the sea salt caramel! It's the candy that launched a thousand artisanal candy-making ships. From candy to sauce, ice cream to frozen yogurt, I'll admit that salty caramel isn't my personal favorite—but that won't keep me from sharing the recipe for QUIN's best-selling candy! A generous amount of kosher salt is cooked into the candy itself, and then the candy is finished with lovely flurries of flake sea salt (see the Resources Guide, page 293, for my recommendations). Sounds beautiful and salty, and it is. When the caramel has set, see pages 164 to 165 for cutting tips, detailed instructions, and illustrations.

SEA SALT CARAMELS

MAKES ABOUT 160 CARAMELS IF MADE IN A FRAME OR 115 CARAMELS IF MADE IN A PAN

438 grams glucose syrup

800 grams granulated sugar

220 grams heavy cream

10 grams kosher salt

3 grams vanilla bean powder (see page 57)

18 grams vanilla extract

330 grams unsalted butter, cut into roughly 1-inch pieces

25 grams flake sea salt

Set up a 12 by 14–inch candy frame or lightly butter a 9 by 13–inch pan (see pages 162 to 163).

Weigh the glucose syrup directly into a heavy-bottomed pot, then set the pot over medium-high heat. Allow the glucose to warm until it liquefies and then starts to bubble. Once the glucose has bubbled a bit in one spot, swirl the pot to distribute the heat.

Add the sugar, about one-third at a time, sprinkling it over the glucose syrup. Using a high-heat spatula or wooden spoon, poke (no stirring) the sugar down into the syrup after each addition. Keep watch to make sure no giant lumps of dry sugar remain before you add the next installment of sugar. If you see lumps, poke them down into the glucose. Once all of the sugar is added and has been poked down into the liquid so it's wet, stop poking.

Pour the cream into a small saucepan and add the kosher salt, vanilla bean powder, and vanilla extract. Stir to mix, then set the pan over low to medium heat. You're not looking to boil the cream; the idea is to simply warm the ingredients so they're not cold when they go into the hot sugar.

Meanwhile, let the glucose and sugar cook, swirling the pot occasionally, until the mixture is dark amber, or the color of a copper penny (see the Caramel Color Chart on page 161). Time-wise, you're looking at 13 to 15 minutes for the caramel to reach the target color. At first the sugar will turn pale brown, then darker brown. This may happen in spots around the pot, so it's important to swirl the pot as the sugar cooks.

Once the sugar is a uniform color, cook it for a second or two longer until you feel good about the color, remembering that you want it to match that dark amber target.

Remove the pot from the heat and very carefully add the warmed cream mixture, immediately followed by the butter. Whisk the candy for 5 minutes, until completely emulsified. This means that the fats have been completely mixed into the sugar with no chance of separating. The mixture will be homogenized, with no oily separation or bits of anything burnt floating around.

Pour the caramel into the prepared candy frame or pan, nudging it into the corners as needed, and allow it to rest for 10 minutes. Shower the sea salt evenly over the top (see page 172) and then allow the candy to sit until cooled and set, at least 3 hours or preferably up to overnight, before cutting.

Without a doubt, this candy combines a pair of great flavors: caramelized sugar and salty popcorn. The popcorn is introduced into the candy in two ways. First, a popcorn-infused cream that basically tastes like popcorn-flavored milk; and second, a layer of popped corn that's pressed directly into the caramel after it's cooked and poured, so that each little square of candy is studded with a kernel or two. Between the flavor and the texture, it's hard to decide what I like best. When the caramel has set, see pages 164 to 165 for cutting tips, detailed instructions, and illustrations.

POPCORN CARAMELS

MAKES ABOUT 160 CARAMELS IF MADE IN A FRAME OR 115 CARAMELS IF MADE IN A PAN

438 grams glucose syrup

800 grams granulated sugar

265 grams Popcorn Cream (see page 52)

7 grams kosher salt

18 grams vanilla extract

295 grams unsalted butter, cut into roughly 1-inch pieces

90 grams Every Day, Popcorn (page 54)

Set up a 12 by 14–inch candy frame or lightly butter a 9 by 13–inch pan (see pages 162 to 163).

Weigh the glucose syrup directly into a heavy-bottomed pot, then set the pot over medium-high heat. Allow the glucose to warm until it liquefies and then starts to bubble. Once the glucose has bubbled a bit in one spot, swirl the pot to distribute the heat.

Add the sugar, about one-third at a time, sprinkling it over the glucose syrup. Using a high-heat spatula or wooden spoon, poke (no stirring) the sugar down into the syrup after each addition. Keep watch to make sure no giant lumps of dry sugar remain before you add the next installment of sugar. If you see lumps, poke them down into the glucose. Once all of the sugar is added and has been poked down into the liquid so it's wet, stop poking.

Pour the cream into a small saucepan and add the salt and vanilla. Stir to mix, then set the pan over low to medium heat. You're not looking to boil the cream; the idea is to simply warm the ingredients so they're not cold when they go into the hot sugar.

Meanwhile, let the glucose and sugar cook, swirling the pot occasionally, until the mixture is dark amber, or the color of a copper penny (see the Caramel Color Chart on page 161). Time-wise, you're looking at 13 to 15 minutes for the caramel to reach the target color. At first the sugar will turn pale brown, then darker brown. This may happen in spots around the pot, so it's important to swirl the pot as the sugar cooks. Once the

CONTINUED

sugar is a uniform color, cook it for a second or two longer until you feel good about the color, remembering that you want it to match that dark amber target.

Remove the pot from the heat and very carefully add the warmed cream mixture, immediately followed by the butter. Whisk the candy for 5 minutes, until completely emulsified. This means that the fats have been completely mixed into the sugar with no chance of separating. The mixture will be homogenized, with no oily separation or bits of anything burnt floating around.

Pour the caramel into the prepared candy frame or pan, nudging it into the corners as needed, and allow it to rest for 5 minutes. Shower the popcorn evenly over the top (see below) and press down lightly to ensure a good stick. Allow the candy to sit until cooled and set, at least 3 hours or preferably up to overnight, before cutting.

TOPPING THE CARAMEL

When topping a slab of candy with an ingredient, whether it's salt, popcorn, seeds, sprinkles, coconut, or shards of chocolate, it's important to shower it from a good height, rather than just an inch or so above the candy. Don't believe me? Try it. Grab a few fingers full of salt and attempt to sprinkle them all over something from an inch or so away. See what happens? The salt all ends up in one big pile. Now, do it again, but sprinkle the salt from 18 inches above the surface. This time the salt is distributed much more evenly, and you've avoided getting too much in any one spot. Knowing how to shower any ingredient is important because you will be sprinkling it on hot candy—and you can't correct your mistake once the sprinkling is done.

I know I said sea salt caramels aren't exactly my favorite. But chocolate caramels? Lock them up when I'm around or they'll all disappear . . . fast. I like these caramels made with all chocolates—light to dark and anywhere in between. That's why you should feel free to experiment with chocolate here. Different chocolates will produce totally different candy, time after time. And, really, don't overlook a milkier chocolate for these. Something around the 38 to 49 percent cacao mark complements the caramelized sugar perfectly.

If you like nuts, don't leave them out. Toasted and chopped hazelnuts are a good choice, but chopped salted peanuts or even chopped fancy smoked almonds are nice, too. Simply mix 150 grams of whatever nut you choose into the candy after the butter and chocolate have fully emulsified into the sugar. When the caramel has set, see pages 164 to 165 for cutting tips, detailed instructions, and illustrations.

CHOCOLATE CARAMELS

MAKES ABOUT 160 CARAMELS IF MADE IN A FRAME OR 115 CARAMELS IF MADE IN A PAN

438 grams glucose syrup

800 grams granulated sugar

220 grams Chocolate Cream (see page 57)

8 grams kosher salt

18 grams vanilla extract

330 grams unsalted butter, cut into roughly 1-inch pieces

70 grams chocolate of your choice, coarsely chopped

Set up a 12 by 14–inch candy frame or lightly butter a 9 by 13–inch pan (see pages 162 to 163).

Weigh the glucose syrup directly into a heavy-bottomed pot, then set the pot over medium-high heat. Allow the glucose to warm until it liquefies and then starts to bubble. Once the glucose has bubbled a bit in one spot, swirl the pot to distribute the heat.

Add the sugar, about one-third at a time, sprinkling it over the glucose syrup. Using a high-heat spatula or wooden spoon, poke (no stirring) the sugar down into the syrup after each addition. Keep watch to make sure no giant lumps of dry sugar remain before you add the next installment of sugar. If you see lumps, poke them down into the glucose. Once all of the sugar is added and has been poked down into the liquid so it's wet, stop poking.

Pour the cream into a small saucepan and add the salt and vanilla. Stir to mix, then set the pan over low to medium heat. You're not looking to boil the cream; the idea is to simply warm the ingredients so they're not cold when they go into the hot sugar.

Meanwhile, let the glucose and sugar cook, swirling the pot occasionally, until the mixture is dark amber or the color of a copper penny (see the Caramel Color Chart on page 161). Time-wise, you're looking at 13 to 15 minutes for the caramel to reach the target color. At first the sugar

will turn pale brown, then darker brown. This may happen in spots around the pot, so it's important to swirl the pot as the sugar cooks. Once the sugar is a uniform color, cook it for a second or two longer until you feel good about the color, remembering that you want it to match that dark amber target.

Remove the pot from the heat and very carefully add the warmed cream mixture, immediately followed by the butter and the chocolate. Whisk the candy for 5 minutes, until completely emulsified. This means that the fats have been completely mixed into the sugar with no chance of separating. All of the chocolate will have disappeared into the caramel and the mixture will be homogenized, with no oily separation or bits of anything burnt floating around.

Pour the caramel into the prepared candy frame or pan, nudging it into the corners as needed. Allow the candy to sit until cooled and set, at least 3 hours or preferably up to overnight, before cutting.

I hate to say it, but for the longest time it really bothered me that my kid preferred vanilla ice cream over all other flavors. Of course, I'm not the best person to ask because I like fudge, peanut butter, nuts, brownie bits, chocolate chunks, and anything else you can cram into a scoop; but his insistence on vanilla being superior never waned. Finally, when pressed to explain his preference, he said, "Vanilla isn't plain. You can taste all the flavors when you eat it." Yes, he was four at the time, but I realized then he was right. Vanilla contains layer upon layer of flavor. From floral and fruity notes to creamy tones, vanilla is anything but plain. When the caramel has set, see pages 164 to 165 for cutting tips, detailed instructions, and illustrations.

VANILLA BEAN CARAMELS

MAKES ABOUT 160 CARAMELS IF MADE IN A FRAME OR 115 CARAMELS IF MADE IN A PAN

438 grams glucose syrup

800 grams granulated sugar

220 grams Vanilla Bean Cream (see page 61)

7 grams kosher salt

5 grams vanilla bean powder (see page 57)

18 grams vanilla extract

330 grams unsalted butter, cut into roughly 1-inch pieces

Set up a 12 by 14–inch candy frame or lightly butter a 9 by 13–inch pan (see pages 162 to 163).

Weigh the glucose syrup directly into a heavy-bottomed pot, then set the pot over medium-high heat. Allow the glucose to warm until it liquefies and then starts to bubble. Once the glucose has bubbled a bit in one spot, swirl the pot to distribute the heat.

Add the sugar, about one-third at a time, sprinkling it over the glucose syrup. Using a high-heat spatula or wooden spoon, poke (no stirring) the sugar down into the syrup after each addition. Keep watch to make sure no giant lumps of dry sugar remain before you add the next installment of sugar. If you see lumps, poke them down into the glucose. Once all of the sugar is added and has been poked down into the liquid so it's wet, stop poking.

Pour the cream into a small saucepan and add the salt, vanilla bean powder, and vanilla extract. Stir to mix, then set the pan over low to medium heat. You're not looking to boil the cream; the idea is to simply warm the ingredients so they're not cold when they go into the hot sugar.

Meanwhile, let the glucose and sugar cook, swirling the pot occasionally, until the mixture is dark amber, or the color of a copper penny (see the Caramel Color Chart on page 161). Time-wise, you're looking at 13 to 15 minutes for the caramel to reach the target color. At first the sugar will turn pale brown, then darker brown. This may happen in spots around the pot, so it's important to swirl the pot as the sugar cooks.

Once the sugar is a uniform color, cook it for a second or two longer until you feel good about the color, remembering that you want it to match that dark amber target.

Remove the pot from the heat and very carefully add the warmed cream mixture, immediately followed by the butter. Whisk the candy for 5 minutes, until completely emulsified. This means that the fats have been completely mixed into the sugar with no chance of separating. The mixture will be homogenized, with no oily separation or bits of anything burnt floating around.

Pour the caramel into the prepared candy frame or pan, nudging it into the corners as needed. Allow the candy to sit until cooled and set, at least 3 hours or preferably up to overnight, before cutting.

EASY CARAMEL SAUCE

Turning caramel candy into caramel sauce is a snap. Most of the recipes in this chapter, save for the truly chunky caramels—like the ones with bits of sugar cone (see page 196) and pretzel (see page 208)—melt beautifully. Then you just add a touch of cream to smooth out everything and transform the melted candy into a sauce that can be poured over just about anything. But I like to dazzle my friends with caramel "*fun*due," served with pieces of fruit (bananas, apples, pears, peaches), crunchy cookies, cake, pretzels, potato chips—whatever sounds like it'd be good dipped in warm caramel. Don't forget fun add-ons like toasted coconut, nuts, sprinkles, or even fancy flake sea salt.

Unwrap 55 caramels you've made. (That's about 490 grams caramel candy before cutting it into 1-inch squares.) Put the caramels in a small saucepan and place over very low heat to melt, taking care to check the bottom of the pan from time to time to ensure the candy isn't scorching. You can stir the caramels a bit to help them melt more evenly.

While the caramels are melting, pour about ¾ cup heavy cream into a second saucepan and set over medium heat until the cream is thinking about steaming.

When the candy has melted and the cream is warm, whisk the cream into the caramel, a little at a time, until the caramel resembles a sauce and the cream is fully incorporated. The sauce is now ready to use.

CHÈVRE CARAMEL SAUCE

This sauce features chèvre, a perfect tangy addition to caramel. It's great with chocolate cake, various flavors of ice cream, and even apple pie.

Unwrap 55 caramels you've made. (That's about 490 grams caramel candy before cutting it into 1-inch squares.) Put the caramels in a small saucepan and place over very low heat to melt, taking care to check the bottom of the pan from time to time to ensure the candy isn't scorching. You can stir the caramels a bit to help them melt more evenly.

While the caramels are melting, pour about ½ cup heavy cream into a second saucepan, add 60 grams chèvre, and set over medium heat. Whisk the chèvre into the cream as it's heating.

When the candy has melted and the cream is warm, whisk the chèvre mixture into the caramel, a little at a time, until the caramel resembles a sauce and the cream is fully incorporated. The sauce is now ready to use.

Using the Vanilla Bean Caramels recipe (see page 176) as a starting point, it's easy to layer in new flavors to create an entirely new treat. Even small whispers of additional flavor can make something wholly original. A great example? Adding roasted fruit purées to caramel. Some of my favorites are raspberry, cherry, and apricot, but any of the fruit purées in chapter two will work.

You'll want to pick a roasted fruit for this caramel and then find the natural flavoring to match the fruit (for example, raspberry flavoring with roasted raspberries). The purée and flavoring are warmed in the cream before pouring the cream into the caramelized sugar. When the caramel has set, see pages 164 to 165 for cutting tips, detailed instructions, and illustrations.

VANILLA BEAN + ROASTED FRUIT CARAMELS

MAKES ABOUT 160 CARAMELS IF MADE IN A FRAME OR 115 CARAMELS IF MADE IN A PAN

438 grams glucose syrup

800 grams granulated sugar

120 grams Vanilla Bean Cream (see page 61)

100 grams roasted fruit purée (see pages 37 to 49)

7 grams kosher salt

6 grams natural flavoring to match fruit purée

5 grams vanilla bean powder (see page 57)

18 grams vanilla extract

330 grams unsalted butter, cut into roughly 1-inch pieces

Set up a 12 by 14–inch candy frame or lightly butter a 9 by 13–inch pan (see pages 162 to 163).

Weigh the glucose syrup directly into a heavy-bottomed pot, then set the pot over medium-high heat. Allow the glucose to warm until it liquefies and then starts to bubble. Once the glucose has bubbled a bit in one spot, swirl the pot to distribute the heat.

Add the sugar, about one-third at a time, sprinkling it over the glucose syrup. Using a high-heat spatula or wooden spoon, poke (no stirring) the sugar down into the syrup after each addition. Keep watch to make sure no giant lumps of dry sugar remain before you add the next installment of sugar. If you see lumps, poke them down into the glucose. Once all of the sugar is added and has been poked down into the liquid so it's wet, stop poking.

Pour the cream into a small saucepan and add the fruit purée, salt, natural flavoring, vanilla bean powder, and vanilla extract. Stir to mix, then set the pan over low to medium heat. You're not looking to boil the cream; the idea is to simply warm the ingredients so they're not cold when they go into the hot sugar.

Meanwhile, let the glucose and sugar cook, swirling the pot occasionally, until the mixture is dark amber, or the color of a copper penny (see the

Caramel Color Chart on page 161). Time-wise, you're looking at 13 to 15 minutes for the caramel to reach the target color. At first the sugar will turn pale brown, then darker brown. This may happen in spots around the pot, so it's important to swirl the pot as the sugar cooks. Once the sugar is a uniform color, cook it for a second or two longer until you feel good about the color, remembering that you want it to match that dark amber target.

Remove the pot from the heat and very carefully add the warmed cream mixture, immediately followed by the butter. Whisk the candy for 5 minutes, or completely emulsified. This means that the fats have been completely mixed into the sugar with no chance of separating. The mixture will be homogenized, with no oily separation or bits of anything burnt floating around.

Pour the caramel into the prepared candy frame or pan, nudging it into the corners as needed. Allow the candy to sit until cooled and set, at least 3 hours or preferably up to overnight, before cutting.

APRICOT + WHITE CHOCOLATE + COCONUT CARAMELS Here's an idea that uses roasted fruit, but also adds in white chocolate and coconut. Use Roasted Apricots with Coconut and Brown Sugar (see page 47) for the roasted fruit purée and natural apricot flavoring for the flavoring. When whisking the cream mixture and butter into the hot sugar, also whisk in 50 grams white chocolate, coarsely chopped. As soon as the caramel is poured into the frame or pan, shower toasted coconut (flake or shredded, sweetened or unsweetened, your choice) all over the top (see page 172). Allow the candy to sit until cooled and set, at least 3 hours or preferably up to overnight, before cutting.

Because we use Oregon honey and Oregon hazelnuts in these caramels at QUIN, they're a huge hit with the tourist set. We've sold millions of these to people who want to take a taste of Oregon home with them. Aside from the Oregon appeal, I love honey and hazelnuts in this caramel. The honey is very mellow but you can still really taste it in the finished product. And the robust hazelnuts add crunch, of course, but they also bring their particular earthiness to the confection. Together? Crunchy, earthy, honey-sweet perfection. When the caramel has set, see pages 164 to 165 for cutting tips, detailed instructions, and illustrations.

HONEY + HAZELNUT CARAMELS

MAKES ABOUT 160 CARAMELS IF MADE IN A FRAME OR 115 CARAMELS IF MADE IN A PAN

438 grams glucose syrup

800 grams granulated sugar

210 grams heavy cream

10 grams kosher salt

2 grams vanilla bean powder (see page 57)

18 grams vanilla extract

30 grams wildflower honey

325 grams unsalted butter, cut into roughly 1-inch pieces

100 grams chopped toasted hazelnuts

1 gram ground cinnamon

Set up a 12 by 14–inch candy frame or lightly butter a 9 by 13–inch pan (see pages 162 to 163).

Weigh the glucose syrup directly into a heavy-bottomed pot, then set the pot over medium-high heat. Allow the glucose to warm until it liquefies and then starts to bubble. Once the glucose has bubbled a bit in one spot, swirl the pot to distribute the heat.

Add the sugar, about one-third at a time, sprinkling it over the glucose syrup. Using a high-heat spatula or wooden spoon, poke (no stirring) the sugar down into the syrup after each addition. Keep watch to make sure no giant lumps of dry sugar remain before you add the next installment of sugar. If you see lumps, poke them down into the glucose. Once all the sugar is added and has been poked down into the liquid so it's wet, stop poking.

Pour the cream into a small saucepan and add the salt, vanilla bean powder, vanilla extract, and honey. Stir to mix, then set the pan over low to medium heat. You're not looking to boil the cream; the idea is to simply warm the ingredients so they're not cold when they go into the hot sugar.

Meanwhile, let the glucose and sugar cook, swirling the pot occasionally, until the mixture is dark amber, or the color of a copper penny (see the Caramel Color Chart on page 161). Time-wise, you're looking at 13 to

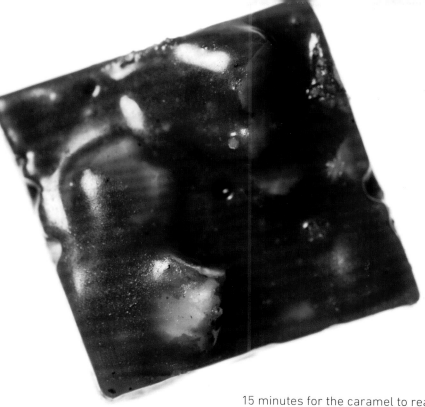

15 minutes for the caramel to reach the target color. At first the sugar will turn pale brown, then darker brown. This may happen in spots around the pot, so it's important to swirl the pot as the sugar cooks. Once the sugar is a uniform color, cook it for a second or two longer until you feel good about the color, remembering that you want it to match that dark amber target.

Remove the pot from the heat and very carefully add the warmed cream mixture, immediately followed by the butter. Whisk the candy for 5 minutes, until completely emulsified. This means that the fats have been completely mixed into the sugar with no chance of separating. The mixture will be homogenized, with no oily separation or bits of anything burnt floating around. Now stir in the hazelnuts and the cinnamon until they are evenly dispersed.

Pour the caramel into the prepared candy frame or pan, nudging it into the corners as needed. Allow the candy to sit until cooled and set, at least 3 hours or preferably up to overnight, before cutting.

The very first treat I learned to bake was pumpkin bread. My Grandma Dot taught me in her Georgia kitchen, and I remember it like it was yesterday. These caramels came about one fall when I was missing my family—my beloved Dot in particular—and wanted to pull some of those pumpkin flavors into a candy. This recipe starts with a pumpkin purée that's cooked with brown sugar and spices almost to mimic a pumpkin pie filling. Once the flavored purée is prepared, it's full steam ahead with the candy. I like to finish this caramel with a sprinkling of crunchy, salted roasted pumpkin seeds. You can buy the pumpkin seeds raw and give them a quick turn on the stove top with some butter and salt until they are toasty and fragrant, or you can buy them already roasted and salted and be done with it. When the caramel has set, see pages 164 to 165 for cutting tips, detailed instructions, and illustrations.

SEA SALT + ROASTED PUMPKIN SEED CARAMELS

MAKES ABOUT 160 CARAMELS IF MADE IN A FRAME OR 115 CARAMELS IF MADE IN A PAN

PUMPKIN PIE PURÉE

160 grams canned plain pumpkin purée (not pumpkin pie filling)

20 grams light brown sugar

1 gram ground cinnamon

1 gram freshly grated nutmeg (see page 92)

1 gram finely ground black pepper

2 grams vanilla bean powder (see page 57)

FOR THE CARAMELS

438 grams glucose syrup

800 grams granulated sugar

To make the pumpkin pie purée, in a medium saucepan, combine all of the purée ingredients and cook over low heat, stirring frequently, for about 20 minutes. The mixture may sputter and steam, and that's fine. When it's done, it will be slightly reduced and look glossy and thick. (You'll end up with about 150 grams of purée that's ready to use immediately or can be refrigerated in a covered container for up to 3 days.)

To make the caramels, set up a 12 by 14–inch candy frame or lightly butter a 9 by 13–inch pan (see pages 162 to 163).

Weigh the glucose syrup directly into a heavy-bottomed pot, then set the pot over medium-high heat. Allow the glucose to warm until it liquefies and then starts to bubble. Once the glucose has bubbled a bit in one spot, swirl the pot to distribute the heat.

Add the sugar, about one-third at a time, sprinkling it over the glucose syrup. Using a high-heat spatula or wooden spoon, poke (no stirring) the sugar down into the syrup after each addition. Keep watch to make sure no giant lumps of dry sugar remain before you add the next installment of sugar. If you see lumps, poke them down into the glucose. Once all of the sugar is added and has been poked down into the liquid so it's wet, stop poking.

120 grams heavy cream

7 grams kosher salt

2 grams vanilla bean powder (see page 57)

1 gram finely ground black pepper

1 gram freshly grated nutmeg (see page 92)

1 gram ground cinnamon

6 grams vanilla extract

About 150 grams prepared Pumpkin Pie Purée (preceding)

120 grams unsalted butter, cut into roughly 1-inch pieces

60 grams salted roasted pumpkin seeds

Pour the cream into a small saucepan and add the salt, vanilla bean powder, pepper, nutmeg, cinnamon, vanilla extract, and pumpkin pie purée. Stir to mix, then set the pan over low to medium heat. You're not looking to boil the cream; the idea is to simply warm the ingredients so they're not cold when they go into the hot sugar.

Meanwhile, let the glucose and sugar cook, swirling the pot occasionally, until the mixture is dark amber, or the color of a copper penny (see the Caramel Color Chart on page 161). Time-wise you're looking at 13 to 15 minutes for the caramel to reach the target color. At first the sugar will turn pale brown, then darker brown. This may happen in spots around the pot, so it's important to swirl the pot as the sugar cooks. Once the sugar is a uniform color, cook it for a second or two longer until you feel good about the color, remembering that you want it to match that dark amber target.

Remove the pan from the heat and very carefully add the warmed cream mixture, immediately followed by the butter. Whisk the candy for 5 minutes, until completely emulsified. This means that the fats have been completely mixed into the sugar with no chance of separating. The mixture will be homogenized, with no oily separation or bits of anything burnt floating around.

Pour the caramel into the prepared candy frame or pan, nudging it into the corners as needed, and allow it to rest for about 5 minutes. Shower the pumpkin seeds evenly over the top (see page 172) and then allow the caramel to sit until cooled and set, at least 3 hours or preferably up to overnight, before cutting.

This caramel is the closest thing to a candy bar that QUIN will ever make. Rich, crunchy, and gooey—three of my favorite words for describing candy—all come into play here.

Stick with coconut milk from a can for this recipe. I always (for everything) prefer full-fat to any reduced-fat version. But there are still lots of ways to change up this recipe. Instead of using toasted pecans, you can toss in candied pecans. The chocolate can range from my suggestion of a very dark chocolate to something a little milkier. You can trade out 200 grams of the granulated sugar for smoked granulated sugar (see page 293). And if you really want to get crazy, allow the caramel to cool in the frame for a minute or so, then sprinkle toasted sweetened shredded coconut evenly over the top for a very pretty and perfectly toothsome candy. When the caramel has set, see pages 164 to 165 for cutting tips, detailed instructions, and illustrations.

COCONUT + TOASTED PECAN + CHOCOLATE CARAMELS

**MAKES ABOUT
160 CARAMELS IF
MADE IN A FRAME
OR 115 CARAMELS
IF MADE IN A PAN**

438 grams glucose syrup

800 grams granulated sugar

200 grams canned full-fat coconut milk

6 grams kosher salt

18 grams vanilla extract

300 grams unsalted butter, cut into roughly 1-inch pieces

50 grams dark chocolate (70 to 80 percent cacao), chopped

100 grams toasted pecans, chopped

Set up a 12 by 14–inch candy frame or lightly butter a 9 by 13–inch pan (see pages 162 to 163).

Weigh the glucose syrup directly into a heavy-bottomed pot, then set the pot over medium-high heat. Allow the glucose to warm until it liquefies and then starts to bubble. Once the glucose has bubbled a bit in one spot, swirl the pot to distribute the heat.

Add the sugar, about one-third at a time, sprinkling it over the glucose syrup. Using a high-heat spatula or wooden spoon, poke (no stirring) the sugar down into the syrup after each addition. Keep watch to make sure no giant lumps of dry sugar remain before you add the next installment of sugar. If you see lumps, poke them down into the glucose. Once all of the sugar is added and has been poked down into the liquid so it's wet, stop poking.

Pour the coconut milk into a small saucepan and add the salt and vanilla extract. Stir to mix, then set the pan over low to medium heat. You're not looking to boil the coconut milk; the idea is to simply warm the ingredients so they're not cold when they go into the hot sugar.

Meanwhile, let the glucose and sugar cook, swirling the pot occasionally, until the mixture is dark amber, or the color of a copper penny (see the Caramel Color Chart on page 161). Time-wise, you're looking at 13 to 15 minutes for the caramel to reach the target color. At first the sugar will turn pale brown, then darker brown. This may happen in spots around the pot, so it's important to swirl the pot as the sugar cooks. Once the sugar is a uniform color, cook it for a second or two longer until you feel good about the color, remembering that you want it to match that dark amber target.

Remove the pot from the heat and very carefully add the warmed coconut milk mixture, immediately followed by the butter and then the chocolate. Whisk the candy for 5 minutes, until completely emulsified. This means that the fats have been completely mixed into the sugar with no chance of separating. All of the chocolate will have disappeared into the caramel and the mixture will be homogenized, with no oily separation or bits of anything burnt floating around. Now stir in the pecans until evenly dispersed.

Pour the caramel into the prepared candy frame or pan, nudging it into the corners as needed. Allow the candy to sit until cooled and set, at least 3 hours or preferably up to overnight, before cutting.

I'm apple-obsessed, and I'm fortunate to know a very skilled apple farmer named Susan Christopherson. Susan lives on a beautiful piece of land in Ridgefield, Washington. The property is dotted with rare and heirloom apple trees—trees with which Susan is so familiar that a walk through the orchard is not unlike flipping through the pages of her family photo album. For me, an afternoon spent at the farm is the perfect getaway. Something about the trees and the sky and Susan herself, I forget about every trouble and doubt, and I find myself feeling completely inspired. (Of course, Susan is a great listener, usually has an apple pie on her kitchen counter, and is a total pro at having a pot of coffee at the ready. These three things definitely add to the "getaway" spirit.)

The key to this recipe is the use of a good-quality apple butter. Homemade is great, but if you use store-bought, the ingredient list on the jar should mention only apples and apple cider. Before you begin the recipe, take a few minutes to remove any extra water content from the apple butter, whether it's homemade or store-bought, by scooping it into a small saucepan and warming it over medium heat until you see steam. Keep the apple butter moving (stir it) so it doesn't scorch and allow it to steam for 5 minutes. Remove it from the heat and proceed with the recipe. When the caramel has set, see pages 164 to 165 for cutting tips, detailed instructions, and illustrations.

APPLE CARAMELS

MAKES ABOUT 160 CARAMELS IF MADE IN A FRAME OR 115 CARAMELS IF MADE IN A PAN

438 grams glucose syrup

800 grams granulated sugar

110 grams heavy cream

7 grams kosher salt

3 grams vanilla bean powder (see page 57)

3 grams ground cinnamon

2 grams freshly grated nutmeg (see page 92)

CONTINUED

Set up a 12 by 14–inch candy frame or lightly butter a 9 by 13–inch pan (see pages 162 to 163).

Weigh the glucose syrup directly into a heavy-bottomed pot, then set the pot over medium-high heat. Allow the glucose to warm until it liquefies and then starts to bubble. Once the glucose has bubbled a bit in one spot, swirl the pot to distribute the heat.

Add the sugar, about one-third at a time, sprinkling it over the glucose syrup. Using a high-heat spatula or wooden spoon, poke (no stirring) the sugar down into the syrup after each addition. Keep watch to make sure no giant lumps of dry sugar remain before you add the next installment of sugar. If you see lumps, poke them down into the glucose. Once all of the sugar is added and has been poked down into the liquid so it's wet, stop poking.

CONTINUED

16 grams vanilla extract

130 grams apple butter, excess moisture removed before weighing (see headnote)

120 grams unsalted butter, cut into roughly 1-inch pieces

Pour the cream into a small saucepan and add the salt, vanilla bean powder, cinnamon, nutmeg, vanilla extract, and apple butter. Stir to mix, then set the pan over low to medium heat. You're not looking to boil the cream; the idea is to simply warm the ingredients so they're not cold when they go into the hot sugar.

Meanwhile, let the glucose and sugar cook, swirling the pot occasionally, until the mixture is dark amber, or the color of a copper penny (see the Caramel Color Chart on page 161). Time-wise, you're looking at 13 to 15 minutes for the caramel to reach the target color. At first the sugar will turn pale brown, then darker brown. This may happen in spots around the pot, so it's important to swirl the pot as the sugar cooks. Once the sugar is a uniform color, cook it for a second or two longer until you feel good about the color, remembering that you want it to match that dark amber target.

Remove the pot from the heat and very carefully add the warmed cream mixture, immediately followed by the butter. Whisk the candy for 5 minutes, until completely emulsified. This means that the fats have been completely mixed into the sugar with no chance of separating. The mixture will be homogenized, with no oily separation or bits of anything burnt floating around.

Pour the caramel into the prepared candy frame or pan, nudging it into the corners as needed. Allow the candy to sit until cooled and set, at least 3 hours or preferably up to overnight, before cutting.

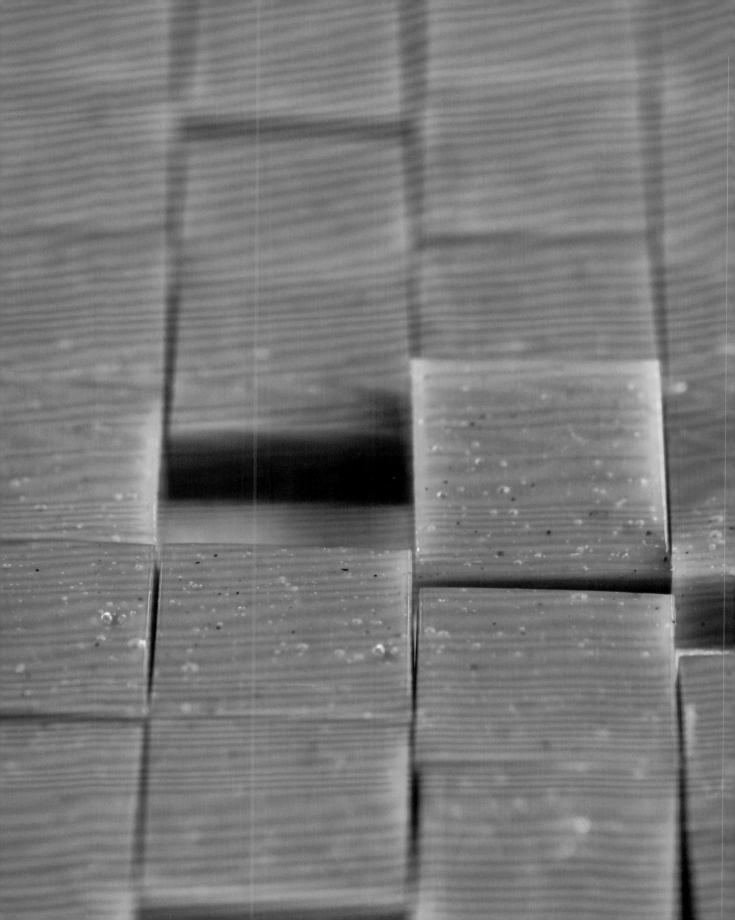

Spicy caramel with chewy raisins—you'll either love it or you won't. That's what I learned the Valentine's Day these hit the shelves at QUIN. I'm crazy about the spicy cream that goes into these caramels; and if you don't care for raisins, you can easily omit them. Overall, I think I'm dedicated to this combination because it's a little daring and a little different. When the caramel has set, see pages 164 to 165 for cutting tips, detailed instructions, and illustrations.

ALEPPO PEPPER + RAISIN CARAMELS

MAKES ABOUT 160 CARAMELS IF MADE IN A FRAME OR 115 CARAMELS IF MADE IN A PAN

438 grams glucose syrup

800 grams granulated sugar

220 grams Pepper Cream (see page 64), made with Aleppo pepper

7 grams kosher salt

3 grams vanilla bean powder (see page 57)

18 grams vanilla extract

330 grams unsalted butter, cut into roughly 1-inch pieces

70 grams raisins

2 grams Aleppo pepper

Set up a 12 by 14–inch candy frame or lightly butter a 9 by 13–inch pan (see pages 162 to 163).

Weigh the glucose syrup directly into a heavy-bottomed pot, then set the pot over medium-high heat. Allow the glucose to warm until it liquefies and then starts to bubble. Once the glucose has bubbled a bit in one spot, swirl the pot to distribute the heat.

Add the sugar, about one-third at a time, sprinkling it over the glucose syrup. Using a high-heat spatula or wooden spoon, poke (no stirring) the sugar down into the syrup after each addition. Keep watch to make sure no giant lumps of dry sugar remain before you add the next installment of sugar. If you see lumps, poke them down into the glucose. Once all of the sugar is added and has been poked down into the liquid so it's wet, stop poking.

Pour the cream into a small saucepan and add the salt, vanilla bean powder, and vanilla extract. Stir to mix, then set the pan over low to medium heat. You're not looking to boil the cream; the idea is to simply warm the ingredients so they're not cold when they go into the hot sugar.

Meanwhile, let the glucose and sugar cook, swirling the pot occasionally, until the mixture is dark amber, or the color of a copper penny (see the Caramel Color Chart on page 161). Time-wise, you're looking at 13 to 15 minutes for the caramel to reach the target color. At first the sugar will turn pale brown, then darker brown. This may happen in spots around the pot, so it's important to swirl the pot as the sugar cooks. Once the sugar is a uniform color, cook it for a second or two longer until you feel good about the color, remembering that you want it to match that dark amber target.

Remove the pot from the heat and very carefully add the warmed cream mixture, immediately followed by the butter. Whisk the candy for 5 minutes, until completely emulsified. This means that the fats have been completely mixed into the sugar with no chance of separating. The mixture will be homogenized, with no oily separation or bits of anything burnt floating around. Now stir in the raisins and the Aleppo pepper until evenly dispersed.

Pour the caramel into the prepared candy frame or pan, nudging it into the corners as needed. Allow the candy to sit until cooled and set, at least 3 hours or preferably up to overnight, before cutting.

I have a deep affection for ice cream. I truly could go on and on, but I'll keep it brief by telling you that this caramel is the exact kind of ice cream I dream of eating—chocolate malt on a sugar cone, thick and rich and dripping all over the place. When the caramel has set, see pages 164 to 165 for cutting tips, detailed instructions, and illustrations.

CHOCOLATE MALT + SUGAR CONE CARAMELS

MAKES ABOUT 160 CARAMELS IF MADE IN A FRAME OR 115 CARAMELS IF MADE IN A PAN

438 grams glucose syrup

800 grams granulated sugar

220 grams Malted Milk Cream (see page 58)

8 grams kosher salt

3 grams vanilla bean powder (see page 57)

18 grams vanilla extract

320 grams unsalted butter, cut into roughly 1-inch pieces

80 grams semisweet chocolate (50 to 60 percent cacao), coarsely chopped

30 grams dark chocolate (more than 70 percent cacao), coarsely chopped

100 grams sugar cones, crushed into walnut-size pieces

Set up a 12 by 14–inch candy frame or lightly butter a 9 by 13–inch pan (see pages 162 to 163).

Weigh the glucose syrup directly into a heavy-bottomed pot, then set the pot over medium-high heat. Allow the glucose to warm until it liquefies and then starts to bubble. Once the glucose has bubbled a bit in one spot, swirl the pot to distribute the heat.

Add the sugar, about one-third at a time, sprinkling it over the glucose syrup. Using a high-heat spatula or wooden spoon, poke (no stirring) the sugar down into the syrup after each addition. Keep watch to make sure no giant lumps of dry sugar remain before you add the next installment of sugar. If you see lumps, poke them down into the glucose. Once all of the sugar is added and has been poked down into the liquid so it's wet, stop poking.

Pour the cream into a small saucepan and add the salt, vanilla bean powder, and vanilla extract. Stir to mix, then set the pan over low to medium heat. You're not looking to boil the cream; the idea is to simply warm the ingredients so they're not cold when they go into the hot sugar.

Meanwhile, let the glucose and sugar cook, swirling the pot occasionally, until the mixture is dark amber, or the color of a copper penny (see the Caramel Color Chart on page 161). Time-wise, you're looking at 13 to 15 minutes for the caramel to reach the target color. At first the sugar will turn pale brown, then darker brown. This may happen in spots around the pot, so it's important to swirl the pot as the sugar cooks. Once the sugar is a uniform color, cook it for a second or two longer until you feel good about the color, remembering that you want it to match that dark amber target.

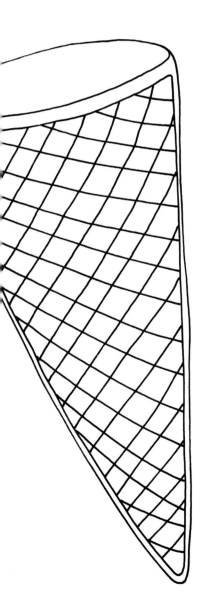

Remove the pot from the heat and very carefully add the warmed cream mixture, immediately followed by the butter and then all of the chocolate. Whisk the candy for 5 minutes, until completely emulsified. This means that the fats have been completely mixed into the sugar with no chance of separating. All of the chocolate will have disappeared into the caramel and the mixture will be homogenized, with no oily separation or bits of anything burnt floating around. Now stir in the sugar cone pieces until evenly dispersed.

Pour the caramel into the prepared candy frame or pan, nudging it into the corners as needed. Allow the candy to sit until cooled and set, at least 3 hours or preferably up to overnight, before cutting.

While this caramel works just fine made with plain granulated sugar, I really do love it best when it's made with smoked sugar. Smoked sugar brings a layer of flavor that nothing else can, and it complements the mysterious flavors of chai perfectly. For tips on finding smoked sugar, see the Resources Guide (page 293). When the caramel has set, see pages 164 to 165 for cutting tips, detailed instructions, and illustrations.

SMOKED CHAI TEA CARAMELS

MAKES ABOUT 160 CARAMELS IF MADE IN A FRAME OR 115 CARAMELS IF MADE IN A PAN

483 grams glucose syrup

600 grams granulated sugar

200 grams smoked granulated sugar

220 grams Chai Tea Cream (see page 63)

9 grams kosher salt

2 grams vanilla bean powder (see page 57)

18 grams vanilla extract

330 grams unsalted butter, cut into roughly 1-inch pieces

Set up a 12 by 14–inch candy frame or lightly butter a 9 by 13–inch pan (see page 162 to 163).

Weigh the glucose syrup directly into a heavy-bottomed pot, then set the pot over medium-high heat. Allow the glucose to warm until it liquefies and then starts to bubble. Once the glucose has bubbled a bit in one spot, swirl the pot to distribute the heat.

Add the sugar, about one-third at a time, sprinkling it over the glucose syrup. Using a high-heat spatula or wooden spoon, poke (no stirring) the sugar down into the syrup after each addition. Keep watch to make sure no giant lumps of dry sugar remain before you add the next installment of sugar. If you see lumps, poke them down into the glucose. Once all of the sugar is added and has been poked down into the liquid so it's wet, stop poking.

Pour the cream into a small saucepan and add the salt, vanilla bean powder, and vanilla extract. Stir to mix, then set the pan over low to medium heat. You're not looking to boil the cream; the idea is to simply warm the ingredients so they're not cold when they go into the hot sugar.

Meanwhile, let the glucose and sugar cook, swirling the pot occasionally, until the mixture is dark amber, or the color of a copper penny (see the Caramel Color Chart on page 161). Time-wise, you're looking at 13 to 15 minutes for the caramel to reach the target color. At first the sugar will turn pale brown, then darker brown. This may happen in spots around the pot, so it's important to swirl the pot as the sugar cooks. Once the sugar is a uniform color, cook it for a second or two longer until you feel good about the color, remembering that you want it to match that dark amber target.

Remove the pot from the heat and very carefully add the warmed cream mixture, immediately followed by the butter. Whisk the candy for 5 minutes, or until completely emulsified. This means that the fats have been completely mixed into the sugar with no chance of separating. The mixture will be homogenized, with no oily separation or bits of anything burnt floating around.

Pour the caramel into the prepared candy frame or pan, nudging it into the corners as needed. Allow the candy to sit until cooled and set, at least 3 hours or preferably up to overnight, before cutting.

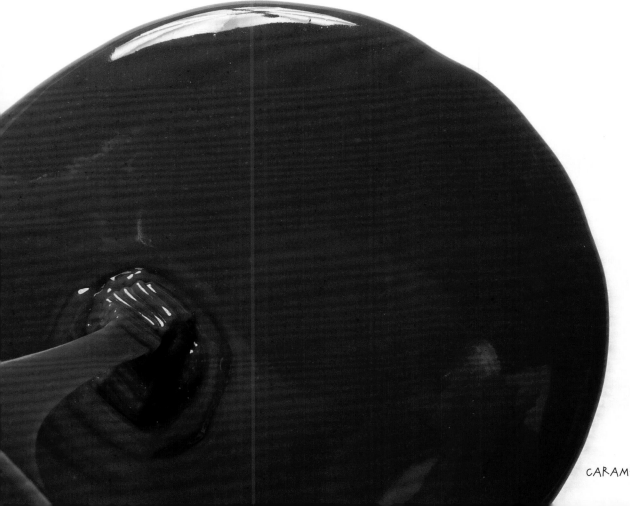

These candies are as sophisticated as they are divine. A tiny tea party in a caramel, the essence of tea is imparted to the candy by way of an infused cream. Once you taste caramel with a hint of orangey-citrusy goodness, you'll never be the same. When the caramel has set, see pages 164 to 165 for cutting tips, detailed instructions, and illustrations.

EARL GREY CARAMELS

MAKES ABOUT 160 CARAMELS IF MADE IN A FRAME OR 115 CARAMELS IF MADE IN A PAN

438 grams glucose syrup

800 grams granulated sugar

220 grams Earl Grey Tea Cream (see page 63)

8 grams kosher salt

2 grams vanilla bean powder (see page 57)

18 grams vanilla extract

330 grams unsalted butter, cut into roughly 1-inch pieces

Set up a 12 by 14-inch candy frame or lightly butter a 9 by 13-inch pan (see pages 162 to 163).

Weigh the glucose syrup directly into a heavy-bottomed pot, then set the pot over medium-high heat. Allow the glucose to warm until it liquefies and then starts to bubble. Once the glucose has bubbled a bit in one spot, swirl the pot to distribute the heat.

Add the sugar, about one-third at a time, sprinkling it over the glucose syrup. Using a high-heat spatula or wooden spoon, poke (no stirring) the sugar down into the syrup after each addition. Keep watch to make sure no giant lumps of dry sugar remain before you add the next installment of sugar. If you see lumps, poke them down into the glucose. Once all of the sugar is added and has been poked down into the liquid so it's wet, stop poking.

Pour the cream into a small saucepan and add the salt, vanilla bean powder, and vanilla extract. Stir to mix, then set the pan over low to medium heat. You're not looking to boil the cream; the idea is to simply warm the ingredients so they're not cold when they go into the hot sugar.

Meanwhile, let the glucose and sugar cook, swirling the pot occasionally, until the mixture is dark amber, or the color of a copper penny (see the Caramel Color Chart on page 161). Time-wise, you're looking at 13 to 15 minutes for the caramel to reach the target color. At first the sugar will turn pale brown, then darker brown. This may happen in spots around the pot, so it's important to swirl the pot as the sugar cooks. Once the sugar is a uniform color, cook it for a second or two longer until you feel good about the color, remembering that you want it to match that dark amber target.

Remove the pot from the heat and very carefully add the warmed cream mixture, immediately followed by the butter. Whisk the candy for 5 minutes, or until completely emulsified. This means that the fats have been completely mixed into the sugar with no chance of separating. The mixture will be homogenized, with no oily separation or bits of anything burnt floating around.

Pour the caramel into the prepared candy frame or pan, nudging it into the corners as needed. Allow the candy to sit until cooled and set, at least 3 hours or preferably up to overnight, before cutting.

These caramels are so good. Don't question it, just make them. And then give them to all of the people you want to impress with your newfound candy-making and flavor-pairing abilities. When the caramel has set, see pages 164 to 165 for cutting tips, detailed instructions, and illustrations.

COFFEE + ORANGE + SMOKED SALT CARAMELS

MAKES ABOUT 160 CARAMELS IF MADE IN A FRAME OR 115 CARAMELS IF MADE IN A PAN

400 grams glucose

70 grams Coffee Syrup (see page 68)

800 grams granulated sugar

200 grams Coffee Cream (see page 55)

6 grams kosher salt

330 grams unsalted butter, cut into roughly 1-inch pieces

15 grams finely grated orange zest

25 grams smoked flake sea salt (see page 293)

Set up a 12 by 14–inch candy frame or lightly butter a 9 by 13–inch pan (see pages 162 to 163).

Weigh the glucose syrup and 40 grams of the coffee syrup directly into a heavy-bottomed pot, then set the pot over medium-high heat. Allow the glucose to warm until it liquefies and then starts to bubble. Once the glucose has bubbled a bit in one spot, swirl the pot to distribute the heat.

Add the sugar, about one-third at a time, sprinkling it over the glucose syrup. Using a high-heat spatula or wooden spoon, poke (no stirring) the sugar down into the syrup after each addition. Keep watch to make sure no giant lumps of dry sugar remain before you add the next installment of sugar. If you see lumps, poke them down into the glucose. Once all of the sugar is added and has been poked down into the liquid so it's wet, stop poking.

Pour the cream into a small saucepan and add the kosher salt and remaining 30 grams coffee syrup. Stir to mix, then set the pan over low to medium heat. You're not looking to boil the cream; the idea is to simply warm the ingredients so they're not cold when they go into the hot sugar.

Meanwhile, let the glucose and sugar cook, swirling the pot occasionally, until the mixture is dark amber, or the color of a copper penny (see the Caramel Color Chart on page 161). Time-wise, you're looking at 13 to 15 minutes for the caramel to reach the target color. At first the sugar will turn pale brown, then darker brown. This may happen in spots around the pot, so it's important to swirl the pot as the sugar cooks.

Once the sugar is a uniform color, cook it for a second or two longer until you feel good about the color, remembering that you want it to match that dark amber target.

Remove the pot from the heat and very carefully add the warmed cream mixture, immediately followed by the butter. Whisk the candy for 5 minutes, until completely emulsified. This means that the fats have been completely mixed into the sugar with no chance of separating. The mixture will be homogenized, with no oily separation or bits of anything burnt floating around. Now stir in the orange zest until evenly dispersed.

Pour the caramel into the prepared candy frame or pan, nudging it into the corners as needed, and allow it to rest for 10 minutes. Shower the smoked sea salt evenly over the top (see page 172). Allow the candy to sit until cooled and set, at least 3 hours or preferably up to overnight, before cutting.

COFFEE CARAMELS Conveniently enough, these orangey caramels can transform into straight coffee caramels with a few simple changes. Prepare the Coffee + Orange + Smoked Salt Caramels as directed, but omit the orange zest and add 5 grams cocoa powder (see page 74) and 3 grams vanilla bean powder (see page 57) to the cream. Leave off the smoked salt, and you've got delicious straight coffee candy on your hands.

CARAMEL APPLE KIT

Here's what you'll need:

* 8 medium apples
* 64 (1-inch) caramels (any flavor)
* 8 caramel-apple sticks
* 8 (12-inch) square cellophane wrappers
* Baker's twine or kitchen twine for securing the cellophane wrappers
* Paper for the instruction card
* Paper bag with handles (apple bag)

Caramel apples. Whenever they're mentioned, people go a little starry-eyed and admit they've never really made one, but definitely enjoy eating one. Let's change that.

This project creates a kit, ready for giving, that includes everything the recipient will need to create perfect caramel apples. You'll make the candy, assemble the kit components, and include a little instruction card to tuck in the bag. I like apple bags (sometimes called market-stand or orchard bags) the best. Details on where to buy the components can be found in the Resources Guide (see page 294).

Write the instruction card (see facing page).

Tuck the apples, caramels, sticks, cellophane, twine, and instruction card inside the bag and you've got your caramel apple kit ready to go.

Of course, I'd be remiss not to point out that you can follow the same instructions to make caramel apples you can eat yourself, and skip giving away the kit.

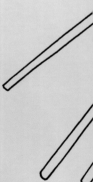

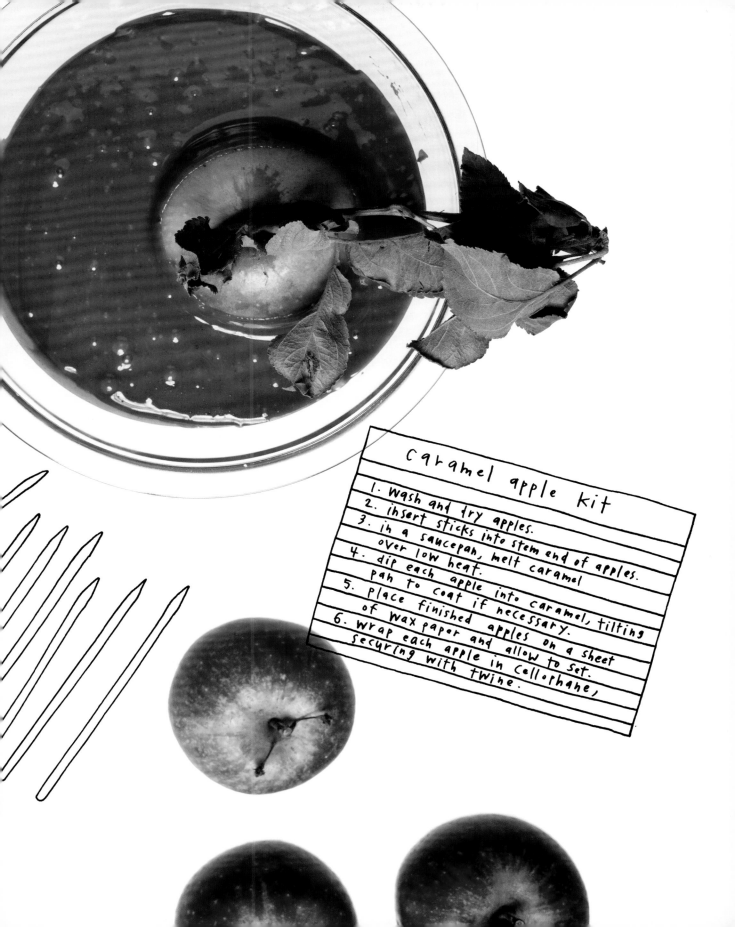

Caramel apple kit

1. Wash and dry apples.
2. Insert sticks into stem end of apples.
3. In a saucepan, melt caramel over low heat.
4. Dip each apple into caramel, tilting pan to coat if necessary.
5. Place finished apples on a sheet of wax paper and allow to set.
6. Wrap each apple in cellophane, securing with twine.

When it comes to candy, it's always been difficult for me to discriminate. From a young age (and probably thanks to my Grandma Dot, who also loved pretty much every candy under the sun), I've really loved black jelly beans. I pick the black ones over the green, yellow, or orange any day. While it's true that black licorice isn't a flavor for everyone, we still sell an awful lot of these caramels at QUIN.

My take on black licorice candy combines anise, molasses, and salt and then cooks them into a caramel. That means it satisfies two major current cravings: salty caramel *and* licorice. One additive this candy is missing? Fake black food coloring. The black dye adds nothing to the candy, so I choose to leave it out. Make this candy and share it with the licorice skeptics. I know you'll win over at least a few. When the caramel has set, see pages 164 to 165 for cutting tips, detailed instructions, and illustrations.

AHOY, MATEY! CARAMELS

MAKES ABOUT 160 CARAMELS IF MADE IN A FRAME OR 115 CARAMELS IF MADE IN A PAN

438 grams glucose syrup

800 grams granulated sugar

210 grams heavy cream

9 grams kosher salt

24 grams natural anise flavoring

30 grams dark (full-flavor) molasses

325 grams unsalted butter, cut into roughly 1-inch pieces

Set up a 12 by 14–inch candy frame or lightly butter a 9 by 13–inch pan (see pages 162 to 163).

Weigh the glucose syrup directly into a heavy-bottomed pot, then set the pot over medium-high heat. Allow the glucose to warm until it liquefies and then starts to bubble. Once the glucose has bubbled a bit in one spot, swirl the pot to distribute the heat.

Add the sugar, about one-third at a time, sprinkling it over the glucose syrup. Using a high-heat spatula or wooden spoon, poke (no stirring) the sugar down into the syrup after each addition. Keep watch to make sure no giant lumps of dry sugar remain before you add the next installment of sugar. If you see lumps, poke them down into the glucose. Once all of the sugar is added and has been poked down into the liquid so it's wet, stop poking.

Pour the cream into a small saucepan and add the salt, anise flavoring, and molasses. Stir to mix, then set the pan over low to medium heat. You're not looking to boil the cream; the idea is to simply warm the ingredients so they're not cold when they go into the hot sugar.

Meanwhile, let the glucose and sugar cook, swirling the pot occasionally, until the mixture is dark amber, or the color of a copper penny (see the Caramel Color Chart on page 161). Time-wise, you're looking at 13 to 15 minutes for the caramel to reach the target color. At first the sugar will turn pale brown, then darker brown. This may happen in spots around the pot, so it's important to swirl the pot as the sugar cooks. Once the sugar is a uniform color, cook it for a second or two longer until you feel good about the color, remembering that you want it to match that dark amber target.

Remove the pot from the heat and very carefully add the warmed cream mixture, immediately followed by the butter. Whisk the candy for 5 minutes, until completely emulsified. This means that the fats have been completely mixed into the sugar with no chance of separating. The mixture will be homogenized, with no oily separation or bits of anything burnt floating around.

Pour the caramel into the prepared candy frame or pan, nudging it into the corners as needed. Allow the candy to sit until cooled and set, at least 3 hours or preferably up to overnight, before cutting.

At QUIN, we have a room that's essentially filled with shelves holding bins of wrapped candy awaiting retail packaging. It's about 1,000 times better than the bulk section of the grocery store, to be certain. When there's an open bin of these Chocolate Pretzel Caramels, I know I'll be going home having eaten too much candy. I simply cannot resist.

When developing this recipe, I wrestled with the texture of the pretzels once they were mixed with hot caramel. I didn't want mush, but I also didn't want something that would disrupt the perfect chew of our caramel. So the pretzels went into the oven for a quick toast before they were stirred into the candy, and it worked. Simply preheat your oven to 400°F, spread the pretzels out on a sheet pan, and let them toast away for 8 to 10 minutes. When the caramel has set, see pages 164 to 165 for cutting tips, detailed instructions, and illustrations.

CHOCOLATE PRETZEL CARAMELS

MAKES ABOUT 160 CARAMELS IF MADE IN A FRAME OR 115 CARAMELS IF MADE IN A PAN

438 grams glucose syrup

800 grams granulated sugar

200 grams Chocolate Cream (see page 57)

8 grams kosher salt

3 grams vanilla bean powder (see page 57)

8 grams cocoa powder (see page 74)

18 grams vanilla extract

320 grams unsalted butter, cut into roughly 1-inch pieces

125 grams semisweet chocolate (50 to 65 percent cacao), chopped

200 grams pretzels, toasted (see headnote) and broken into bite-size pieces

Set up a 12 by 14–inch candy frame or lightly butter a 9 by 13–inch pan (see pages 162 to 163).

Weigh the glucose syrup directly into a heavy-bottomed pot, then set the pot over medium-high heat. Allow the glucose to warm until it liquefies and then starts to bubble. Once the glucose has bubbled a bit in one spot, swirl the pot to distribute the heat.

Add the sugar, about one-third at a time, sprinkling it over the glucose syrup. Using a high-heat spatula or wooden spoon, poke (no stirring) the sugar down into the syrup after each addition. Keep watch to make sure no giant lumps of dry sugar remain before you add the next installment of sugar. If you see lumps, poke them down into the glucose. Once all of the sugar is added and has been poked down into the liquid so it's wet, stop poking.

Pour the cream into a small saucepan and add the salt, vanilla bean powder, cocoa powder, and vanilla extract. Stir to mix, then set the pan over low to medium heat. You're not looking to boil the cream; the idea is to simply warm the ingredients so they're not cold when they go into the hot sugar.

Meanwhile, let the glucose and sugar cook, swirling the pot occasionally, until the mixture is dark amber, or the color of a copper penny (see the Caramel Color Chart on page 161). Time-wise, you're looking at 13 to 15 minutes for the caramel to reach the target color. At first the sugar will turn pale brown, then darker brown. This may happen in spots around the pot, so it's important to swirl the pot as the sugar cooks. Once the sugar is a uniform color, cook it for a second or two longer until you feel good about the color, remembering that you want it to match that dark amber target.

Remove the pot from the heat and very carefully add the warmed cream mixture, immediately followed by the butter and then the chocolate. Whisk the candy for 5 minutes, until completely emulsified. This means that the fats have been completely mixed into the sugar with no chance of separating. All of the chocolate will have disappeared into the caramel and the mixture will be homogenized, with no oily separation or bits of anything burnt floating around. Now stir in the pretzels until evenly dispersed.

Pour the caramel into the prepared candy frame or pan, nudging it into the corners as needed. Allow the candy to sit until cooled and set, at least 3 hours or preferably up to overnight, before cutting.

Maybe it's just my Ohio upbringing talking, but I love candy turtles. In fact, I don't know anyone who grew up in the Midwest who doesn't love a good turtle. Pecans (always my nut of choice), chocolate, and caramel together in one candy that looks like a reptile? Sounds crazy, but I actually drool just thinking about eating one. This recipe combines toasty pecans, two varieties of chocolate, and a good amount of salt. The finished candy is quite stunning, with the glossy caramel giving way to the pecan bits and pieces. When the caramel has set, see pages 164 to 165 for cutting tips, detailed instructions, and illustrations.

TURTLE CARAMELS

MAKES ABOUT 160 CARAMELS IF MADE IN A FRAME OR 115 CARAMELS IF MADE IN A PAN

438 grams glucose syrup

800 grams granulated sugar

220 grams heavy cream

9 grams kosher salt

2 grams vanilla bean powder (see page 57)

18 grams vanilla extract

320 grams unsalted butter, cut into roughly 1-inch pieces

81 grams dark milk chocolate (about 49 percent cacao), coarsely chopped

30 grams semisweet chocolate (55 to 60 percent cacao), coarsely chopped

175 grams pecans, toasted and chopped

Set up a 12 by 14–inch candy frame or lightly butter a 9 by 13–inch pan (see pages 162 to 163).

Weigh the glucose syrup directly into a heavy-bottomed pot, then set the pot over medium-high heat. Allow the glucose to warm until it liquefies and then starts to bubble. Once the glucose has bubbled a bit in one spot, swirl the pot to distribute the heat.

Add the sugar, about one-third at a time, sprinkling it over the glucose syrup. Using a high-heat spatula or wooden spoon, poke (no stirring) the sugar down into the syrup after each addition. Keep watch to make sure no giant lumps of dry sugar remain before you add the next installment of sugar. If you see lumps, poke them down into the glucose. Once all of the sugar is added and has been poked down into the liquid so it's wet, stop poking.

Pour the cream into a small saucepan and add the salt, vanilla bean powder, and vanilla extract. Stir to mix, then set the pan over low to medium heat. You're not looking to boil the cream; the idea is to simply warm the ingredients so they're not cold when they go into the hot sugar.

Meanwhile, let the glucose and sugar cook, swirling the pot occasionally, until the mixture is dark amber or the color of a copper penny (see the Caramel Color Chart on page 161). Time-wise, you're looking at 13 to 15 minutes for the caramel to reach the target color. At first the sugar will turn pale brown, then darker brown. This may happen in spots around the pot, so it's important to

swirl the pot as the sugar cooks. Once the sugar is a uniform color, cook it for a second or two longer until you feel good about the color, remembering that you want it to match that dark amber target.

Remove the pot from the heat and very carefully add the warmed cream mixture, immediately followed by the butter and then all of the chocolate. Whisk the candy for 5 minutes, until completely emulsified. This means that the fats have been completely mixed into the sugar with no chance of separating. All of the chocolate will have disappeared into the caramel and the mixture will be homogenized, with no oily separation or bits of anything burnt floating around. Now stir in the pecans until evenly dispersed.

Pour the caramel into the prepared candy frame or pan, nudging it into the corners as needed. Allow the candy to sit until cooled and set, at least 3 hours or preferably up to overnight, before cutting.

Black pepper and maple syrup—anyone who's ever swiped a piece of pepper bacon through a puddle of syrup on a nearly empty breakfast plate will understand this combination. These caramels are familiar and warming, with bright sparks of coarsely ground black pepper guiding the way.

For baking and candy making, I prefer the more robust flavor of grade B maple syrup. But if you stock only grade A in your pantry, that will do just fine. When the caramel has set, see pages 164 to 165 for cutting tips, detailed instructions, and illustrations.

MAPLE + CRACKED BLACK PEPPER CARAMELS

MAKES ABOUT 160 CARAMELS IF MADE IN A FRAME OR 115 CARAMELS IF MADE IN A PAN

438 grams glucose syrup

800 grams granulated sugar

200 grams heavy cream

7 grams kosher salt

1 gram vanilla bean powder (see page 57)

18 grams vanilla extract

11 grams coarsely ground black pepper

100 grams grade B maple syrup

250 grams unsalted butter, cut into roughly 1-inch pieces

Set up a 12 by 14–inch candy frame or lightly butter a 9 by 13–inch pan (see pages 162 to 163).

Weigh the glucose syrup directly into a heavy-bottomed pot, then set the pot over medium-high heat. Allow the glucose to warm until it liquefies and then starts to bubble. Once the glucose has bubbled a bit in one spot, swirl the pot to distribute the heat.

Add the sugar, about one-third at a time, sprinkling it over the glucose syrup. Using a high-heat spatula or wooden spoon, poke (no stirring) the sugar down into the syrup after each addition. Keep watch to make sure no giant lumps of dry sugar remain before you add the next installment of sugar. If you see lumps, poke them down into the glucose. Once all of the sugar is added and has been poked down into the liquid so it's wet, stop poking.

Pour the cream into a small saucepan and add the salt, vanilla bean powder, vanilla extract, pepper, and maple syrup. Stir to mix, then set the pan over low to medium heat. You're not looking to boil the cream; the idea is to simply warm the ingredients so they're not cold when they go into the hot sugar.

Meanwhile, let the glucose and sugar cook, swirling the pot occasionally, until the mixture is dark amber, or the color of a copper penny (see the Caramel Color Chart on page 161). Time-wise, you're looking at 13 to

15 minutes for the caramel to reach the target color. At first the sugar will turn pale brown, then darker brown. This may happen in spots around the pot, so it's important to swirl the pot as the sugar cooks. Once the sugar is a uniform color, cook it for a second or two longer until you feel good about the color, remembering that you want it to match that dark amber target.

Remove the pot from the heat and very carefully add the warmed cream mixture, immediately followed by the butter. Whisk the candy for 5 minutes, until completely emulsified. This means that the fats have been completely mixed into the sugar with no chance of separating. The mixture will be homogenized, with no oily separation or bits of anything burnt floating around.

Pour the caramel into the prepared candy frame or pan, nudging it into the corners as needed. Allow the candy to sit until cooled and set, at least 3 hours or preferably up to overnight, before cutting.

Very simple and even more fun, a Candy Pow Wow is a great way to package and present candy. You're essentially stuffing paper tubes with candy and then wrapping them up like presents. You can make the pow wow work for any occasion by just switching up the wrapping paper. I like to use them as gift toppers, place cards, teacher gifts, and totally unexpected surprises. For information on finding supplies, see the Resources Guide (page 291).

CANDY POW

Here's what you'll need:

Empty toilet-paper or paper-towel tubes

Confetti (very fun but completely optional)

Candy (assorted favorites of your choice)

Double-sided tape

Ribbon (your choice)

Wrapping paper, tissue paper, or kraft paper (your choice)

1 Stuff a tube with candy. Sprinkle in some confetti (if you're a confetti person).

2 Lay a sheet of wrapping paper on a work surface and set the candy-filled tube at one end of it. The paper should be long enough to fully wrap around the tube and wide enough so that the paper that goes past the ends of the tube can be gathered into a bit of flair.

3 Roll the paper around the tube, then secure the paper in place with double-sided tape.

4 Working carefully to avoid rips, gather the paper at each end of the tube and tie closed with a bit of ribbon.

CHAPTER FIVE

DREAMS COME CHEW

CANDY DREAMS

At this point in my professional candy-making career, the Dreams Come Chew story has been told so many times that it has reached legend status. This recipe came to me in a dream: I was in a laboratory wearing a white lab coat and I was standing behind one of those lab tables covered with all sorts of bubbling, steaming, spewing lab equipment. I looked down at the tabletop and saw a notebook opened to a page with some ratios scribbled on it—and that's when I woke up. I keep a notebook by my bed, so I scribbled down what I could remember from the page in the dream and then went back to sleep. The next day at work I fooled around with what I had scratched down in the middle of the night, eventually landing on the recipe for what is, without a doubt, QUIN's most popular candy ever: Dreams Come Chew.

We make Dreams Come Chew (or Dreams, as we refer to them at the factory) in a variety of flavor profiles, all of which someone out there claims to be the best of the bunch. I've never been able to settle on one favorite, so I'll keep coming up with new flavors while the Dreams fans keep debating.

DREAMS COME CHEW TECHNIQUE

You set up your workspace for making Dreams the same way you do for caramels. Once the candy is cooked, it can be, as with caramels, poured into a 12 by 14-inch candy frame (see pages 162 to 163) or a 9 by 13-inch pan.

Dreams also take the same journey as a pot of caramel; ingredients are combined and cooked for a while, other ingredients are added, and then everything is whisked and whisked until the candy is ready to be poured into a frame. The only difference in the journey is that you definitely need to use a thermometer when making Dreams. From there, Dreams are cut and wrapped the same way you cut and wrap caramels. When the Dreams have set, see pages 164 to 165 for cutting tips, detailed instructions, and illustrations.

FRUITY DREAMS

All fruity Dreams begin the same way: with glucose syrup, sugar, and butter in a pot. These three ingredients are cooked to a specific temperature (yes, you'll use a thermometer) and then flavoring, citric acid, and coloring are added.

What follows is the base recipe for Dreams. Stick to it for the initial cooking, then see the flavor guide for exactly how much flavoring, citric acid, and coloring you should add for the Dream flavor of your choice. You can make Dreams in single flavors, like cherry or orange, or flavors can be combined, like pineapple and coconut, to create something entirely new.

EVEN DREAMIER

The recipes on pages 228 to 234 stray a bit from the standard Dreams recipe because some ingredients are removed from the basic recipe and some added. But the method remains exactly the same as for Cherry Dreams Come Chew (see page 222).

CANDY ROPES

Once you've made a few batches of Dreams, you'll start to realize that they're actually pretty soft once the're set. This kind of malleable candy is ideal for rolling into ropes. You can even twist two different-flavored ropes together to create an entirely new candy. A nonstick mat can help make the rolling easier, but the rest is up to you, so use your imagination to create interesting combinations. You can also cut your ropes into 1-inch lengths and create multilayered candies that look as amazing as they taste. (Pssst, this works with caramel, too!)

One question I am asked over and over is one of the toughest questions to answer: What's your favorite QUIN candy? And while the answer depends greatly on my mood, Cherry Dreams Come Chew are generally at the top of the list. The experience begins when I untwist the wrapper—that cherry scent starts my mouth watering, and from there I almost feel as if I can't eat the candy fast enough. And I don't think I'm alone; when we sample a variety of Dreams at QUIN, these bright pink gems are the fastest to disappear. This is the candy that wins popularity contests, for certain.

CHERRY DREAMS COME CHEW

MAKES ABOUT 160 CANDIES IF MADE IN A FRAME OR 115 CANDIES IF MADE IN A PAN

616 grams glucose syrup

644 grams granulated sugar

200 grams unsalted butter, cut into ½-inch cubes

24 grams natural cherry flavoring

10 grams citric acid

7 grams natural red coloring (brighter pink to red)

Set up a 12 by 14–inch candy frame or lightly butter a 9 by 13–inch pan (see pages 162 to 163).

Weigh the glucose syrup, sugar, and butter directly into a heavy-bottomed pot, then set the pot over medium-high heat and watch as the ingredients start to melt together. Grab a high-heat spatula or a wooden spoon and use it to ease the candy from the outer edges of the pot into the center. You're not stirring; instead, you're gently scooting the candy so it will cook evenly.

Continue scooting the candy to ensure even cooking until it reaches 248°F, which will take about 10 minutes.

Remove the pot from the heat and allow the candy to rest for a handful of seconds until the furious bubbling ceases. Once that happens, add the cherry flavoring, citric acid, and red coloring. (If you are making one of the variations, add the substitutions at this point.) Now, grab a whisk and start whisking. (Much like the approach to caramel making, Dreams need a good whisking at the end to emulsify the fat into the candy and to ensure an even flavor.) Whisk for a full 4 minutes. The candy will be very smooth and slightly thickened. Another good reason for all that whisking? It incorporates air, which results in a lovely texture when the Dreams are cool and ready to cut (and eat).

When you've finished whisking, pour the candy into the prepared candy frame or pan, using the whisk to ease it into the corners as needed. Allow the candy to sit until cooled and set, at least 3 hours or preferably up to overnight, before cutting.

FLAVOR GUIDE

Use the this guide to create new Dream flavors by substituting the following ingredients for the flavoring and coloring used to create Cherry Dreams Come Chew.

STRAWBERRY DREAMS

24 grams natural strawberry flavoring

3 grams natural red coloring (pale pink)

TANGERINE DREAMS

24 grams natural tangerine or orange flavoring

3 grams natural orange coloring (medium-bright orange)

LEMON DREAMS

24 grams natural lemon flavoring

6 grams natural yellow coloring (bright yellow)

PINEAPPLE + COCONUT DREAMS

12 grams natural pineapple flavoring

12 grams natural coconut flavoring

(Don't add coloring here, for a nice creamy white result.)

WATERMELON + LIME DREAMS

12 grams natural watermelon flavoring

12 grams natural lime flavoring

4 grams natural red coloring (bright pale pink)

FRUIT PUNCH DREAMS

6 grams natural cherry flavoring

3 grams natural tangerine flavoring

3 grams natural pineapple flavoring

3 grams natural raspberry flavoring

3 grams natural coconut flavoring

3 grams natural red coloring plus 1 gram natural orange coloring (sunset colored)

INSTABRATION

What on Earth is an Instabration? An instant celebration in a bag all ready for party time, that's what! Picture this: a bag filled with all of the trinkets you need to celebrate something big, small, great, kind of great—all the occasions. The key ingredient? Candy. (And if it's a birthday you're instabrating, might I suggest the Vanilla Cake with Sprinkles candy on page 234.) I've included information on where to buy most of the items listed here in the handy Resources Guide (see page 295), but don't let my list limit your imagination.

You'll need a sack for each party-time participant. Even a cute paper lunch sack will do the trick. Now, you take that sack and you add to it tiny trinkets to enhance any celebration. Here's a list to get you started:

* Tiny sparklers
* Balloon ready to be blown up (the bigger the balloon, the better)
* Tissue-paper crown
* Many wrapped pieces of candy
* Fortune card (or paper slip–type fortune) with pleasant news and perhaps lucky numbers.

If you want to get extra crafty, you can decorate the bags with the names of the recipients or some other celebration-type designs. Or you can leave them a bit plain so the contents really shine. It's all up to you.

tiny
sparklers

fortune card

FORTUNE
I see a great
deal of happiness in
store for you. Love and
happiness, second chances, dreams
fulfilled, mistakes realized. It
will all be yours.
LUCKY NUMBERS: 7, 27, 75, 3, 29, 7

PARTY TIME

tissue-paper crown

balloon

wrapped candies

These Dreams are super pretty and full of flavor. The coloring that's added gives them a lovely slightly purple hue (I love it), but you can leave the coloring out if you'd like. And, of course, you can make these Dreams with almost any fruit purée you'd like, just be sure to match the purée with the same flavoring.

BLACKBERRY + TANGERINE DREAMS

MAKES ABOUT 160 CANDIES IF MADE IN A FRAME OR 115 CANDIES IF MADE IN A PAN

616 grams glucose syrup

644 grams granulated sugar

180 grams unsalted butter, cut into ½-inch cubes

20 grams roasted blackberry purée (see page 42)

20 grams natural blackberry flavoring

4 grams natural tangerine or orange flavoring

10 grams citric acid

2 grams natural red coloring plus 1 gram natural blue coloring

Set up a 12 by 14–inch candy frame or lightly butter a 9 by 13–inch pan (see pages 162 to 163).

Weigh the glucose syrup, sugar, butter, and blackberry purée directly into a heavy-bottomed pot, then set the pot over medium-high heat and watch as the ingredients start to melt together. Grab a high-heat spatula or a wooden spoon and use it to ease the candy from the outer edges of the pot into the center. You're not stirring; instead, you're gently scooting the candy so it will cook evenly.

Continue scooting the candy to ensure even cooking until it reaches 248°F, which will take about 10 minutes. Then remove the pot from the heat and allow the candy to rest for a handful of seconds until the furious bubbling ceases. Once that happens, add the blackberry and tangerine flavorings, citric acid, and red and blue colorings. Now, grab a whisk and start whisking. (Much like the approach to caramel making, Dreams need a good whisking at the end to emulsify the fat into the candy and to ensure an even flavor.) Whisk for a full 4 minutes. Another good reason for all of that whisking? It incorporates air, which results in a lovely smooth texture.

When you've finished whisking, pour the candy into the prepared candy frame or pan, using the whisk to ease it into the corners as needed. Allow the candy to sit until cooled and set, at least 3 hours or preferably up to overnight, before cutting.

If you like minty, chewy candy, these Dreams are for you. They're great on their own, and they're also great as the surprise center of a chocolate lollipop (see page 138 for a how-to). I like to leave these uncolored so you can see the pretty vanilla bean specks peeking out, but if color is your thing, go for it. And, of course, if you'd rather have a plain old vanilla candy? Leave out the mint flavoring and that's what you've got.

VANILLA MINT DREAMS

MAKES ABOUT 160 CANDIES IF MADE IN A FRAME OR 115 CANDIES IF MADE IN A PAN

616 grams glucose syrup

644 grams granulated sugar

200 grams unsalted butter, cut into ½-inch cubes

3 grams vanilla bean powder (see page 57)

12 grams natural mint flavoring

Set up a 12 by 14-inch candy frame or lightly butter a 9 by 13-inch pan (see pages 162 to 163).

Weigh the glucose syrup, sugar, butter, and vanilla bean powder directly into a heavy-bottomed pot, then set the pot over medium-high heat and watch as the ingredients start to melt together. Grab a high-heat spatula or a wooden spoon and use it to ease the candy from the outer edges of the pot into the center. You're not stirring; instead, you're gently scooting the candy so it will cook evenly.

Continue scooting the candy to ensure even cooking until it reaches 248°F, which will take about 10 minutes. Then remove the pot from the heat and allow the candy to rest for a handful of seconds until the furious bubbling ceases. Once that happens, add the mint flavoring. Now, grab a whisk and start whisking. (Much like the approach to caramel making, Dreams need a good whisking at the end to emulsify the fat into the candy and to ensure an even flavor.) Whisk for a full 3 minutes. Another good reason for all that whisking? It incorporates air, which results in a lovely smooth texture.

When you've finished whisking, pour the candy into the prepared candy frame or pan, using the whisk to ease it into the corners as needed. Allow the candy to sit until cooled and set, at least 3 hours or preferably up to overnight, before cutting.

These Dreams are chewy, chocolaty, and minty all at once. And while those three things go together really well, this candy can also be made into simpler Chocolate Dreams by omitting the mint flavoring. They also require no coloring, because of that beautiful, rich cocoa powder. When the Dreams have set, see pages 164 to 165 for cutting tips, detailed instructions, and illustrations.

CHOCOLATE MINT DREAMS

MAKES ABOUT 160 CANDIES IF MADE IN A FRAME OR 115 CANDIES IF MADE IN A PAN

616 grams glucose syrup

644 grams granulated sugar

200 grams unsalted butter, cut into ½-inch cubes

24 grams cocoa powder (see page 74)

2 grams vanilla bean powder (see page 57)

9 grams natural mint flavoring

Set up a 12 by 14–inch candy frame or lightly butter a 9 by 13–inch pan (see pages 162 to 163).

Weigh the glucose syrup, sugar, butter, cocoa powder, and vanilla bean powder directly into a heavy-bottomed pot, then set the pot over medium-high heat and watch as the ingredients start to melt together. Grab a high-heat spatula or a wooden spoon and use it to ease the candy from the outer edges of the pot into the center. You're not stirring; instead, you're gently scooting the candy so it will cook evenly.

Continue scooting the candy to ensure even cooking until it reaches 240°F, which will take about 10 minutes. Then remove the pot from the heat and allow the candy to rest for a handful of seconds until the furious bubbling ceases. Once that happens, add the mint flavoring. Now, grab a whisk and start whisking. (Much like the approach to caramel making, Dreams need a good whisking at the end to emulsify the fat into the candy and to ensure an even flavor.) Whisk for 3 minutes. The candy will be very smooth and slightly thickened. Another good reason for all of that whisking? It incorporates air, which results in a lovely smooth texture.

When you've finished whisking, pour the candy into the prepared candy frame or pan, using the whisk to ease it into the corners as needed. Allow the candy to sit until cooled and set, at least 3 hours or preferably up to overnight, before cutting.

These smooth and stretchy, pale pink Dreams have a bright cinnamon spark that's a bit creamy thanks to the butter and vanilla in the recipe. Because it delivers a more saturated flavor and disperses more evenly, I prefer natural cinnamon flavoring to ground cinnamon here. When the Dreams have set, see pages 164 to 165 for cutting tips, detailed instructions, and illustrations.

CINNAMON DREAMS

MAKES ABOUT 160 CANDIES IF MADE IN A FRAME OR 115 CANDIES IF MADE IN A PAN

616 grams glucose syrup

644 grams granulated sugar

200 grams unsalted butter, cut into ½-inch cubes

1 gram vanilla bean powder (see page 57)

18 grams natural cinnamon flavoring

1 gram natural red coloring

Set up a 12 by 14–inch candy frame or lightly butter a 9 by 13–inch pan (see pages 162 to 163).

Weigh the glucose syrup, sugar, butter, and vanilla bean powder directly into a heavy-bottomed pot, then set the pot over medium-high heat and watch as the ingredients start to melt together. Grab a high-heat spatula or a wooden spoon and use it to ease the candy from the outer edges of the pot into the center. You're not stirring; instead, you're gently scooting the candy so it will cook evenly.

Continue scooting the candy to ensure even cooking until it reaches 248°F, which will take about 10 minutes. Then remove the pot from the heat and allow the candy to rest for a handful of seconds until the furious bubbling ceases. Once that happens, add the cinnamon flavoring and red coloring. Now, grab a whisk and start whisking. (Much like the approach to caramel making, Dreams need a good whisking at the end to emulsify the fat into the candy and to ensure an even flavor.) Whisk for 3 minutes. Another good reason for all of that whisking? It incorporates air, which results in a lovely, smooth texture.

When you've finished whisking, pour the candy into the prepared candy frame or pan, using the whisk to ease it into the corners as needed. Allow the candy to sit until cooled and set, at least 3 hours or preferably up to overnight, before cutting.

Tiny Piñata

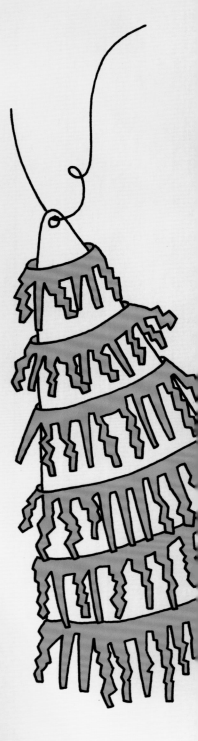

It may seem like a crazy idea, but making tiny piñatas really is a great party activity. It never ceases to amaze people, young or old. I plop all of the supplies on a table, give a quick tutorial, and let the partygoers go wild.

I make the entire process easy by using a paper drinking cone for the piñata base. There are no complicated shapes to cut and piece together. All of the candy (and confetti!) gets stuffed into the paper cone, the cone is strung on a string and then covered in tissue paper that has been made all fringy with scissors.

Here is what you'll need:

* 6-ounce paper drinking cone (see page 296)
* Card stock (or any handy repurposed cardboard, like the back of a cereal box or the lid of a shoebox)
* Pencil
* Scissors
* String or yarn, 12 inches or longer
* Scotch tape
* Candy (as much as you want to stuff in your piñata)
* Confetti (optional)
* Tissue paper, multicolored
* Glue
* Paintbrush

1. MAKE A LID

Place the paper cone, opened side down, on the piece of card stock. Using the pencil, trace around the opening to make a circle and then cut out the circle. You now have a lid that can be taped over the cone opening to enclose the candy inside. But do not close up that candy yet! Instead, set the round aside until it's ready to join the piñata party.

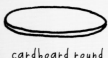

cardboard round

2. ATTACH THE STRING

Tip the cone over and poke a hole into its pointed top. (The tip of the pencil is a good hole-poking device to use here.) Thread the string through the hole, tie a knot in the end inside the cone, and then tape that end to the inside of the cone to secure it. You now have an empty cone dangling on a string.

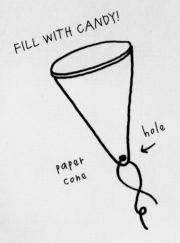

FILL WITH CANDY!

paper cone

hole

3. STUFF THE CONE

Fill the cone with candies and confetti. The confetti can be glitter, scraps of paper, or even all of the stuff you clean out of your hole punch. If you are like me and the idea of confetti gives you the I-just-cleaned-the-house sweats, skip it.

4. CLOSE THAT CONE

Hold the candy-filled cone in one hand and place the lid over the opening with the other hand. Now use a lot of tape to close it up tight. Tape it up, tape it shut.

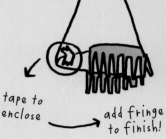

tape to enclose

add fringe to finish!

5. DECORATE IT

Using scissors, cut the tissue paper into strips about 6 inches long and 2 inches wide. Then, cut into the tissue leaving a ½-inch border uncut. This is your fringe.

Starting at the bottom, swipe a little glue around the edge of the cone using the paintbrush. Adhere a strip of fringe and then repeat until you've completely encircled the cone and can start a new layer of tissue. Continue layering the fringe so it covers the cone completely, keeping in mind that you can glue on as many layers of fringe as you like. I like a lot of fringe in multiple colors, but do whatever seems right to you. Once the entire cone is covered in fringe, cover the lid (and your tape job!) with even more tissue fringe. Now, set the piñata aside and let it dry.

Once the glue has dried, fluff up the fringe by separating and crumpling up the layers of tissue. Done!

I suggest crafting these Dreams in a variety of beautiful colors, from pale pink to creamy yellow. A spectrum of pastels make these candies even more captivating. Use up to 2 grams of any natural coloring of your choice to achieve the shade of your Dreams. Anything you choose will look divine. When the Dreams have set, see pages 164 to 165 for cutting tips, detailed instructions, and illustrations.

VANILLA CAKE DREAMS

MAKES ABOUT 160 CANDIES IF MADE IN A FRAME OR 115 CANDIES IF MADE IN A PAN

616 grams glucose syrup

644 grams granulated sugar

200 grams unsalted butter, cut into ½-inch cubes

3 grams vanilla bean powder (see page 57)

50 grams full-fat sour cream

2 grams natural coloring of your choice

Set up a 12 by 14–inch candy frame or lightly butter a 9 by 13–inch pan (see pages 162 to 163).

Weigh the glucose syrup, sugar, butter, and vanilla bean powder directly into a heavy-bottomed pot, then set the pot over medium-high heat and watch as the ingredients start to melt together. Grab a high-heat spatula or a wooden spoon and use it to ease the candy from the outer edges of the pot into the center. You're not stirring; instead, you're gently scooting the candy so it will cook evenly.

Continue scooting the candy to ensure even cooking until it reaches 248°F, which will take about 10 minutes. Then remove the pot from the heat and allow the candy to rest for a handful of seconds until the furious bubbling ceases. Once that happens, add the sour cream and coloring. Now, grab a whisk and start whisking. (Much like the approach to caramel making, Dreams need a good whisking at the end to emulsify the fat into the candy and to ensure an even flavor.) Whisk for 3 minutes. Another good reason for all of that whisking? It incorporates air, which results in a lovely smooth texture.

When you've finished whisking, pour the candy into the prepared candy frame or pan, using the whisk to ease it into the corners as needed. Allow the candy to sit until cooled and set, at least 3 hours or preferably up to overnight, before cutting.

VANILLA CAKE WITH SPRINKLES Vanilla Cake Dreams are practically begging to be coated in sprinkles. The crystal sprinkles (tinted but not flavored) from page 95 would be perfect. Individual pieces of candy that taste like cake with a layer of colorful sprinkles? That's exactly what I want to see through a cellophane wrapper.

SUPER SWEET ORNAMENT ORBS

I have a complicated relationship with craft stores. If I didn't insist on holding all of my craft supplies in my own hands when mapping out a project, I'd just buy everything on the Internet and skip the mix of magic and misery only the craft store can conjure. Lucky for you, I've hunted down all of the key ingredients for making these ornament orbs and put the details on how to find them in the Resources Guide (page 296).

What we've got here is a crystal-clear ornament that can be stuffed with candy, dangled on a bit of fancy string (with perhaps some bells and giant shiny sequins to pretty it up), and then given away, hung on your tree, tied to the top of a gift, or tucked into a stocking. Here's what you'll need:

* Clear fillable ornaments
* Candy (caramels, see pages 168 to 212, and Dreams Come Chew, see pages 222 to 234, work best)
* Ribbon
* Bells, sequins, beads, or other flair
* To/From tags

1. FILL THE ORNAMENTS

The two-part ornaments can be taken apart, filled with candy, and then snapped back together. Do that now.

2. ADD FLAIR

Each ornament has a little hole on top. Thread a length of ribbon through the hole. Slip bells, sequins, beads, or whatever you like onto the ribbon, securing each addition in place with a little knot, if you like—or just let them dangle free and collect around the ornament however gravity dictates. Add a To/From tag and you're done.

SUPER SWEET
ORNAMENT ORBS

FOR YOU

MERRY
HAPPY
JOY!

CHAPTER SIX

MARSHMALLOWS

CANDY CLOUDS

Light and fluffy, sweet and puffy—quality marshmallows are the cumulonimbus clouds of the candy world. Incredibly versatile, marshmallows know no season, turning up in summer s'mores and winter hot chocolate. Indeed, there's always room for marshmallows.

At QUIN, we make heaps of marshmallows and package them by the foot. Of course, eating a marshmallow—by the foot or any other way—is a delight, but what's best about the following magnificent marshmallows is that they are made with great ingredients, taste incredibly fresh, and can be turned into a dizzying array of other treats.

MARSHMALLOW TECHNIQUE

In general, marshmallows are easy to make, but you do need to pay attention to what I'm saying here. So, read these words carefully, do what they say, and you'll have outrageous marshmallows on your hands in no time.

INGREDIENTS

Marshmallows are made with gelatin, which they rely on for their signature texture. Gelatin is a hydrocolloid (a technical term that means it forms a gel when combined with water). It's an ingredient that can both thicken and gel. This thickening and gelling is key in marshmallows because it helps produce that bouncy-soft texture that then gives way to an almost creamy texture in your mouth.

Gelatin is thermoreversible, which means it's a gel when cooled and a very thick liquid when heated. And that transition is not permanent. Simply because you've made the candy and it looks perfect now doesn't mean it won't melt if subjected to heat later. That's why I say that you should never leave candies like marshmallows (or gumdrops, which are also made with gelatin) in your car on a hot day. Even shipping them during the summer can get tricky. The gel that's formed by gelatin will melt at temperatures right around 86°F. That translates into gelatin being responsible for the best melt-in-your-mouth sensation you could ever hope to achieve. Basically, the minute these marshmallows hit your mouth, they begin melting, and then the melty sensation gives way to flavor. And great flavor is what you want, especially after the pouf of the marshmallow has melted in your mouth.

The recipes that follow call for leaf gelatin, the kind of gelatin that comes in sheets. I make marshmallows with leaf gelatin because it produces stellar results and has no lingering flavors that can get in the way of the candy. In my work, gelatin sheets have always bloomed in water more evenly than powdered gelatin does. They melt nicely with no granules left behind, unlike what often happens when I use powdered gelatin. They also don't require weighing because I use them in specific numbers. I always love finding ways to increase my odds of success in a recipe, and because these marshmallows rely so heavily on gelatin, the exactness of counting sheets rather than fussing with a scale means something to me. Leaf gelatin, sometimes called *sheet gelatin*, comes in four types, all named after precious metals: bronze, silver, gold, and platinum. All of the recipes that follow call for silver leaf gelatin, which is the same type we use at QUIN. For tips on where to find silver leaf gelatin, see the Resources Guide (page 292).

EQUIPMENT

First, you'll need something to contain the candy while it sets. I like to use a 12 by 14–inch candy frame (see page 162 to 163), but a 9 by 13–inch pan will work in a pinch. A marshmallow frame is made the same way as the caramels and Dreams Come Chew frames. After the frame is built, however, marshmallows take a different turn. All four bars and the work surface on which the frame is built need a light sheen of vegetable oil applied to them prior to the candy going in.

Second, you'll need a stand mixer fitted with the whisk attachment to achieve a light and fluffy result and to cool the marshmallow adequately. (If you don't have a stand mixer, a handheld mixer and a mixing bowl will work.) Inadequate cooling prior to scooping the oozy marshmallow into a frame or pan will result in a soggy-bottomed marshmallow (and no person I know enjoys a soggy-bottomed marshmallow).

Third, you'll need a thermometer to check the temperature a few times along the way.

BASIC STEPS

Marshmallow creation happens in a few distinct steps. Here's a quick rundown: There's gelatin to bloom (in a bowl), gelatin to melt (the bowl in which it was bloomed now sits atop a double boiler), a sugar syrup to cook to a specific temperature (in a pot on the stove), and a mixer bowl containing additional ingredients. The mixer bowl will eventually contain everything—the melted gelatin, the hot sugar syrup, and the ingredients that you put into it in the first place.

Once everything has been whipped into fluffy oblivion, the marshmallow is scooped out of the bowl into a frame or pan to cool and set. When it has set, it's cut and dusted with marshmallow powder, which is equal parts cornstarch and powdered sugar sifted together. The powder prevents the finished candy from sticking together and forming a crazy (but delicious) mass.

This is the most versatile marshmallow of the bunch, and while you may consider vanilla too plain to be exciting, I urge you to give these surprisingly flavorful, bouncy vanilla bean–speckled treats a try, especially if you're accustomed to eating old marshmallows from a plastic bag.

In the method, I suggest cutting the marshmallows into 1-inch squares, but I always think 1-inch marshmallows are a little small. (Of course, sometimes you shouldn't take my advice on size or amount of treats because my ability to eat large volumes with zero complaints isn't actually a talent or a blessing. It's really more of a circus sideshow kind of spectacle.) If you agree, feel free to cut the marshmallows into 2-inch squares, or whatever feels and looks right when you're wielding your knife.

VANILLA BEAN MARSHMALLOWS

MAKES ABOUT 160 (1-INCH) SQUARES IF MADE IN A FRAME OR 115 (1-INCH) SQUARES IF MADE IN A PAN

FOR THE BLOOM
20 sheets silver leaf gelatin

108 grams ice-cold water

FOR THE MIXER BOWL
98 grams glucose syrup

9 grams vanilla bean powder (see page 57)

FOR THE COOKING POT
600 grams granulated sugar

255 grams water

FOR THE MARSHMALLOW POWDER
114 grams cornstarch

114 grams powdered sugar

Set up a 12 by 14–inch candy frame but instead of buttering the work surface, lightly coat it and the inside surfaces of the acrylic frame with vegetable oil, or lightly oil a 9 by 13–inch pan.

The Bloom Place the gelatin sheets in a shallow heat-proof bowl and place the bowl on your scale. Slowly drizzle *exactly* 108 grams of ice-cold water over the top. Allow the water to settle, then lift, shift, and nudge the gelatin sheets apart so that each of them has a fair chance of becoming uniformly wet and soaking up an equal amount of water. The gelatin will absorb all 108 grams of water, but you'll want to help it along a bit to make sure no rough patches remain. It should take 8 to 10 minutes for the gelatin to soak up the water.

The Mixer Bowl While the gelatin is absorbing the water, place the mixer bowl on the scale and weigh the glucose syrup and vanilla bean powder directly into it. Set the bowl aside, as you won't need it until a little later.

CONTINUED

The Cooking Pot Weigh the granulated sugar directly into a heavy-bottomed pot and sprinkle the water over it. Set the pot over medium-high heat and allow the sugar to begin to melt, poking it into the water with a high-heat spatula or a wooden spoon here and there only if necessary. Cook the sugar and water to a temperature of 225°F, which will take about 6 minutes.

Back to the Bloom While the sugar syrup is cooking, set up a double boiler for the gelatin. Select a pot that will hold the bowl of gelatin snugly in its rim. Pour water to a depth of a few inches into the bottom of the pot, place the pot on the stove top, and rest the bowl in the rim, making sure the bottom of the bowl is not touching the water. Turn on the heat to medium-high and bring the water to a simmer. The gelatin will melt into a thick liquid in 4 to 6 minutes. When it has melted, remove the pot from the heat, but leave the bowl resting in the rim so the gelatin stays warm.

Back to the Cooking Pot By now the sugar syrup should be close to 225°F. Test the temperature with a thermometer. If it has reached its target, it's time to return to the mixer bowl and prepare to add the melted gelatin and the sugar syrup to the glucose syrup and vanilla bean powder that have been waiting in the bowl.

Back to the Mixer Bowl Fit the mixer with the whisk attachment and pour the hot sugar syrup in a slow stream into the mixer bowl. Once all of the sugar syrup has been added, pick up the bowl of melted gelatin and ease that oozy stuff into the mixer bowl. To review: The mixer bowl now contains the glucose syrup, vanilla bean powder, the hot sugar syrup, and the melted gelatin. Take care, because everything is hot.

Starting the mixer on low speed and gradually increasing the speed to high, whip the marshmallow for 8 to 10 minutes, until it becomes a beautiful vanilla bean–speckled, fluffy, sticky white mass that's roughly three times greater in volume than when you started. When the marshmallow is sufficiently whipped, its temperature should have cooled to between 90° and 95°F.

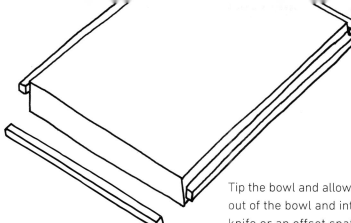

Remove the frame from the slab of marshmallow. Have a knife and damp towel at the ready!

Tip the bowl and allow gravity to help you push the sticky marshmallow out of the bowl and into the prepared candy frame or pan. Use a butter knife or an offset spatula to ease the marshmallow into the corners of the frame or pan, spreading it as evenly as you can. The top of the marshmallow will look like beautiful, smooth snowdrifts, unless you get fussy and attempt (crazily) to get it perfectly smooth (I don't recommend it). Allow the candy to cool and then set completely, keeping in mind that gelatin doesn't fully set until it cools to 68°F. Translation: Wait for at least a few hours or up to overnight before cutting.

To Make the Marshmallow Powder Sift together the cornstarch and powdered sugar into a bowl. (The powder can be stored in an airtight container in a cool, dry place indefinitely.)

To Finish If using a candy frame, remove the bars. If your marshmallows are in a pan, ease the candy out of it and set it on a cutting surface. Cut the marshmallow slab into 1-inch squares by first cutting it into 1-inch-wide rows and then cutting across the rows at 1-inch intervals. You may want to use a ruler (if you seek perfection) and either a good knife or a metal bench scraper. You may need to wipe the knife or scraper with a damp kitchen towel once or twice during cutting, as it can get quite messy, which makes cutting more difficult than it needs to be. Once the marshmallows are cut, toss them in the marshmallow powder, taking care to coat them completely.

The marshmallows are now ready to eat, to add to another recipe, or to store in an airtight container in a dry, cool place, for up to 4 weeks, keeping in mind that the fresher they are, the more delightful they will be.

CONTINUED

Cut the marshmallow into 1-inch squares: cut long rows first, then cut those rows into smaller pieces.

Once cut, toss the pieces in marshmallow powder.

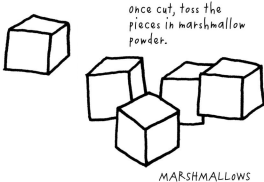

MINT MARSHMALLOWS A mint marshmallow in a mug of hot chocolate? You shouldn't need much more convincing than that to make this candy. Follow the recipe for Vanilla Bean Marshmallows (see page 244), adding 12 grams natural mint flavoring to the mixer bowl with the glucose syrup and vanilla bean powder.

TOASTED COCONUT MARSHMALLOWS There once was a time when I was absolutely neutral about coconut. I'm not sure how that's possible, because now I can't imagine not at least considering coconut when creating treats. To make coconut marshmallows, spread 115 grams sweetened shredded dried coconut on a sheet pan and slide the pan into a preheated 350°F oven. Toast for about 10 minutes, until the coconut is fragrant and begins to turn golden brown. Follow the recipe for Vanilla Bean Marshmallows (see page 244), adding the toasted coconut to the mixer bowl with the glucose syrup and vanilla bean powder.

CINNAMON MARSHMALLOWS Cinnamon adds a little spark to a marshmallow that's especially good when the marshmallow is warmed up. S'mores become tastier and hot chocolate somehow becomes warmer. To make these cinnamon-scented marshmallows, follow the Vanilla Bean Marshmallows recipe (see page 244), adding 12 grams ground cinnamon to the mixer bowl with the glucose syrup and vanilla bean powder.

S'MORES BAR

I've never not had fun putting together a s'mores bar and working behind the table at an event. From weddings to birthdays, the s'mores bar packs in a ton of "wow" for a modest amount of up-front work.

Start with a head count; and from there you'll pull together everything you'll need for that many people to make their own s'mores. Your new amazing skills as a marshmallow maker will be front and center, of course, and you'll need graham crackers, chocolate (use the Hot Fudge recipe on page 86), and a gaggle of toppings, ranging from toasted coconut to sprinkles, chopped pretzels to salty peanuts.

Arrange for a fire pit, get some metal skewers, set up a display of bowls filled with the marshmallows, graham crackers, and more, and your s'mores bar is ready to go. Don't have access to a fire pit? You can put the bar together in the comfort of your home kitchen. Swap out the fire pit for a kitchen torch, torch the marshmallows until they're nice and golden, and then proceed with the s'mores making.

Keep in mind that homemade marshmallows melt much faster than their come-in-a-plastic-bag-and-last-for-years counterparts. We're really talking about just a few moments in the hot flames, and that's all they need to get gooey. You've been warned.

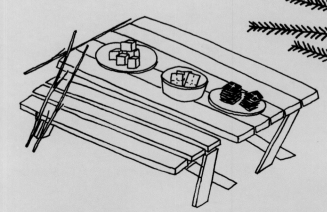

MARSHMALLOW SAUCE (OR BEST EVER ICE CREAM SAUCE)

This recipe makes a single serving of sauce, which means it's ideal for a night in—just you and a marshmallow ice cream sundae and that show you love so much that everyone's talking about. Or you can double the amounts listed, invite a friend, and call it anything but "date night" (because who needs a date to eat a sundae?).

In the top of a double boiler, combine 8 (1-inch) marshmallows and 2 teaspoons heavy cream. Allow the marshmallows to melt, then give them a stir to incorporate the cream. Spoon the sauce over ice cream and top with nuts or sprinkles or crumbled cookies or brownie bits or anything else your ice-cream-sundae-buffet dreams are made of. (If this is your first ice-cream-sundae-buffet dream, I'm happy to be with you on this inaugural experience.)

MARSHMALLOW BROWNIES

Grab your favorite brownie recipe and let's get started!

Once you've poured your brownie batter into the pan, sink 10 to 20 (½-inch or so) marshmallow pieces into the brownie batter, dotting the entire expanse of batter with the candy. Bake the brownies as you usually do, taking care not to plunge your toothpick into a marshmallow when you test for doneness.

Might I suggest a half-and-half option? Plunk caramel pieces (any flavor; recipes begin on page 168) on one side of the pan and marshmallow pieces on the other. Or mix them up. I don't think either way would be a mistake.

SKILLET S'MORES

SERVES 8

12 to 15 whole graham
crackers

½ cup Hot Fudge
(see page 86), or more
as needed

20 to 24 (1-inch)
Vanilla Bean Marshmallows
(see page 244)

I love this dessert because it's simple to prepare yet requires
interaction when it's time to eat. With everyone sharing the same
skillet, you can't help but have messy, gooey fun. If you don't like
sharing, you can doll these up in mini skillets. I'm trying to think
of something cuter than s'mores in tiny skillets, and right now
I really can't.

Preheat the broiler (to the highest setting if your broiler has settings).
Grab your 8- or 9-inch cast-iron skillet and line it with aluminum foil
(this is to keep cleanup to a minimum later).

Place the graham crackers in the bottom of the prepared skillet,
breaking them into pieces as needed to make them fit. Spoon the hot
fudge over the graham crackers and then nestle the marshmallows
into the fudge.

Slide the skillet under the broiler and toast the marshmallows to your
liking. This will take 3 to 7 minutes, depending on your broiler and how
much toasting you like.

Carefully remove the skillet from the oven and place it on a trivet in the
center of the table.

Serve warm (be careful—the skillet will be hot), with a stack of spoons
(and maybe some bowls of ice cream).

In a very clever moment, I figured out that the same Chocolate Magic Dust that makes a truly outrageous mug of hot chocolate can also be used to make a truly outrageous chocolate marshmallow. Once you've made Vanilla Bean Marshmallows (see page 244), this recipe will be easy for you.

CHOCOLATE MARSHMALLOWS

MAKES ABOUT 160 (1-INCH) SQUARES IF MADE IN A FRAME OR 115 (1-INCH) SQUARES IF MADE IN A PAN

FOR THE BLOOM
20 sheets silver leaf gelatin

120 grams ice-cold water

FOR THE MIXER BOWL
98 grams glucose syrup

3 grams vanilla bean powder (see page 57)

125 grams Chocolate Magic Dust (see page 74)

5 grams kosher salt

FOR THE COOKING POT
500 grams granulated sugar

155 grams water

FOR THE MARSHMALLOW POWDER
114 grams cornstarch

114 grams powdered sugar

Set up a 12 by 14–inch candy frame but instead of buttering the work surface, lightly coat it and the inside surfaces of the acrylic frame with vegetable oil, or lightly oil a 9 by 13–inch pan.

The Bloom Place the gelatin sheets in a shallow heat-proof bowl and place the bowl on your scale. Slowly drizzle *exactly* 120 grams of ice-cold water over the top. Allow the water to settle, then lift, shift, and nudge the gelatin sheets apart so that each of them has a fair chance of becoming uniformly wet and soaking up an equal amount of water. The gelatin will absorb all 120 grams of water, but you'll want to help it along a bit to make sure no rough patches remain. It should take 8 to 10 minutes for the gelatin to soak up the water.

The Mixer Bowl While the gelatin is absorbing the water, place the mixer bowl on the scale and weigh the glucose syrup, vanilla bean powder, magic dust, and salt directly into it. Set the bowl aside, as you won't need it until a little later.

The Cooking Pot Weigh the granulated sugar directly into a heavy-bottomed pot and sprinkle the water over it. Set the pot over medium-high heat and allow the sugar to begin to melt, poking it into the water with a high-heat spatula or a wooden spoon here and there only if necessary. Cook the sugar and water to a temperature of 225°F, which will take about 6 minutes.

Back to the Bloom While the sugar syrup is cooking, set up a double boiler for the gelatin. Select a pot that will hold the bowl of gelatin snugly in its rim. Pour water to a depth of a few inches into the bottom of the pot, place the pot on the stove top, and rest the bowl in the rim, making sure the bottom of the bowl is not touching the water. Turn on the heat to medium-high and bring the water to a simmer. The gelatin will melt into a thick liquid in 4 to 6 minutes. When it has melted, remove the pot from the heat, but leave the bowl resting in the rim so the gelatin stays warm.

Back to the Cooking Pot By now the sugar syrup should be close to 225°F. Test the temperature with a thermometer. If it has reached its target, it's time to return to the mixer bowl and prepare to add the melted gelatin and the sugar syrup to the glucose syrup, vanilla bean powder, and magic dust that have been waiting in the bowl.

Back to the Mixer Bowl Fit the mixer with the whisk attachment and pour the hot sugar syrup in a slow stream into the mixer bowl. Once all of the sugar syrup has been added, pick up the bowl of melted gelatin and ease that oozy stuff into the mixer bowl. To review: The mixer bowl now contains the glucose syrup, vanilla bean powder, magic dust, the hot sugar syrup, and the melted gelatin. Take care because everything is hot.

Starting the mixer on low speed and gradually increasing the speed to high, whip the marshmallow for 8 to 10 minutes, until it becomes a fluffy, sticky mass that's roughly three times greater in volume than when you started. When the marshmallow is sufficiently whipped, its temperature should have cooled to between 90° and 95°F.

Tip the bowl and allow gravity to help you push the sticky marshmallow out of the bowl and into the prepared candy frame or pan. Use a butter knife or an offset spatula to ease the marshmallow into the corners of the frame or pan, spreading it as evenly as you can. The top of the marshmallow will look like beautiful, smooth chocolate snowdrifts, unless you get fussy and attempt (crazily) to get it perfectly smooth (I don't recommend it). Allow the candy to cool and then set completely, keeping in mind that gelatin doesn't fully set until it cools to 68°F. Translation: Wait for at least a few hours or up to overnight before cutting.

To Make the Marshmallow Powder See directions on page 247.

To Finish See directions on page 247.

MARSHMALLOWS SET FREE

The shape of a finished marshmallow is an area where you have full creative freedom. Instead of using a frame to create a slab of marshmallow for cutting, you can use a spoon to scoop marshmallow out of the mixer bowl, then slide each scoop onto a sheet pan that has been dusted with marshmallow powder (see page 243). Allow the marshmallows to cool and set completely, then dust with more marshmallow powder so they won't stick together. You can also spoon the marshmallow directly from the mixer bowl into a piping bag fitted with a large plain tip and pipe out little mounds of marshmallow onto a marshmallow powder–dusted sheet pan. Again, allow the piped mounds to cool and set completely, then dust with more powder.

If you use a frame or 9 by 13–inch pan, you can let the marshmallow cool and set and then use cookie cutters to cut the marshmallows into the shapes of your choice. Dust the shapes in marshmallow powder and they're ready to go. Just make sure you have a plan for the scraps. They can go into a ziplock bag and wait in your pantry for hot chocolate, brownies, cookies, or ice cream topping (see page 251). Whatever you do, just promise me you won't waste the scraps!

Here, lovely petal-pink marshmallows come to life thanks to roasted strawberries. These sweet things are perfect on their own or as part of a s'more alternative—swap out the chocolate for peanut butter (or keep the chocolate and add peanut butter), then roast the berry marshmallows and layer everything on a graham cracker (or shortbread cookie, if you're fancy).

STRAWBERRY MARSHMALLOWS

MAKES ABOUT 160 (1-INCH) SQUARES IF MADE IN A FRAME OR 115 (1-INCH) SQUARES IF MADE IN A PAN

FOR THE BLOOM
20 sheets silver leaf gelatin

108 grams ice-cold water

FOR THE MIXER BOWL
98 grams glucose syrup

12 grams natural strawberry flavoring

3 grams vanilla bean powder (see page 57)

FOR THE COOKING POT
600 grams granulated sugar

155 grams water

100 grams roasted strawberry purée (see page 37)

FOR THE MARSHMALLOW POWDER
114 grams cornstarch

114 grams powdered sugar

Set up a 12 by 14–inch candy frame but instead of buttering the work surface, lightly coat it and the inside surfaces of the acrylic frame with vegetable oil, or lightly oil a 9 by 13–inch pan.

The Bloom Place the gelatin sheets in a shallow heat-proof bowl and place the bowl on your scale. Slowly drizzle *exactly* 108 grams of ice-cold water over the top. Allow the water to settle, then lift, shift, and nudge the gelatin sheets apart so each of them has a fair chance of becoming uniformly wet and soaking up an equal amount of water. The gelatin will absorb all 108 grams of water, but you'll want to help it along a bit to make sure no rough patches remain. It should take 8 to 10 minutes for the gelatin to soak up the water.

The Mixer Bowl While the gelatin is absorbing the water, place the mixer bowl on a scale and weigh the glucose syrup, strawberry flavoring, and vanilla bean powder directly into it. Set the bowl aside, as you won't need it until a little later.

The Cooking Pot Weigh the granulated sugar, water, and strawberry purée directly into a heavy-bottomed pot. Set the pot over medium-high heat and allow the sugar to begin to melt, poking it into the water with a high-heat spatula or a wooden spoon here and there only if necessary. Cook the contents of the pot to a temperature of 225°F, which will take about 6 minutes.

Back to the Bloom While the sugar syrup is cooking, set up a double boiler for the gelatin. Select a pot that will hold the bowl of gelatin snugly in its rim. Pour water to a depth of a few inches into the bottom of the pot, place the pot on the stove top, and rest the bowl in the rim, making sure the bottom of the bowl is not touching the water. Turn on the heat to medium-high and bring the water to a simmer. The gelatin will melt into a thick liquid in 4 to 6 minutes. When it has melted, remove the pot from the heat, but leave the bowl resting in the rim so the gelatin stays warm.

Back to the Cooking Pot By now the sugar syrup should be close to 225°F. Test the temperature with a thermometer. If it has reached its target, it's time to return to the mixer bowl and prepare to add the melted gelatin and the sugar syrup with the glucose syrup, strawberry flavoring, and vanilla bean powder that have been waiting in the mixer bowl.

Back to the Mixer Bowl Fit the mixer with the whisk attachment and pour the hot sugar syrup in a slow stream into the mixer bowl. Once all of the sugar syrup has been added, pick up the bowl of melted gelatin and ease that oozy stuff into the mixer bowl. To review: The mixer bowl now contains the glucose syrup, strawberry flavoring, vanilla bean powder, the hot sugar syrup, and the melted gelatin. Take care because everything is hot.

Starting the mixer on low speed and gradually increasing the speed to high, whip the marshmallow for 8 to 10 minutes, until it becomes a beautiful fluffy, sticky pale pink mass that's roughly three times greater in volume than when you started. When the marshmallow is sufficiently whipped, its temperature should have cooled to between 90° and 95°F.

Tip the bowl and allow gravity to help you push the sticky marshmallow out of the bowl and into the prepared candy frame or pan. Use a butter knife or an offset spatula to ease the marshmallow into the corners of the frame or pan, spreading it as evenly as you can. The top of the marshmallow will look like beautiful, smooth snowdrifts, unless you get fussy and attempt (crazily) to get it perfectly smooth (I don't recommend it). Allow the candy to cool and then set completely, keeping in mind that gelatin doesn't fully set until it cools to 68°F. Translation: Wait for at least a few hours or up to overnight before cutting.

To Make the Marshmallow Powder See directions on page 247.

To Finish See directions on page 247.

Figuring out how to make a successful caramel marshmallow has been a real (professional) struggle of mine. Yes, I could whip up a basic vanilla marshmallow, cook a pot of caramel sauce, and swirl the two together, but that can be quite messy. If the caramel is too hot, it will melt the temperature-sensitive marshmallow, which leads to a sticky situation that's best avoided. And even if the marshmallow does set up with the caramel intact, I've found that the two different candies eventually find a way to slide apart. It finally struck me that a praline syrup makes a really good caramel marshmallow without being a caramel at all. The syrup mimics the flavors of caramel because it contains brown sugar and salt, two nice flavor profiles often present in caramel. And the syrup is easily added to the marshmallow during the candy-making process (rather than after), which results in a marshmallow that's caramel flavored rather than a marshmallow that simply contains caramel.

CARAMEL MARSHMALLOWS

MAKES ABOUT 160 (1-INCH) SQUARES IF MADE IN A FRAME OR 115 (1-INCH) SQUARES IF MADE IN A PAN

FOR THE BLOOM
20 sheets silver leaf gelatin

108 grams ice-cold water

FOR THE MIXER BOWL
98 grams glucose syrup

100 grams Praline Syrup (see page 70), at room temperature

9 grams vanilla bean powder (see page 57)

8 grams flake sea salt

FOR THE COOKING POT
400 grams granulated sugar

100 grams light brown sugar

155 grams water

CONTINUED

Set up a 12 by 14–inch candy frame but instead of buttering the work surface, lightly coat it and the inside surfaces of the acrylic frame with vegetable oil, or lightly oil a 9 by 13–inch pan.

The Bloom Place the gelatin sheets in a shallow heat-proof bowl and place the bowl on your scale. Slowly drizzle *exactly* 108 grams of ice-cold water over the top. Allow the water to settle, then lift, shift, and nudge the gelatin sheets apart so that each of them has a fair chance of becoming uniformly wet and soaking up an equal amount of water. The gelatin will absorb all 108 grams of water, but you'll want to help it along a bit to make sure no rough patches remain. It should take 8 to 10 minutes for the gelatin to soak up the water.

The Mixer Bowl While the gelatin is absorbing the water, place the mixer bowl on a scale and weigh the glucose syrup, praline syrup, vanilla bean powder, and salt directly into it. Set the bowl aside, as you won't need it until a little later.

The Cooking Pot Weigh the granulated sugar and brown sugar directly into a heavy-bottomed pot and then sprinkle the water over the sugars. Set the pot over medium-high heat and allow the sugar to begin to melt, poking it into the water with a high-heat spatula or a wooden spoon

CONTINUED

FOR THE MARSHMALLOW POWDER

114 grams cornstarch

114 grams powdered sugar

here and there only if necessary. Cook the sugars and water to a temperature of 225°F, which will take about 6 minutes.

Back to the Bloom While the sugar syrup is cooking, set up a double boiler for the gelatin. Select a pot that will hold the bowl of gelatin snugly in its rim. Pour water to a depth of a few inches into the bottom of the pot, place the pot on the stove top, and rest the bowl in the rim, making sure the bottom of the bowl is not touching the water. Turn on the heat to medium-high and bring the water to a simmer. The gelatin will melt into a thick liquid in 4 to 6 minutes. When it has melted, remove the pot from the heat, but leave the bowl resting in the rim so the gelatin stays warm.

Back to the Cooking Pot By now the sugar syrup should be close to 225°F. Test the temperature with a thermometer. If it has reached its target, it is time to return to the mixer bowl and prepare to add the melted gelatin and the sugar syrup with the glucose syrup, praline syrup, vanilla bean powder, and salt that have been waiting in the mixer bowl.

Back to the Mixer Bowl Fit the mixer with the whisk attachment and pour the hot sugar syrup in a slow stream into the mixer bowl. Once all of the sugar syrup has been added, pick up the bowl of melted gelatin and ease that oozy stuff into the mixer bowl. To review: The mixer bowl now contains the glucose syrup, praline syrup, vanilla bean powder, salt, the hot sugar syrup, and the melted gelatin. Take care because everything is hot.

Starting the mixer on low speed and gradually increasing the speed to high, whip the marshmallow for 8 to 10 minutes, until it becomes a beautiful fluffy, sticky off-white mass that's roughly three times greater in volume than when you started. When the marshmallow is sufficiently whipped, its temperature should have cooled to between 90° and 95°F.

Tip the bowl and allow gravity to help you push the sticky marshmallow out of the bowl and into the prepared candy frame or pan. Use a butter knife or an offset spatula to ease the marshmallow into the corners of the frame or pan, spreading it as evenly as you can. The top of the marshmallow will look like beautiful, smooth snowdrifts, unless you get fussy and attempt (crazily) to get it perfectly smooth (I don't recommend it). Allow the candy to cool and then set completely, keeping in mind that gelatin doesn't fully set until it cools to 68°F. Translation: Wait for at least a few hours or up to overnight before cutting.

To Make the Marshmallow Powder See directions on page 247.

To Finish See directions on page 247.

CHOCOLATE CARAMEL COCONUT MARSHMALLOWS If you combine the best parts of Chocolate Marshmallows (see page 254) and Toasted Coconut Marshmallows (see page 248) with Caramel Marshmallows, you'll create some pretty outrageous marshmallows. Here's how to do it.

Follow the recipe for Caramel Marshmallows, adding 125 grams Chocolate Magic Dust (see page 74) and 115 grams toasted coconut to the mixer bowl along with the glucose syrup, praline syrup, vanilla bean powder, and salt. Proceed with the recipe as directed, adding the hot sugar syrup and melted gelatin and whipping the whole concoction for about 8 minutes. Finish as you would the other marshmallows.

Delicate and beautiful, honey-flavored marshmallows are a breath of fresh candy air. To make your own honey marshmallows, start with a great honey. Fruity honey, such as orange blossom or raspberry, is splendid, but something a little more robust like buckwheat honey could make these really special (imagine one of these roasted over a campfire!).

HONEY + SEA SALT MARSHMALLOWS

MAKES ABOUT 160 (1-INCH) SQUARES IF MADE IN A FRAME OR 115 (1-INCH) SQUARES IF MADE IN A PAN

FOR THE BLOOM
20 sheets silver leaf gelatin

108 grams ice-cold water

FOR THE MIXER BOWL
98 grams glucose syrup

100 grams honey

8 grams flake sea salt

FOR THE COOKING POT
500 grams granulated sugar

155 grams water

FOR THE MARSHMALLOW POWDER
114 grams cornstarch

114 grams powdered sugar

Set up a 12 by 14–inch candy frame but instead of buttering the work surface, lightly coat it and the inside surfaces of the acrylic frame with vegetable oil, or lightly oil a 9 by 13–inch pan.

The Bloom Place the gelatin sheets in a shallow heat-proof bowl and place the bowl on your scale. Slowly drizzle *exactly* 108 grams of ice-cold water over the top, taking care not to let any ice cubes slip into the mix. Allow the water to settle, then lift, shift, and nudge the gelatin sheets apart so that each of them has a fair chance of becoming uniformly wet and soaking up an equal amount of water. The gelatin will absorb all 108 grams of water, but you'll want to help it along a bit to make sure no rough patches remain. It should take 8 to 10 minutes for the gelatin to soak up the water.

The Mixer Bowl While the gelatin is absorbing the water, place the mixer bowl on a scale and weigh the glucose syrup, honey, and salt directly into it. Set the bowl aside, as you won't need it until a little later.

The Cooking Pot Weigh the granulated sugar directly into a heavy-bottomed pot and then sprinkle the water over it. Set the pot over medium-high heat and allow the sugar to begin to melt, poking it into the water with a high-heat spatula or a wooden spoon here and there only if necessary. Cook the sugar and water to a temperature of 225°F, which will take about 6 minutes.

Back to the Bloom While the sugar syrup is cooking, set up a double boiler for the gelatin. Select a pot that will hold the bowl of gelatin snugly in its rim. Pour water to a depth of a few inches into the bottom of the pot, place the pot on the stove top, and rest the bowl in the rim, making sure the bottom of the bowl is not touching the water. Turn on the heat to medium-high and bring the water to a simmer. The gelatin will melt into a thick liquid in 4 to 6 minutes. When it has melted, remove the pot from the heat, but leave the bowl resting in the rim so the gelatin stays warm.

Back to the Cooking Pot By now the sugar syrup should be close to 225°F. Test the temperature with a thermometer. If it has reached its target, it is time to return to the mixer bowl and prepare to add the melted gelatin and the sugar syrup with the glucose syrup, honey, and salt that have been waiting in the mixer bowl.

Back to the Mixer Bowl Fit the mixer with the whisk attachment and pour the hot sugar syrup in a slow stream into the mixer bowl. Once all of the sugar syrup has been added, pick up the bowl of melted gelatin and ease that oozy stuff into the mixer bowl. To review: The mixer bowl now contains the glucose syrup, honey, salt, the hot sugar syrup, and the melted gelatin. Take care because everything is hot.

Starting the mixer on low speed and gradually increasing the speed to high, whip the marshmallow for 8 to 10 minutes, until it becomes a beautiful fluffy, sticky off-white mass that's roughly three times greater in volume than when you started. When the marshmallow is sufficiently whipped, its temperature should have cooled to between 90° and 95°F.

Tip the bowl and allow gravity to help you push the sticky marshmallow out of the bowl and into the prepared candy frame or pan. Use a butter knife or an offset spatula to ease the marshmallow into the corners of the frame or pan, spreading it as evenly as you can. The top of the marshmallow will look like beautiful, smooth snowdrifts, unless you get fussy and attempt (crazily) to get it perfectly smooth (I don't recommend it). Allow the candy to cool and then set completely, keeping in mind that gelatin doesn't fully set until it cools to 68°F. Translation: Wait for at least a few hours or up to overnight before cutting.

To Make the Marshmallow Powder See directions on page 247.

To Finish See directions on page 247.

Of course coffee marshmallows are stupendous when suspended in a mug of hot chocolate, but they're also an incredible addition to s'mores, bake beautifully into brownies, and make a pretty great treat all on their own.

COFFEE MARSHMALLOWS

MAKES ABOUT 160 (1-INCH) SQUARES IF MADE IN A FRAME OR 115 (1-INCH) SQUARES IF MADE IN A PAN

FOR THE BLOOM
20 sheets silver leaf gelatin

108 grams ice-cold water

FOR THE MIXER BOWL
98 grams glucose syrup

20 grams Coffee Syrup (see page 68)

5 grams kosher salt

FOR THE COOKING POT
600 grams granulated sugar

215 grams brewed coffee (see page 81)

FOR THE MARSHMALLOW POWDER
114 grams cornstarch

114 grams powdered sugar

Set up a 12 by 14–inch candy frame but instead of buttering the work surface, lightly coat it and the inside surfaces of the acrylic frame with vegetable oil, or lightly oil a 9 by 13–inch pan.

The Bloom Place the gelatin sheets in a shallow heat-proof bowl and place the bowl on your scale. Slowly drizzle *exactly* 108 grams of ice-cold water over the top. Allow the water to settle, then lift, shift, and nudge the gelatin sheets apart so that each of them has a fair chance of becoming uniformly wet and soaking up an equal amount of water. The gelatin will absorb all 108 grams of water, but you'll want to help it along a bit to make sure no rough patches remain. It should take 8 to 10 minutes for the gelatin to soak up the water.

The Mixer Bowl While the gelatin is absorbing the water, place the mixer bowl on a scale and weigh the glucose, coffee syrup, and salt directly into it. Set the bowl aside, as you won't need it until a little later.

The Cooking Pot Weigh the granulated sugar into a heavy-bottomed pot and then sprinkle the coffee over the sugar. Set the pot over medium-high heat and allow the sugar to begin to melt, poking it into the water with a high-heat spatula or a wooden spoon here and there only if necessary. Cook the sugar and coffee to a temperature of 225°F, which will take about 6 minutes.

Back to the Bloom While the sugar is cooking, set up a double boiler for the gelatin. Select a pot that will hold the bowl of gelatin snugly in its rim. Pour water to a depth of a few inches into the bottom of the pot, place the pot on the stove top, and rest the bowl in the rim, making sure the bottom of the bowl is not touching the water. Turn on the heat to medium-high and bring the water to a simmer. The gelatin will melt into a thick liquid in 4 to 6 minutes. When it has melted, remove the pot from the heat, but leave the bowl resting in the rim so the gelatin stays warm.

Back to the Cooking Pot By now the sugar syrup should be close to 225°F. Test the temperature with a thermometer. If it has reached its target, it is time to return to the mixer bowl and prepare to add the melted gelatin and the hot sugar syrup with the glucose syrup, coffee syrup, and salt that have been waiting in the mixer bowl.

Back to the Mixer Bowl Fit the mixer with the whisk attachment and pour the hot sugar syrup in a slow stream into the mixer bowl. Once all of the sugar syrup has been added, pick up the bowl of melted gelatin and ease that oozy stuff into the mixer bowl. To review: The mixer bowl now contains the glucose syrup, coffee syrup, salt, the hot sugar syrup, and the melted gelatin. Take care because everything is hot.

Starting the mixer on low speed and gradually increasing the speed to high, whip the marshmallow for 8 to 10 minutes, until it becomes a beautiful fluffy, sticky cream-colored mass that's roughly three times greater in volume than when you started. When the marshmallow is sufficiently whipped, its temperature should have cooled to between 90° and 95°F.

Tip the bowl and allow gravity to help you push the sticky marshmallow out of the bowl and into the prepared candy frame or pan. Use a butter knife or an offset spatula to ease the marshmallow into the corners of the frame or pan, spreading it as evenly as you can. The top of the marshmallow will look like beautiful, smooth snowdrifts, unless you get fussy and attempt (crazily) to get it perfectly smooth (I don't recommend it). Allow the candy to cool and then set completely, keeping in mind that gelatin doesn't fully set until it cools to 68°F. Translation: Wait for at least a few hours or up to overnight before cutting.

To Make the Marshmallow Powder See directions on page 247.

To Finish See directions on page 247.

CHAPTER SEVEN

GUMDROPS

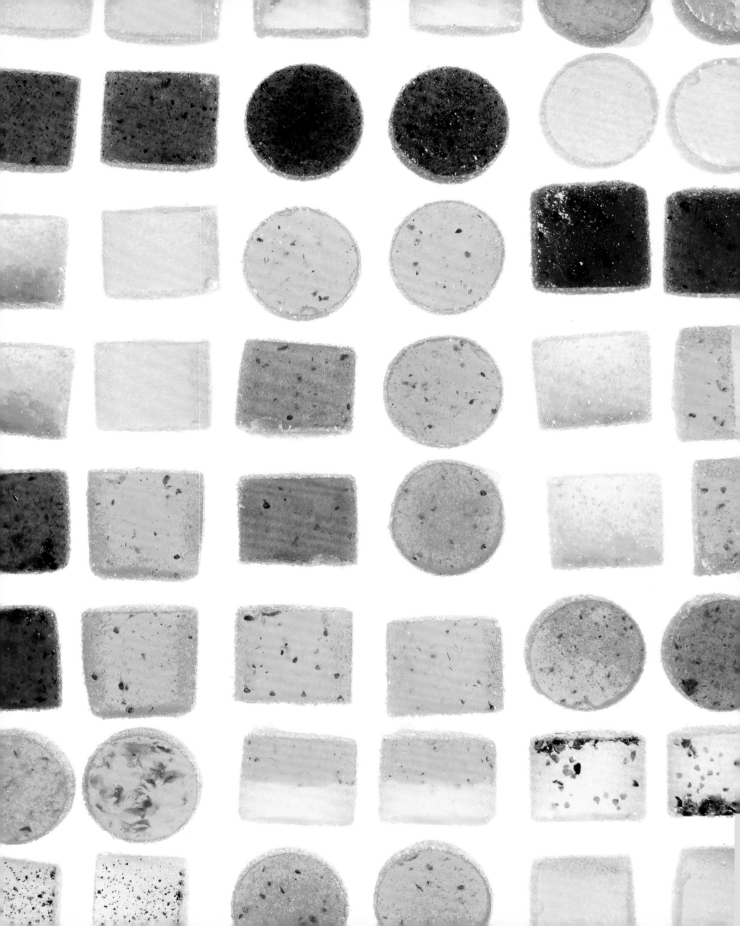

GUMMY GALORE

I'd be willing to bet that very few of you have ever rejoiced in the sensational experience of eating a fresh gumdrop. Instead, you've been saddled with the kind that are tossed into an Easter basket; the red ones being gobbled up first, then the green ones, and the black ones sitting around for weeks. Regular gumdrops just aren't good. What should be bouyant, bouncy, and flavorful is more like tough, chewy, and fake-tasting. And, let's face it, commercially made gumdrops are truly built to last, filled with who knows what to give them a multiyear shelf life. Compared to this, fresh gumdrops are a revelation.

Fresh gumdrops are fun to eat and are nearly limitless in variations. And they're just as much fun to make because they're definitely overachievers in terms of candy wizardry. A hot, oozy concoction is transformed into a candy that's not solid and not liquid but is instead gummy. Think about that! It sure sounds like sugary magic to me.

GUMDROP TECHNIQUE

Gumdrops rely on gelatin for their signature bounce. And if you've already tried marshmallow making, you know that gelatin can be persnickety. For example, if gelatin is heated improperly, acidic fruit ingredients, such as lemon, orange, or lime, will cause it to break down and liquefy a bit. This reaction results in gumdrops that will start to look weepy. In other words, they will go from being completely great, bouncy little candies to, just a few days later, looking as if someone accidently spilled a glass of water on them or, worse yet, dropped them into a puddle. My advice is that if you're set on crafting citrusy gumdrops, use a natural flavoring rather than a fruit juice or more than 5 grams finely grated zest.

Another thing to keep in mind about gelatin is that it's thermoreversible, or a gel when cooled and a thick liquid when hot. Yes, I know I explained this in the marshmallow section, but I think it bears repeating. If gummy candies get hot, they will melt, and the temperature at which they will melt will always be lower than you think (around 86°F). So, as I said before, no hot cars, and if you want to surprise your aunt with a bundle of gumdrops for her mid-August birthday, be sure to use cold packs when shipping them so your sweet gesture arrives intact.

BASIC STEPS

Making gummy candies involves three simple steps. You'll begin with combining leaf gelatin (see page 242) and ice-cold water, and while the gelatin is blooming, you'll begin cooking a pot of glucose syrup, sugar, and a few other ingredients. Once this sugar syrup is cooking, the gelatin will be ready to melt over simmering water. When the gelatin has melted and the syrup has cooled to a specific temperature, you will combine the gelatin and the syrup and then mix in some flavoring and perhaps some citric acid. At this point, the concoction is ready to be funneled or poured into a silicone mold.

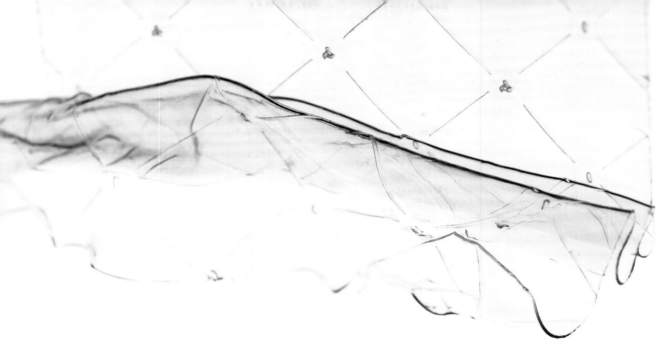

Silicone mold? I know we talked a little about molds in chapter one
(see page 24), but now that you're here preparing to make gumdrops, it's
time to get more specific. To make gummy candies, I suggest you get your
hands on silicone molds into which the candy can be directly funneled. The
molds come in a variety of sizes and their cavities in all kinds of shapes.
Once the candies have cooled and set, you'll pop them out of the mold and
then let them rest in some sugar.

The sugar coating prevents the gumdrops from sticking together. You can
use either granulated sugar or powdered sugar. Granulated sugar will
produce a toothsome and crystalline finish, while powdered sugar will give
the candy a kind of dull-looking but sweet patina. To coat the candy, pour
granulated sugar or powdered sugar into a large bowl, and as you remove
the gumdrops from the molds, plop them into the sugar. Let them sit for a
while, then toss to coat, pluck them out, and admire their sugary coatings.
You can then package them as you like. Gumdrops should be kept in a cool,
dry place and will be good for 6 months (although the fresher they are,
the more enjoyable they will be).

At QUIN, we use silicone molds that produce a piece of candy that's sort of
cylindrical and about ¾ inch tall and ¾ inch wide. Of course, you can use
whatever mold you'd like, but I prefer gumdrops that are between ¾ inch
and 1 inch. Any larger than 1 inch and they're a pretty big mouthful.

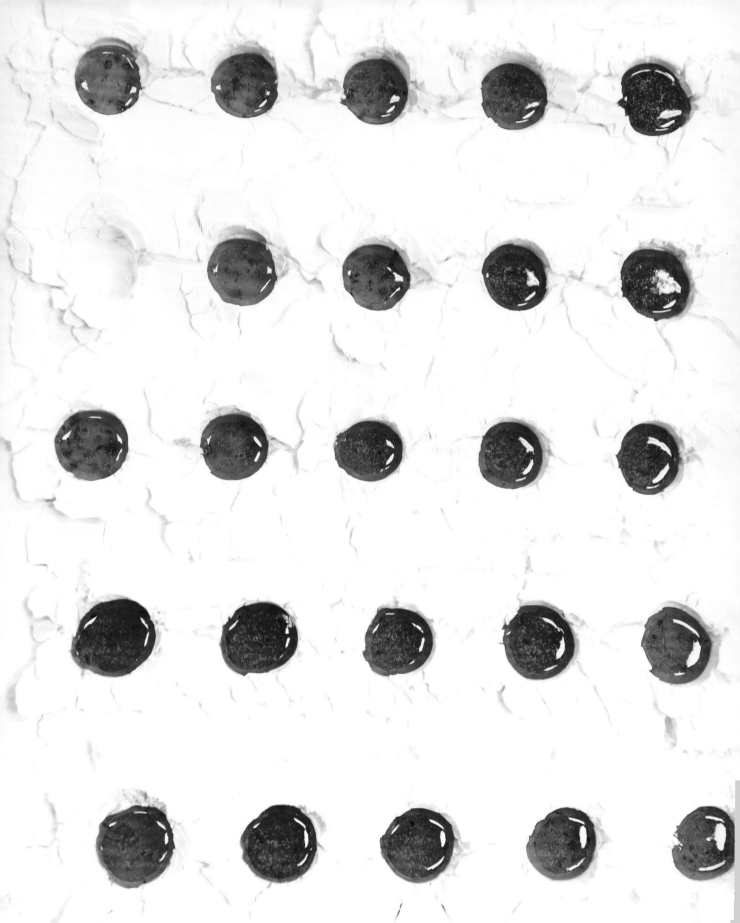

BUILD YOUR OWN MOLDS

Yes, it's possible to make gumdrops without using a silicone mold, but you'll have to get crafty and make a mold. Cornstarch molds require some work and are a bit of a mess but are very useful if you want to create candy in a specific shape. Here's what you will need:

* 8 pounds cornstarch
* 3 half sheet pans
* Wooden spoon or whisk with a handle ½ to ¾ inch in diameter
* Coconut oil, for coating candy

First, preheat the oven to 250°F. Next, pour 4 pounds of the cornstarch into a half sheet pan, then pack the cornstarch down by rapping the pan on the countertop. Set a second sheet pan on top of the cornstarch and press down on the pan to pack and level the cornstarch. If any cornstarch falls out of the pan, scoop it up, return it to the pan, and smooth it out again. Pour the remaining 4 pounds cornstarch into the third sheet pan and pack and level it the same way. Bake the cornstarch-filled sheet pans in the oven for 1½ hours.

Remove the pans from the oven. The cornstarch will be dry. Using the wooden spoon, move the cornstarch around within each pan to speed up the cooling, then tamp it down again by rapping the pans on the countertop and then topping with the empty pan and pressing down on them again.

Use the wooden spoon make repeated impressions in the cornstarch by sticking the end of the handle into it. Take care not to press all the way through to the bottom of the pan and be careful to make the impressions uniform. A good way to ensure precision is to draw a line on the handle to indicate how deeply to bury it into the cornstarch.

Once the impressions are made in both pans, pour the hot candy into a funnel (it will work much better than a spouted cup here), and fill each cavity to the rim. Allow the candy to sit for 2 hours, until cooled and set.

Reach into the cornstarch, pull out the candies, and dust them off. Place all of the candies in a large bowl, add 1 or 2 drops of coconut oil, and mix until each piece is a tiny bit shiny with oil. Now sink the gummies into granulated or powdered sugar as directed on page 273 and toss to coat.

The same cornstarch can be used over and over without baking it again. Pack it into ziplock bags and store it in a cool, dry place, then repack into the sheet pans when you make candy again.

I still get a thrill out of seeing bits of cherries or the seeds of a blackberry suspended in gummy candy goodness. This master recipe and the variations in the flavor guide use roasted fruit purées from chapter two and natural flavorings. What I've included here are my fruit gumdrop greatest hits—along with some suggestions for using more than one flavor in a candy, such as blackberry + orange gumdrops. But you can combine any fruit purée and complementary flavoring in gumdrops to originate you own flavors. Just make sure that you stick to the exact weight of each ingredient in the master recipe and follow the directions precisely.

In terms of yield, it's tough to pinpoint exactly how many individual candies you'll get from one batch of gummy syrup. This is mostly because I don't know what kind of mold you're using. This recipe makes about 650 grams of gumdrop syrup, and if you make candies that weigh 10 grams apiece, you'll end up with about 65 candies. But if you make candies that weigh only 5 grams each, you're looking at around 130 pieces. (At QUIN, we make gumdrops on the larger size, 10 grams each, which is about twice the size of a standard gummy bear.)

BLACKBERRY GUMDROPS

**MAKES ABOUT
650 GRAMS SYRUP;
ABOUT 65 (10-GRAM)
CANDIES**

FOR THE BLOOM
16 sheets silver leaf gelatin

110 grams ice-cold water

FOR THE SUGAR SYRUP
215 grams glucose syrup

260 grams granulated sugar

25 grams water

25 grams roasted blackberry purée (see page 42)

CONTINUED

Bloom the Gelatin Place the gelatin sheets in a shallow heat-proof bowl and place the bowl on your scale. Slowly drizzle *exactly* 110 grams of ice-cold water over the top. Allow the water to settle, then lift, shift, and nudge the gelatin sheets apart so that each of them has a fair chance of becoming uniformly wet and soaking up an equal amount of water. The gelatin will absorb all 110 grams of water, but you'll want to help it along a bit to make sure no rough patches remain. It should take 10 to 12 minutes for the gelatin to soak up the water.

Cook the Sugar Syrup While the gelatin is absorbing the water, weigh the glucose syrup, granulated sugar, water, and blackberry purée directly into a 2-quart cooking pot and set the pot over medium-high heat. Watch the pot as the ingredients begin to cook, and if they appear to be cooking unevenly, use a high-heat spatula or a wooden spoon to poke them gently and then give the pot a swirl or two to even them out. Cook the sugar mixture to a temperature of 278°F, which will take 8 to 10 minutes.

CONTINUED

FOR THE FLAVORING

9 grams natural blackberry flavoring

2 grams citric acid

Granulated or powdered sugar, for coating (see page 273)

Melt the Gelatin While the sugar syrup is cooking, set up a double boiler for the gelatin. Select a pot that will hold the bowl of gelatin snugly in its rim. Pour water to a depth of a few inches into the bottom of the pot, place the pot on the stove top, and rest the bowl in the rim, making sure the bottom of the bowl is not touching the water. Turn on the heat to medium-high and bring the water to a simmer. The gelatin will melt into a thick liquid in 4 to 6 minutes. When it has melted, remove the pot from the heat, but leave the bowl resting in the rim so the gelatin stays warm.

Finish the Sugar Syrup By now the sugar syrup should be close to 278°F. Test the temperature with a thermometer. If it has reached its target, remove the pot from the heat and set it aside until the syrup cools to 242°F. This will take about 7 minutes. Keep an eye on the syrup and test the temperature occasionally so you hit it right at 242°F.

Flavor the Gelatin and Sugar Syrup When the sugar syrup has cooled to 242°F, using a high-heat spatula or a wooden spoon, stir in the melted gelatin, natural flavoring, and citric acid, mixing thoroughly. (You don't want to use a whisk here because you're not trying to incorporate air into the candy.)

To Finish The candy syrup is complete and ready to be poured into a funnel and deposited into silicone molds or cornstarch molds (see page 275). Because you're making candy with real fruit, the funnel may get clogged with seeds or skins and trick you into thinking something has gone wrong. Don't fret. Just use the plunger to help ease the seedy candy through the hole. Once the molds are filled, allow the candies to cool for 2 hours, until fully cooled and completely set.

Pop the candies out of the silicone molds or pluck them from the cornstarch molds, coat them in sugar, and package them in cellophane bags, ziplock bags, or tightly capped jars.

Use the following guide to create new gumdrop flavors
by substituting these ingredients for the roasted fruit purée
and flavoring used to make Blackberry Gumdrops.

BLACKBERRY + ORANGE GUMDROPS

For a vibrant addition to blackberry gummy candies, add 6 grams natural orange flavoring and 10 grams finely grated orange zest with the blackberry flavoring and citric acid.

STRAWBERRY GUMDROPS

For the 25 grams roasted fruit purée, use roasted strawberry purée (see page 37). For the 9 grams natural fruit flavoring, use natural strawberry flavoring.

STRAWBERRY + LEMON GUMDROPS

Make the Strawberry Gumdrops (previous) as directed, adding 6 grams natural lemon flavoring and 5 grams finely grated lemon zest with the strawberry flavoring and citric acid.

BLUEBERRY GUMDROPS

For the 25 grams roasted fruit purée, use roasted blueberry purée (see page 46). For the 9 grams natural fruit flavoring, use natural blueberry flavoring.

BLUEBERRY + CINNAMON GUMDROPS

Make the Blueberry Gumdrops (previous) as directed, adding 3 grams ground cinnamon with the blueberry flavoring and citric acid. Warm cinnamon with the cool blueberries is a pretty great combination of two opposites.

APRICOT GUMDROPS

For the 25 grams roasted fruit purée, use roasted apricot purée (see page 47). For the 9 grams natural fruit flavoring, use natural apricot flavoring.

APRICOT + ALMOND + NUTMEG GUMDROPS

Make the Apricot Gumdrops (previous) as directed, adding a few scrapes of nutmeg and a quick dash of almond extract with the apricot flavoring and citric acid.

RASPBERRY GUMDROPS

For the 25 grams roasted fruit purée, use roasted raspberry purée (see page 43). For the 9 grams natural fruit flavoring, use natural raspberry flavoring.

RASPBERRY + VANILLA GUMDROPS

Make the Raspberry Gumdrops (previous) as directed, adding 2 or 3 grams vanilla bean powder (see page 57; I love the creaminess it adds) with the raspberry flavoring and citric acid.

PEACH GUMDROPS

For the 25 grams roasted fruit purée, use roasted peach purée (see page 49). For the 9 grams natural fruit flavoring, use natural peach flavoring.

PEACH + GINGER + BLACK PEPPER GUMDROPS

Make the Peach Gumdrops (previous) as directed, adding 2 grams ground ginger and, 1 gram ground black pepper with the peach flavoring and citric acid.

CHERRY GUMDROPS

For the 25 grams roasted fruit purée, use roasted cherry purée (see page 44). For the 9 grams natural fruit flavoring, use natural cherry flavoring.

CHERRY COLA GUMDROPS

Make the Cherry Gumdrops (previous) as directed, adding 9 grams natural cola flavoring with the cherry flavoring and citric acid.

While I definitely love a gumdrop that tastes like a piece of fresh fruit, I also love the flavors of cola or root beer, vanilla or coffee, tea or wine. There's a lot of room for variation here. Start with vanilla and what else can you do? Add root beer and you've got a candy that tastes like a root beer float. Or add black pepper and you've got a spicy, creamy concoction. Get solid on this basic recipe and then see what else can happen.

VANILLA GUMDROPS

MAKES ABOUT 650 GRAMS SYRUP; ABOUT 65 (10-GRAM) CANDIES

FOR THE BLOOM
16 sheets silver leaf gelatin

110 grams ice-cold water

FOR THE SUGAR SYRUP
215 grams glucose syrup

260 grams granulated sugar

95 grams water

FOR THE FLAVORING
5 grams vanilla bean powder (see page 57)

Granulated or powdered sugar, for coating (see page 273)

Bloom the Gelatin Place the gelatin sheets in a shallow heat-proof bowl and place the bowl on your scale. Slowly drizzle *exactly* 110 grams of ice-cold water over the top. Allow the water to settle, then lift, shift, and nudge the gelatin sheets apart so that each of them has a fair chance of becoming uniformly wet and soaking up an equal amount of water. The gelatin will absorb all 110 grams of water, but you'll want to help it along a bit to make sure no rough patches remain. It should take 10 to 12 minutes for the gelatin to soak up the water.

Cook the Sugar Syrup While the gelatin is absorbing the water, weigh the glucose syrup, granulated sugar, and water directly into a 2-quart cooking pot and set the pot over medium-high heat. Watch the pot as the ingredients begin to cook, and if they appear to be cooking unevenly, use a high-heat spatula or a wooden spoon to poke them gently and then give the pot a swirl or two to even them out. Cook the sugar mixture to a temperature of 278°F, which will take 8 to 10 minutes.

Melt the Gelatin While the sugar syrup is cooking, set up a double boiler for the gelatin. Select a pot that will hold the bowl of gelatin snugly in its rim. Pour water to a depth of a few inches into the bottom of the pot, place the pot on the stove top, and rest the bowl in the rim, making sure the bottom of the bowl is not touching the water. Turn on the heat to medium-high and bring the water to a simmer. The gelatin will melt into a thick liquid in 4 to 6 minutes. When it has melted, remove the pot from the heat, but leave the bowl resting in the rim so the gelatin stays warm.

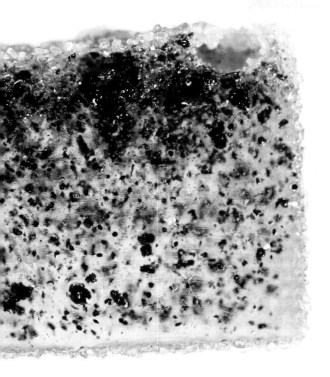

Finish the Sugar Syrup By now the sugar syrup should be close to 278°F. Test the temperature with a thermometer. If it has reached its target, remove the pot from the heat and set it aside until the syrup cools to 242°F. This will take about 7 minutes. Keep an eye on the syrup and test the temperature occasionally so you hit it right at 242°F.

Flavor the Gelatin and Sugar Syrup When the sugar syrup has cooled to 242°F, using a high-heat spatula or a wooden spoon, stir in the melted gelatin and vanilla bean powder, mixing thoroughly. (You don't want to use a whisk here because you're not trying to incorporate air into the candy.)

To Finish The candy syrup is complete and ready to be poured into a funnel and deposited into silicone molds or cornstarch molds (see page 275). Once the molds are filled, allow the candies to cool for 2 hours, until fully cooled and completely set.

Pop the candies out of the silicone molds or pluck them from the cornstarch molds, coat them in sugar, and package them in cellophane bags, ziplock bags, or tightly capped jars.

CONTINUED

FLAVOR GUIDE

Now that you've got a handle on Vanilla Gumdrops (page 280), you can use the recipe as the launching pad for a few new great flavors. And yes, I know the idea of black pepper in candy seems a little daring, but you have to trust me.

BLACK PEPPER GUMDROPS

Follow the Vanilla Gumdrops recipe, substituting 6 grams cracked black pepper for the vanilla bean powder.

CINNAMON GUMDROPS

Follow the Vanilla Gumdrops recipe, adding 5 grams ground cinnamon with the vanilla bean powder.

COLA OR ROOT BEER GUMDROPS

Follow the Vanilla Gumdrops recipe, substituting 9 grams natural cola or natural root beer flavoring for the vanilla bean powder.

CITRUS GUMDROPS

Follow the Vanilla Gumdrops recipe, omitting the vanilla bean powder and adding 12 grams natural citrus flavoring (orange, lemon, lime, or grapefruit) and 5 grams finely grated citrus zest (to match the flavoring). You might instead combine a couple of flavors, such as orange and grapefruit or lemon and lime. If you leave all or even a little of the vanilla bean powder in the recipe, you'll create a citrus candy with a pleasing layer of creaminess.

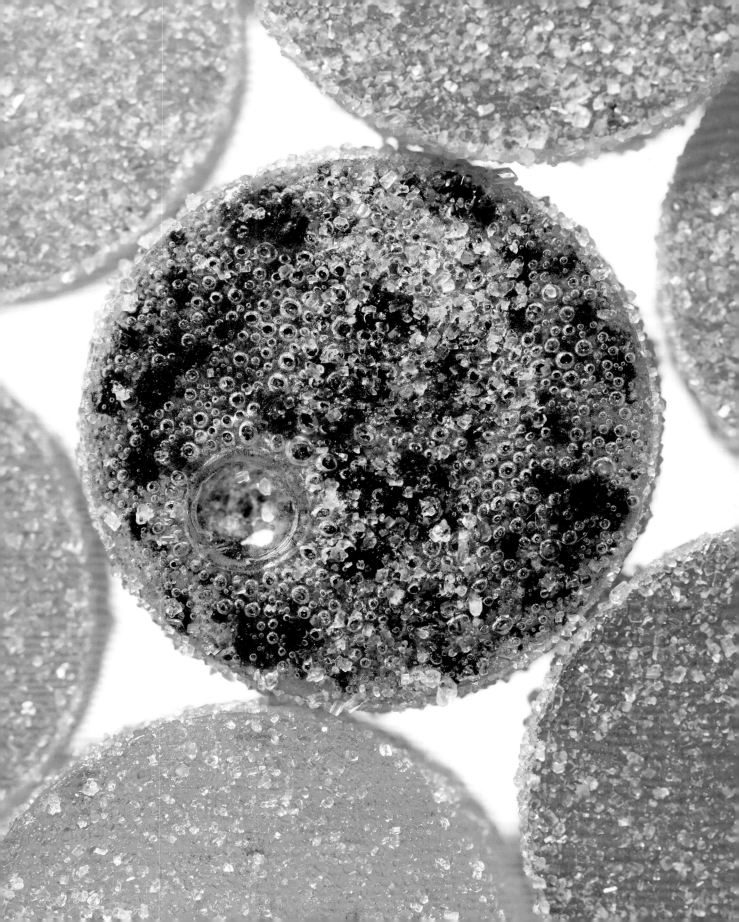

Oh, these gumdrops! I truly love them, especially when made with a deep, rich dark roasted coffee. All of those toasty notes translate perfectly to candy, and you can really taste the results in these little gems. Yes, you're eating candy and not sipping from a mug, but that hasn't stopped coffee devotees from falling in love.

If you're feeling fresh, add a little orange zest (5 to 10 grams) to the candy when you add the coffee syrup. Something about that zest really makes the coffee flavor sing.

COFFEE GUMDROPS

**MAKES ABOUT
650 GRAMS SYRUP;
ABOUT 65 (10-GRAM)
CANDIES**

FOR THE BLOOM
16 sheets silver leaf gelatin

110 grams ice-cold water

FOR THE SUGAR SYRUP
215 grams glucose syrup

260 grams granulated sugar

95 grams brewed coffee
(see page 81)

FOR THE FLAVORING
43 grams Coffee Syrup
(see page 68)

1 gram kosher salt

Granulated or powdered
sugar, for coating
(see page 273)

Bloom the Gelatin Place the gelatin sheets in a shallow heat-proof bowl and place the bowl on your scale. Slowly drizzle *exactly* 110 grams of ice-cold water over the top. Allow the water to settle, then lift, shift, and nudge the gelatin sheets apart so that each of them has a fair chance of becoming uniformly wet and soaking up an equal amount of water. The gelatin will absorb all 110 grams of water, but you'll want to help it along a bit to make sure no rough patches remain. It should take 10 to 12 minutes for the gelatin to soak up the water.

Cook the Sugar Syrup While the gelatin is absorbing the water, weigh the glucose syrup, granulated sugar, and brewed coffee directly into a 2-quart cooking pot and set the pot over medium-high heat. Watch the pot as the ingredients begin to cook, and if they appear to be cooking unevenly, use a high-heat spatula or a wooden spoon to poke them gently and then give the pot a swirl or two to even them out. Cook the sugar mixture to a temperature of 278°F, which will take 8 to 10 minutes.

Melt the Gelatin While the sugar syrup is cooking, set up a double boiler for the gelatin. Select a pot that will hold the bowl of gelatin snugly in its rim. Pour water to a depth of a few inches into the bottom of the pot, place the pot on the stove top, and rest the bowl in the rim, making sure the bottom of the bowl is not touching the water. Turn on the heat to medium-high and bring the water to a simmer. The gelatin will melt into a thick liquid in 4 to 6 minutes. When it has melted, remove the pot from the heat, but leave the bowl resting in the rim so the gelatin stays warm.

Finish the Sugar Syrup By now the sugar syrup should be close to 278°F. Test the temperature with a thermometer. If it has reached its target, remove the pot from the heat and set it aside until the syrup cools to 242°F. This will take about 7 minutes. Keep an eye on the syrup and test the temperature occasionally so you hit it right at 242°F.

Flavor the Gelatin and Sugar Syrup When the sugar syrup has cooled to 242°F, using a high-heat spatula or a wooden spoon, stir in the melted gelatin, coffee syrup, and salt, mixing thoroughly. (You don't want to use a whisk here because you're not trying to incorporate air into the candy.)

To Finish The candy syrup is complete and ready to be poured into a funnel and deposited into silicone molds or cornstarch molds (see page 275). Once the molds are filled, allow the candies to cool for 2 hours, until fully cooled and completely set.

Pop the candies out of the silicone molds or pluck them from the cornstarch molds, coat them in sugar, and package them in cellophane bags, ziplock bags, or tightly capped jars.

Whether you refer to it as Arnold Palmer, Fifty-Fifty, Half 'n' Half, or simply tea with lemonade, this drink-inspired candy is as full of flavor as it is swimming in nicknames. The recipe, of course, makes use of actual tea and bright lemon zest—which is as close to the real thing as you can get.

ICED TEA + LEMONADE GUMDROPS

**MAKES ABOUT
650 GRAMS SYRUP;
ABOUT 65 (10-GRAM)
CANDIES**

FOR THE BLOOM
16 sheets silver leaf gelatin

110 grams ice-cold water

FOR THE SUGAR SYRUP
415 grams glucose syrup

260 grams granulated sugar

90 grams Tea Syrup
(see page 69)

FOR THE FLAVORING
5 grams Tea Syrup
(see page 69)

5 grams finely grated
lemon zest

2 grams citric acid

Granulated or powdered
sugar, for coating
(see page 273)

Bloom the Gelatin Place the gelatin sheets in a shallow heat-proof bowl and place the bowl on your scale. Slowly drizzle *exactly* 110 grams of ice-cold water over the top. Allow the water to settle, then lift, shift, and nudge the gelatin sheets apart so that each of them has a fair chance of becoming uniformly wet and soaking up an equal amount of water. The gelatin will absorb all 110 grams of water, but you'll want to help it along a bit to make sure no rough patches remain. It should take 10 to 12 minutes for the gelatin to soak up the water.

Cook the Sugar Syrup While the gelatin is absorbing the water, weigh the glucose syrup, granulated sugar, and tea syrup directly into a 2-quart cooking pot and set the pot over medium-high heat. Watch the pot as the ingredients begin to cook, and if they appear to be cooking unevenly, use a high-heat spatula or a wooden spoon to poke them gently and then give the pot a swirl or two to even them out. Cook the sugar mixture to a temperature of 278°F, which will take 8 to 10 minutes.

Melt the Gelatin While the sugar syrup is cooking, set up a double boiler for the gelatin. Select a pot that will hold the bowl of gelatin snugly in its rim. Pour water to a depth of a few inches into the bottom of the pot, place the pot on the stove top, and rest the bowl in the rim, making sure the bottom of the bowl is not touching the water. Turn on the heat to medium-high and bring the water to a simmer. The gelatin will melt into a thick liquid in 4 to 6 minutes. When it has melted, remove the pot from the heat, but leave the bowl resting in the rim so the gelatin stays warm.

Finish the Sugar Syrup By now the sugar syrup should be close to 278°F. Test the temperature with a thermometer. If it has reached its target, remove the pot from the heat and set it aside until the syrup cools to 242°F. This will take about 7 minutes. Keep an eye on the syrup and test the temperature occasionally so you hit it right at 242°F.

Flavor the Gelatin and Sugar Syrup When the sugar syrup has cooled to 242°F, using a high-heat spatula or a wooden spoon, stir in the melted gelatin, tea syrup, lemon zest, and citric acid, mixing thoroughly. (You don't want to use a whisk here because you're not trying to incorporate air into the candy.)

To Finish The candy syrup is complete and ready to be poured into a funnel and deposited into silicone molds or cornstarch molds (see page 275). Once the molds are filled, allow the candies to cool for 2 hours, until fully cooled and completely set.

Pop the candies out of the silicone molds or pluck them from the cornstarch molds, coat them in sugar, and package them in cellophane bags, ziplock bags, or tightly capped jars.

Bright, fruity, and sweet, rosé is a total natural when it comes to candy making. Using the wine reduction from chapter two, these gumdrops make fantastic party favors. Baby showers, bridal showers, birthday parties, and even engagement celebrations all are the perfect occasions for turning your favorite wine into a bouncy treat.

ROSÉ GUMDROPS

**MAKES ABOUT
650 GRAMS SYRUP;
ABOUT 65 (10-GRAM)
CANDIES**

FOR THE BLOOM
16 sheets silver leaf gelatin

110 grams ice-cold water

FOR THE SUGAR SYRUP
215 grams glucose syrup

260 grams granulated sugar

25 grams rosé reduction
(see page 71)

FOR THE FLAVORING
3 grams natural strawberry
flavoring

3 grams natural pineapple
flavoring

3 grams natural watermelon
flavoring

2 grams instant yeast

Granulated or powdered
sugar, for coating
(see page 273)

Bloom the Gelatin Place the gelatin sheets in a shallow heat-proof bowl and place the bowl on your scale. Slowly drizzle *exactly* 110 grams of ice-cold water over the top. Allow the water to settle, then lift, shift, and nudge the gelatin sheets apart so that each of them has a fair chance of becoming uniformly wet and soaking up an equal amount of water. The gelatin will absorb all 110 grams of water, but you'll want to help it along a bit to make sure no rough patches remain. It should take 10 to 12 minutes for the gelatin to soak up the water.

Cook the Sugar Syrup While the gelatin is absorbing the water, weigh the glucose syrup, granulated sugar, and wine reduction directly into a 2-quart cooking pot and set the pot over medium-high heat. Watch the pot as the ingredients begin to cook, and if they appear to be cooking unevenly, use a high-heat spatula or a wooden spoon to poke them gently and then give the pot a swirl or two to even them out. Cook the sugar mixture to a temperature of 278°F, which will take 8 to 10 minutes.

Melt the Gelatin While the sugar syrup is cooking, set up a double boiler for the gelatin. Select a pot that will hold the bowl of gelatin snugly in its rim. Pour water to a depth of a few inches into the bottom of the pot, place the pot on the stove top, and rest the bowl in the rim, making sure the bottom of the bowl is not touching the water. Turn on the heat to medium-high and bring the water to a simmer. The gelatin will melt into a thick liquid in 4 to 6 minutes. When it has melted, remove the pot from the heat, but leave the bowl resting in the rim so the gelatin stays warm.

Finish the Sugar Syrup By now the sugar syrup should be close to 278°F. Test the temperature with a thermometer. If it has reached its target, remove the pot from the heat and set it aside until the syrup cools to 242°F. This will take about 7 minutes. Keep an eye on the syrup and test the temperature occasionally so you hit it right at 242°F.

Flavor the Gelatin and Sugar Syrup When the sugar syrup has cooled to 242°F, using a high-heat spatula or a wooden spoon, stir in the melted gelatin, all of the natural flavorings, and the yeast, mixing thoroughly. (You don't want to use a whisk here because you're not trying to incorporate air into the candy.)

To Finish The candy syrup is complete and ready to be poured into a funnel and deposited into silicone molds or cornstarch molds (see page 275). Once the molds are filled, allow the candies to cool for 2 hours, until fully cooled and completely set.

Pop the candies out of the silicone molds or pluck them from the cornstarch molds, coat them in sugar, and package them in cellophane bags, ziplock bags, or tightly capped jars.

LAYERS OF FLAVOR

If you're really excelling at gumdrop creation, here's a suggestion: Make two batches of gumdrops in flavors that pair well together, such as cherry and cola, vanilla and orange, or coffee and black pepper. Cook the first flavor and funnel it into your molds, filling the cavities only half full, and set the molds aside. Whip up the second flavor, finish filling the molds with this new flavor, and set the molds aside until the candies are fully cooled and completely set, around 2 hours. When you pop or pluck the candies out of the molds, you'll see two very distinct layers of flavor and color. This takes a little more effort than the regular method, but it's definitely worth the wow factor.

RESOURCES GUIDE

I'll be the first to admit that I take a kind of scrappy/shoestring-budget/how-can-we-do-it-for-less approach when starting new projects. I begin by looking at what I already have and (fingers crossed) put it to use. And for the things I don't already have? I go shopping. Most of the ingredients and supplies we use at QUIN come in extreme bulk amounts (a typical minimum order of custom-printed cellophane for wrapping candy is one million feet!) but because every QUIN recipe started very small, I have many tips on where to buy exactly what you need for even the smallest of candy-making operations. Many supplies can be purchased from a well-stocked grocery store, kitchen-supply shop, or craft store. For the rest of it? The Internet has it (and I've included the search terms here in *italic*).

INGREDIENTS

Berries You should be able to find high-quality frozen berries at almost any well-stocked grocery store. Plus, because you'll be roasting the berries and adding sugar and other ingredients, they will pop back to life with a nice vibrancy.

Chai Tea Concentrate A great ingredient for making lollipops (see page 149), chai tea concentrate should be in the tea aisle of your grocery store. Can't find it there? An Internet search for *chai tea concentrate* will provide a nice group of choices.

Chocolate My two favorite chocolate brands are Felchlin and Valrhona (*see* Cocoa Powder, page 292); search for *felchlin chocolate* or *valrhona chocolate*.

Cinnamon As I noted on page 89, I favor Ceylon cinnamon for candy making. Penzeys Spices and King Arthur Flour are good online sources for this particular type.

Citric Acid Great for adding either a little or a lot of pucker to candy, food-grade citric acid is widely available online and in the bulk-food section of some grocery stores. A quick online search for *citric acid* will bring up many options, but you can also find it at your local brewing supply shop.

Cocoa Powder For the correct results, I insist you treat yourself to a supply of high-quality cocoa powder. My preferred brand is Felchlin, made in Switzerland, with the French-made Valrhona coming in a close second. Felchlin can be found online; search for *felchlin cacaopulver* or *felchlin cocoa powder*. Valrhona cocoa powder is sold in higher-end grocery stores and through many online sources; search for *valrhona cocoa powder*.

Colorings It's relatively easy to find natural colorings these days, but the key for candy making is that, as with flavorings (see entry), the colorings must be stable enough to withstand high heat. If the colorings lack heat stability, your candies will not turn out looking the way you imagined they would. Don't think that what you use doesn't matter, because I've learned the hard way that it does. Pick a natural coloring made for high-heat applications and you'll happy with the candy; search for *heat stable natural coloring*.

Crystal Sugar Buying this large-crystal sugar in small repackaged containers from cake-decorating supply shops can be expensive. So if you are committing to many projects involving crystal sugar, go ahead and spring for a larger amount, which will definitely save you money in the long run. At QUIN, we purchase C&H crystal sugar from our local food-service supply company. Hot tip: If you will-call products and go pick them up yourself (and are ready to pay when you get there), your local specialty foods supply company will let you buy what they sell, from crystal sugar to olive oil.

Flavorings Finding the right natural flavorings for your candy can be tricky. Lucky for you, I've been through most of the natural flavorings on the market, and I have two brands that I like a lot. LorAnn manufactures a line of natural flavorings made for high-heat applications. That specific characteristic is a must. Many flavorings exist, of course, but you must be sure to use a product that's meant for hard candy. If you don't, the flavor will dissipate during cooking, and you'll be left with flavorless candy. In general, flavorings created specifically for high-heat applications will be called flavor emulsions. Nature's Flavors, which is based in California, makes a good product. The Nature's Flavors website very clearly explains which of their wide selection of unique flavorings work for high-heat applications.

Gelatin You'll need leaf gelatin, also known as sheet gelatin, for the recipes in this book. It comes in four different strengths, and I recommend silver strength. You may be able to find it in a well-stocked kitchen store or a specialty foods store. If you look online, search for *silver leaf gelatin* or *silver sheet gelatin*.

Glucose Syrup Glucose can be purchased at your local cake-decorating store, some well-stocked craft stores (in the cake-decorating section), or online. At QUIN, we use Pastry 1 brand glucose syrup, but there are several other brands on the market. A good way to search for glucose syrup is by using the phrase *buy glucose syrup*.

Malted Milk Powder Available at your grocery store and online, this is the stuff you can mix with milk (or into a milk shake) and make malted milk (or a malted milk shake.) Search for *malted milk powder*.

Salts You'll need three types of salt for the recipes. All of the salt that's cooked into candy is kosher salt. I prefer Diamond Crystal brand kosher salt, which is widely available in grocery stores. If you have trouble finding it, you can buy it online; search for *diamond crystal kosher salt*.

When I'm sprinkling salt on cooked candy, I look to a flaky sea salt. Penzeys and The Meadow are good online resources, but well-stocked grocery stores usually stock Maldon (which is an excellent choice).

Finally, smoked flake sea salt is another good finishing salt. And again, Maldon makes an especially nice one; search for *maldon smoked sea salt flakes*.

Smoked Granulated Sugar Adding smoked sugar to a candy recipe lends a note of mystery and deep richness. I love smoked ingredients, and now that smoked sugar is readily available online, I can skip the chore of setting up a cold smoker to produce it myself; search for *buy smoked sugar*.

Tea I love both a good cup of tea and tea-flavored candy, and the teas from Steven Smith Teamaker never disappoint. Every recipe that calls for tea in this book was made with a Steven Smith tea; search for *steven smith teamaker*.

Vanilla Bean Powder At QUIN, we buy our vanilla bean powder online from Beanilla, but quality brands are also available through Amazon and other sites; search for *vanilla bean powder*. Make sure that you buy a quality powder, rather than one made from exhausted beans (see page 57). True vanilla bean powder isn't cheap, so if the price seems too good to be true, the product is likely inferior.

EQUIPMENT

See pages 22 to 25 for a list of important candy-making tools.

WRAPPING AND PACKAGING SUPPLIES

Apple Bags These paper bags, which are sometimes called orchard bags, are perfect for packing up Caramel Apple Kits (page 204) or for containing any number of sweet surprises you've made for someone. I prefer unprinted bags (and I just can't resist that crosswise handle!). Well-stocked restaurant-supply stores carry these bags, but you'll likely have better luck locating them online; search for *1 peck paper bags*.

Caramel-Apple Sticks You can use regular Popsicle-type sticks for caramel apples (easily found at your local craft store), or you can go the more dowel-shaped bamboo-skewer route. I prefer the classic look of a wooden dowel, but in a pinch, I've used what I've had on hand. For the perfect sticks, search for *wood candy apple sticks*.

Cellophane Wrappers Cellophane is the best wrapping material I've found for all of the types of candy we make at QUIN. Candy tends to stick to wax paper, traditional twisting paper for taffy doesn't let the beauty of the candy peek through, and candy doesn't release cleanly from parchment paper. My wrappers of choice are 5-inch-square cellophane sheets; and for caramel apples, I like 12-inch-square cellophane sheets. Precut cellophane is widely available; search for *cellophane candy wrappers*.

Jars Uline stocks jars that are perfect for containing Chocolate Magic Dust (page 74) and more. Simply head to Uline online and search for *16-ounce jars*.

Lollipop Sticks These sturdy paper sticks come in a variety of lengths. I like a lollipop stick that's 4 to 5 inches long; search for *lollipop sticks*.

To/From Tags I prefer the clean look of a manila tag with a simple hole on top for threading twine or ribbon. Uline stocks a great assortment of tags on its website, but you can usually find similar tags at an office-supply store or your favorite craft store. If you prefer to shop online, search for *manila shipping tags*.

Twist Ties At QUIN, we still wrap our lollipops by hand and use twist ties to secure the cellophane. Luckily, these produce-aisle staples have been refreshed and now come in all sorts of colors, from red to clear to sparkly metallic; buy online and search for *twist ties*.

PROJECT SUPPLIES

Candy Garland & Countdown (page 146) Both of these projects require a quick trip to the craft store or an equally quick Internet search, where you can pick up or order all of the following:

* **Bolt Bags** These bags are essentially tiny cloth bags with a drawstring. For a candy countdown, I prefer them on the small side, about 2 by 3 inches. Smaller bags are perfect for marking with numbers and for filling with candy or small surprises. You may not be able to find these bags at a craft store, but Uline carries a great variety of parts bags; search for *bolt bags* or *cloth parts bags*.

* **Grosgrain Ribbon** This is the ribbon on which you will build your garland. You'll want a minimum of 2 yards of ribbon per garland, in any color you like. It's nice for countdowns, too, with the length depending on the number of days you're counting.

* **Jingly Bells** Big or small, silver or gold, these little guys add a lot of life to a garland.

* **Metallic Pipe Cleaners** Of course, you can decide to use nonmetallic pipe cleaners to add pizzazz to a garland, but I prefer the extra sparkle that metallic ones, in a rainbow of colors, bring to the project.

* **Numbered Rubber Stamp Set and Stamp Pad** Although this stamp set is not necessary, it will give your countdown a tidy flair.

* **Wooden Beads** Any color is good, as long as the beads have a hole large enough to push ribbon through.

INSTABRATION (PAGE 224)

* **Fortune Cards** I love the idea of giving someone the gift of good feelings for the coming year. Fortune cards, the kind that come out of fortune-telling machines, are an easy way to spread those good feelings. I've never seen them in the wilds of any store at which I shop, so I'd suggest buying these online; search for *fortune telling machine cards*.

* **Paper Crowns** Tissue-paper crowns liven up any celebration, birthday or not. These are easiest to find online; search for *tissue paper crowns*.

* **Tiny Sparklers** Nothing on Earth screams Surprise! or Happy Birthday! or You Did It! like a tiny sparkler. You can find these sparklers in odd places—near the register of a bookstore, in the candle section of a kitchen-supply store, in the quirky gift shop in town—or you can skip all the guesswork and order them online; search for *mini sparklers*.

MISCELLANEOUS PROJECT SUPPLIES

Baker's Twine I'd wrap the world in this stuff if I could. It's perfect for attaching hangtags and so much more. You'll pay a lot more if you buy it in a kitchen-supply store, so my suggestion is to buy a giant skein of it online (it'll last forever and cost pennies on the dollar when compared to what you could pay for a few feet at a kitchen-supply store); search for *baker's twine*.

Candy Say you want to make the Dark Chocolate Bunny Cake (page 82) but you're pinched for time? I know exactly where you can get the candy you need to create the cutest little bunny face: Quin! Quincandy.com

Fillable Ornaments You'll need these clear acrylic ornaments for the Super Sweet Ornament Orbs project on page 236. If you can't find them at your local craft store, you can easily find them on the Internet; search for *acrylic fillable ball ornaments*. For other supplies for this project, see the list for Candy Garland & Countdown on page 295.

Paper Cones The tiny piñatas on page 232 are made using 6- to 8-ounce paper drinking cones, which can be purchased online by searching for *paper drinking cones*.

Paper Tubes I like to package Candy Pow Wows (page 214) in paper tubes for gifts or party favors. You can collect your empty paper-towel and toilet-paper tubes before they hit the recycling bin, or you can turn to the Internet to scoop some up; search for *paper tubes for crafts*.

BECAUSE of YOU

I could dedicate several pages to the experiences that have made me Jami Curl and to the people who have helped me (directly and indirectly) write this book. I can only do the work I do and live the life I love because of the history, support, help, guidance, love, fun times, last-minute childcare, and real talk the following people so generously provide (or provided) to me. Dear reader, while I wish you happy times with lots of sugar, I mostly hope that you are surrounded by as much love and happiness as I am.

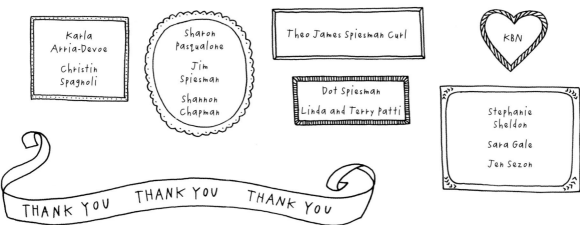

Karla Arria-Devoe
Christin Spagnoli

Sharon Pasqualone
Jim Spiesman
Shannon Chapman

Theo James Spiesman Curl

Dot Spiesman
Linda and Terry Patti

KBN

Stephanie Sheldon
Sara Gale
Jen Sezon

THANK YOU   THANK YOU   THANK YOU

I have always adored words, writing, teaching, and explaining. Turns out a book is the ideal place to put all of that into action.

ALISON FARGIS—none of this would be happening without you.

JENNY WAPNER AND TEN SPEED PRESS—you gave me the freedom to make the book of my dreams. I'm so thankful.

CHRISTIN SPAGNOLI—you have always understood my mind better than anyone else. You are able to take what I see in my head and make it real (which is actual magic).

MAGGIE KIRKLAND, MICHELLE OTT, STEPHANIE SHELDON-NEVAREZ—I never ever want to do anything without the three of you by my side. You worked on this book as if it were your own and I cannot ever thank you enough.

And to MEGAN ANDERSON, ASHLEY LIMA, the QUIN team, THOM NEVAREZ, JENNIFER BATCHELOR, the Ohio University Department of English, WILLY AND CHARLIE, LAURIE COLWIN, summertime in Ohio, CHEF KEN NORRIS, THOM YORKE, BRUCE SPRINGSTEEN, and all the books I've ever read, thank you for supporting my past and present life in candy and for inspiring me to do the things I love in the exact way I want to do them. I actually cannot believe any of this is really real. (I am forever grateful.)

INDEX

A

Ahoy, Matey! Caramels, 206–7
Aleppo pepper
    Aleppo Pepper + Raisin
        Caramels, 194–95
    Pepper Cream, 64
Almonds
    Apricot + Almond + Nutmeg
        Gumdrops, 279
    Roasted Cherries with
        Almond, 44
Ancho Chile, Chocolate +,
    Ice Cream, 105
Apples
    Apple Caramels, 191–92
    Caramel Apple Kit, 204
    Doughnut Magic Dust
        Glazed Apples, 91
    Sniffle Slayer Lollipops, 148
    Sour Apple Lollipops, 127
Apricots
    Apricot + Almond + Nutmeg
        Gumdrops, 279
    Apricot Gumdrops, 279
    Apricot Lollipops, 119
    Apricot + White Chocolate
        + Coconut Caramels, 183
    Roasted Apricots with
        Coconut and Brown
        Sugar, 47

B

Berries, 291
Blackberries
    Blackberry Gumdrops, 276–78
    Blackberry Lollipops, 119
    Blackberry + Orange
        Gumdrops, 279
    Blackberry + Tangerine
        Dreams, 228
    Blackberry + Tangerine
        Lollipops, 119
    Roasted Blackberries with
        Lime and Nutmeg, 42
Black pepper
    Black Pepper Gumdrops, 282
    Maple + Cracked Black
        Pepper Caramels, 212–13
    Pepper Cream, 64
Blueberries
    Blueberry + Cinnamon
        Gumdrops, 279
    Blueberry Gumdrops, 279
    Blueberry Lollipops, 119
    Roasted Blueberries with
        Vanilla and Orange, 46
Brownies, Marshmallow, 251
Butter, Doughnut Magic
    Dust, 91
Buttercream
    Infused-Cream
        Buttercream, 59
    Peanut Butter
        Buttercream, 82–83
Butter Pecan Ice Cream, 100
Butterscotch Hard Candy, 155

C

Cake, Dark Chocolate Bunny,
    82–85
Candy frames, 24–25
Candy funnels, 24, 113
Candy making
    approach to, 11–12
    flavor development
        and, 12, 27–31
    ingredients for, 15–21, 291–93
    tools for, 12, 22–25
Candy thermometers, 23, 113
Caramel
    Ahoy, Matey! Caramels, 206–7
    Aleppo Pepper + Raisin
        Caramels, 194–95
    Apple Caramels, 191–92
    Apricot + White Chocolate +
        Coconut Caramels, 183
    Caramel Apple Kit, 204
    Caramel Lollipops, 153
    Caramel Marshmallows,
        260–63
    Chèvre Caramel Sauce, 180
    Chocolate Caramel Coconut
        Marshmallows, 263
    Chocolate Caramels, 174–75
    Chocolate Malt + Sugar Cone
        Caramels, 196–97
    Chocolate Pretzel
        Caramels, 208–9
    Coconut + Toasted Pecan +
        Chocolate Caramels, 188–89
    Coffee Caramels, 203
    Coffee + Orange + Smoked
        Salt Caramels, 202–3
    color chart for, 161
    Earl Grey Caramels, 200–201
    Easy Caramel Sauce, 179
    Honey + Hazelnut
        Caramels, 184–85
    Maple + Cracked Black
        Pepper Caramels, 212–13
    Popcorn Caramels, 171–72
    Sea Salt Caramels, 168–69
    Sea Salt + Roasted Pumpkin
        Seed Caramels, 186–87
    Smoked Chai Tea Caramels,
        198–99
    techniques for, 159–66, 172
    Turtle Caramels, 210–11
    Vanilla Bean Caramels, 176–77
    Vanilla Bean + Roasted Fruit
        Caramels, 182–83
Chai tea
    Chai Tea Cream, 63
    Chai Tea Ice Cream, 106
    Chai Tea Lollipops, 149
    concentrate, 291
    Smoked Chai Tea
        Caramels, 198–99
Champagne
    Champagne Hard Candy, 155
    Strawberry Bubbly, 41
Cherries
    Cherry Cola Gumdrops, 279

Cherry Dreams Come
  Chew, 222
Cherry Gumdrops, 279
Cherry Honey Vanilla
  Lollipops, 145
Cherry Lollipops, 119
pitting, 45
Roasted Cherries with
  Almond, 44
Roasted Fruit Whipped
  Cream, 45
Sour Cherry Lollipops, 126
Chèvre Caramel Sauce, 180
Chiles
  Chocolate + Ancho Chile Ice
    Cream, 105
  Pepper Cream, 64
Chocolate, 291, 292
  Chocolate Caramel Coconut
    Marshmallows, 263
  Chocolate Caramels, 174–75
  Chocolate Cream, 57
  Chocolate for Breakfast, 78
  Chocolate Lollipops, 151
  Chocolate Magic Dust, 74
  Chocolate Magic Dust Ice
    Cream, 104
  Chocolate Magic Dust
    Whipped Cream, 80
  Chocolate Malt + Sugar Cone
    Caramels, 196–97
  Chocolate Marshmallows,
    254–57
  Chocolate Mint Dreams, 230
  Chocolate + Olive Oil + Sea
    Salt Lollipops, 152
  Chocolate Pretzel
    Caramels, 208–9
  Chocolate Sauce, 81
  Chocolate Swirl Ice
    Cream, 103
  Coconut + Toasted Pecan +
    Chocolate Caramels, 188–89
  Dark Chocolate Bunny
    Cake, 82–85

Hot Chocolate and
  Marshmallow Kit, 77
Hot Chocolate Bar!, 79
Hot Chocolate with Vanilla
  Bean Marshmallows and
  Mint Crystal Sugar, 78
Hot Fudge, 86
Hot or Cold Chocolate, 76
Malted Chocolate Magic
  Dust, 88
Marshmallow Brownies, 251
Peanut Butter Hot Fudge, 86
Skillet S'mores, 252
S'mores Bar, 249
Turtle Caramels, 210–11
Cinnamon, 99, 291
  Blueberry + Cinnamon
    Gumdrops, 279
  Cinnamon Dreams, 231
  Cinnamon Gumdrops, 282
  Cinnamon Hard Candy, 155
  Cinnamon Marshmallows,
    248
Citric acid, 291
Citrus Gumdrops, 282
Clouds of Candy, 140
Cocoa powder, 74, 292
Coconut
  Apricot + White Chocolate +
    Coconut Caramels, 183
  Chocolate Caramel Coconut
    Marshmallows, 263
  Coconut + Toasted Pecan +
    Chocolate Caramels, 188–89
  Pineapple + Coconut
    Dreams, 223
  Roasted Apricots with
    Coconut and Brown
    Sugar, 47
  Toasted Coconut
    Marshmallows, 248
Coffee
  Chocolate + Coffee
    Ice Cream, 105
  Coffee Caramels, 203
  Coffee Cream, 55

Coffee Gumdrops, 284–85
Coffee Ice Cream, 100
Coffee Lollipops, 130
Coffee Marshmallows, 266–67
Coffee + Orange + Smoked
  Salt Caramels, 202–3
Coffee Syrup, 86
Coffee Whipped Cream, 56
saving leftover, 81
Cola
  Cherry Cola Gumdrops, 279
  Cola Gumdrops, 282
Colorings, 292
Cookies, Doughnut Magic
  Dust, 92
Cotton candy machines, 140
Crystal blockers, 15, 16–18
Cups, spouted, 24, 113

D

Doughnut Magic Dust, 91
  Doughnut Magic Dust
    Butter, 91
  Doughnut Magic Dust
    Cookies, 92
  Doughnut Magic Dust Glazed
    Apples, 91
  Doughnut Magic Dust
    Ice Cream, 101
Dreams
  Blackberry + Tangerine
    Dreams, 228
  Cherry Dreams Come
    Chew, 222
  Chocolate Mint Dreams, 230
  Cinnamon Dreams, 231
  Fruit Punch Dreams, 223
  history of, 219
  Lemon Dreams, 223
  Pineapple + Coconut
    Dreams, 223
  Strawberry Dreams, 223
  Tangerine Dreams, 223
  techniques for, 219, 221
  Vanilla Cake Dreams, 234

Dreams, continued
    Vanilla Mint Dreams, 229
    Watermelon + Lime
        Dreams, 223

E

Earl Grey tea
    Earl Grey Caramels, 200–201
    Earl Grey Tea Cream, 63
    Earl Grey Tea Whipped
        Cream, 56

F

Fat, 15, 19
Five-spice powder
    Five-Spice Magic Dust, 89
    Five-Spice Magic Dust
        Ice Cream, 101
Flavor development, 12, 27–31
Flavorings, 292
Fruit
    Fruit Punch Dreams, 223
    Fruit Punch Hard Candy, 155
    juice, leftover, 39
    Roasted Fruit Whipped
        Cream, 45
    roasting, 35
    Vanilla Bean + Roasted Fruit
        Caramels, 182–83
    See also individual fruits
Fudge
    Hot Fudge, 86
    Peanut Butter Hot Fudge, 86

G

Garland, Candy, 146–47
Gelatin, 292
Ginger
    Peach + Ginger + Black
        Pepper Gumdrops, 279
    Roasted Peaches with
        Ginger, 49
Glucose syrup, 16–18, 161, 293
Graham crackers
    Skillet S'mores, 252

S'mores Bar, 249
Grapefruit
    Citrus Gumdrops, 282
Gumdrops
    Apricot + Almond + Nutmeg
        Gumdrops, 279
    Apricot Gumdrops, 279
    Blackberry Gumdrops,
        276–78
    Blackberry + Orange
        Gumdrops, 279
    Black Pepper Gumdrops, 282
    Blueberry + Cinnamon
        Gumdrops, 279
    Blueberry Gumdrops, 279
    Cherry Cola Gumdrops, 279
    Cherry Gumdrops, 279
    Cinnamon Gumdrops, 282
    Coffee Gumdrops, 284–85
    Cola Gumdrops, 282
    Iced Tea + Lemonade
        Gumdrops, 286–87
    Peach + Ginger + Black
        Pepper Gumdrops, 279
    Peach Gumdrops, 279
    Raspberry Gumdrops, 279
    Raspberry + Vanilla
        Gumdrops, 279
    Root Beer Gumdrops, 282
    Rosé Gumdrops, 288–89
    Strawberry Gumdrops, 279
    Strawberry + Lemon
        Gumdrops, 279
    techniques for, 272–73, 275
    with two flavors, 289
    Vanilla Gumdrops, 280–81

H

Hard Candy
    Butterscotch Hard Candy,
        155
    Champagne Hard Candy, 155
    Cinnamon Hard Candy, 155
    Fruit Punch Hard Candy, 155
    Root Beer Hard Candy, 155

Hazelnuts
    Honey + Hazelnut Caramels,
        184–85
Honey
    Cherry Honey Vanilla
        Lollipops, 145
    Honey + Hazelnut Caramels,
        184–85
    Honey + Sea Salt
        Marshmallows, 264–65
    Honey Vanilla Lollipops, 144

I

Ice cream
    Butter Pecan Ice Cream, 100
    Chai Tea Ice Cream, 106
    Chocolate + Ancho Chile
        Ice Cream, 105
    Chocolate + Coffee Ice
        Cream, 105
    Chocolate Magic Dust
        Ice Cream, 104
    Chocolate + Malted Milk
        Ice Cream, 105
    Chocolate + Orange
        Ice Cream, 105
    Chocolate + Peppermint
        Ice Cream, 105
    Chocolate Swirl Ice
        Cream, 103
    Coffee Ice Cream, 100
    Doughnut Magic Dust
        Ice Cream, 101
    Easy Vanilla Bean Ice
        Cream, 100
    Five-Spice Magic Dust
        Ice Cream, 101
    Popcorn Ice Cream, 107
    Strawberry Ice Cream, 102
    techniques for, 99, 101
Iced Tea + Lemonade
    Gumdrops, 286–87
Infused creams
    Chai Tea Cream, 63
    Chocolate Cream, 57
    Coffee Cream, 55

Earl Grey Tea Cream, 63
Infused-Cream
    Buttercream, 59
Infused-Cream Whipped
    Creams, 56
Malted Milk Cream, 58
Orange Cream, 60
Pepper Cream, 64
Peppermint Tea Cream, 63
Popcorn Cream, 52
techniques for, 51
Vanilla Bean Cream, 61
Instabration, 224
Interfering agents, 16–18

L

Lemons
    Citrus Gumdrops, 282
    Iced Tea + Lemonade
        Gumdrops, 286–87
    Lemon Dreams, 223
    Lemon Lollipops, 123
    Roasted Strawberries with
        Lemon, 37
    Sniffle Slayer Lollipops, 148
    Sour Lemon Lollipops, 127
    Strawberry + Lemon
        Gumdrops, 279
    Sweet Tea with Lemon
        Lollipops, 131
Limes
    Citrus Gumdrops, 282
    Lime Lollipops, 123
    Roasted Blackberries with
        Lime and Nutmeg, 42
    Watermelon + Lime Dreams,
        223
Lollipops
    alternatives to, 155
    Apricot Lollipops, 119
    Blackberry Lollipops, 119
    Blackberry + Tangerine
        Lollipops, 119
    Blueberry Lollipops, 119
    Caramel Lollipops, 153

Chai Tea Lollipops, 149
Cherry Honey Vanilla
    Lollipops, 145
Cherry Lollipops, 119
with chewy centers, 138–39
Chocolate Lollipops, 151
Chocolate + Olive Oil + Sea
    Salt Lollipops, 152
Coffee Lollipops, 130
Honey Vanilla Lollipops, 144
Lemon Lollipops, 123
Lime Lollipops, 123
Lollipop Bouquet, 132
Mint Lollipops, 150
Orange Lollipops, 122
Peach Lollipops, 119
Pecan Praline Lollipops, 136
Pinot Gris Lollipops, 133
Pinot Noir Lollipops, 134
Raspberry Lollipops, 119
Rosé Lollipops, 135
Sniffle Slayer Lollipops, 148
Sour Apple Lollipops, 127
Sour Cherry Lollipops, 126
Sour Lemon Lollipops, 127
Sour Orange Lollipops, 127
Sour Raspberry Lollipops, 127
Strawberry Lollipops, 118
Sweet Tea with Lemon
    Lollipops, 131
techniques for, 111–15, 117,
    121, 125

M

Magic dusts
    Chocolate Magic Dust, 74
    Doughnut Magic Dust, 91
    Five-Spice Magic Dust, 89
    Malted Chocolate Magic
        Dust, 88
    Sweet + Sour Magic Dust, 93
Magic Sugar Crystals
    Flavored Variety, 94
    Tinted Variety, 95

Malted milk powder, 293
    Chocolate Malt + Sugar Cone
        Caramels, 196–97
    Chocolate + Malted Milk
        Ice Cream, 105
    Malted Chocolate Magic
        Dust, 88
    Malted Milk Cream, 58
Maple + Cracked Black Pepper
    Caramels, 212–13
Marshmallows
    Caramel Marshmallows,
        260–63
    Chocolate Caramel Coconut
        Marshmallows, 263
    Chocolate Marshmallows,
        254–57
    Cinnamon Marshmallows,
        248
    Coffee Marshmallows,
        266–67
    Honey + Sea Salt
        Marshmallows, 264–65
    Hot Chocolate and
        Marshmallow Kit, 77
    Hot Chocolate with Vanilla
        Bean Marshmallows and
        Mint Crystal Sugar, 78
    Marshmallow Brownies, 251
    Marshmallow Sauce, 251
    Mint Marshmallows, 248
    shapes of, 257
    Skillet S'mores, 252
    S'mores Bar, 249
    Strawberry Marshmallows,
        258–59
    techniques for, 242–43
    Toasted Coconut
        Marshmallows, 248
    Vanilla Bean Marshmallows,
        244–47
Mats, nonstick, 24, 113
"Medium-high heat," meaning
    of, 149

Mint
    Chocolate Mint Dreams, 230
    Mint Lollipops, 150
    Mint Marshmallows, 248
    Vanilla Mint Dreams, 229
    See also Peppermint
Molds, 24, 113, 275

N

Nutmeg, 92

O

Olive oil
    Chocolate + Olive Oil + Sea
      Salt Lollipops, 152
Oranges
    Blackberry + Orange
      Gumdrops, 279
    Chocolate + Orange Ice
      Cream, 105
    Citrus Gumdrops, 282
    Coffee + Orange + Smoked
      Salt Caramels, 202–3
    Orange Cream, 60
    Orange Lollipops, 122
    Orange Whipped Cream, 56
    Roasted Blueberries with
      Vanilla and Orange, 46
    Sour Orange Lollipops, 127
Ornament Orbs, Super
    Sweet, 236

P

Pans. *See* Pots and pans
Peaches
    Peach + Ginger + Black
      Pepper Gumdrops, 279
    Peach Gumdrops, 279
    Peach Lollipops, 119
    Roasted Peaches with
      Ginger, 49
Peanut butter
    Peanut Butter Buttercream,
      82–83
    Peanut Butter Hot Fudge, 86

Pecans
    Butter Pecan Ice Cream, 100
    Coconut + Toasted Pecan
      + Chocolate Caramels,
      188–89
    Pecan Praline Lollipops, 136
    Turtle Caramels, 210–11
Pepper. *See* Aleppo pepper;
    Black pepper; Chiles
Peppermint
    Chocolate + Peppermint Ice
      Cream, 105
    Peppermint Tea Cream, 63
Piñata, Tiny, 232–33
Pineapple + Coconut
    Dreams, 223
Pinot Gris
    Pinot Gris Lollipops, 133
    Wine Reduction, 71
Pinot Noir
    Pinot Noir Lollipops, 134
    Wine Reduction, 71
Popcorn
    Every Day, Popcorn, 54
    Popcorn Caramels, 171–72
    Popcorn Cream, 52
    Popcorn Ice Cream, 107
Pots and pans, 22–23, 24–25
Pow Wow, Candy, 214–15
Praline Syrup, 70
Pretzel Caramels, Chocolate,
    208–9
Pumpkin
    Pumpkin Pie Purée, 186
    Sea Salt + Roasted Pumpkin
      Seed Caramels, 186–87

R

Raisins
    Aleppo Pepper + Raisin
      Caramels, 194–95
Raspberries
    Raspberry Gumdrops, 279
    Raspberry Lollipops, 119
    Raspberry + Vanilla
      Gumdrops, 279

    Roasted Raspberries with
      Two Sugars, 43
    Sour Raspberry Lollipops, 127
Root beer
    Root Beer Gumdrops, 282
    Root Beer Hard Candy, 155
Rosé
    Rosé Gumdrops, 288–89
    Rosé Lollipops, 135
    Wine Reduction, 71

S

Salt, 15, 19–20, 21, 293
Sauces
    Chèvre Caramel Sauce, 180
    Chocolate Sauce, 81
    Easy Caramel Sauce, 179
    Hot Fudge, 86
    Marshmallow Sauce, 251
    Peanut Butter Hot Fudge, 86
Scales, 22
Sea Salt Caramels, 168–69
Sea Salt + Roasted Pumpkin
    Seed Caramels, 186–87
S'mores
    Skillet S'mores, 252
    S'mores Bar, 249
Sniffle Slayer Lollipops, 148
Soda, Strawberry Cream, 40
Spatulas, 23
Spoons, wooden, 23
Sprinkles, 107
Strawberries
    Roasted Strawberries with
      Lemon, 37
    Roasted Strawberry Simple
      Syrup, 40
    Strawberry Bubbly, 41
    Strawberry Cream Soda, 40
    Strawberry Dreams, 223
    Strawberry Gumdrops, 279
    Strawberry Ice Cream, 102
    Strawberry + Lemon
      Gumdrops, 279

Strawberry Lollipops, 118
Strawberry Marshmallows,
    258–59
Sugar, 11, 15–16
    crystal, 292
    Magic Sugar Crystals, 94–5
    smoked granulated, 293
    vanilla, 39
Sugar cones
    Chocolate Malt + Sugar Cone
        Caramels, 196–97
Supplies, 294–96
Sweet + Sour Magic Dust, 93
Syrups
    Coffee Syrup, 68
    Praline Syrup, 70
    Roasted Strawberry Simple
        Syrup, 40
    Tea Syrup, 69
    techniques for, 67

T

Tangerines
    Blackberry + Tangerine
        Dreams, 228
    Blackberry + Tangerine
        Lollipops, 119
    Tangerine Dreams, 223
Tea, 293
    Iced Tea + Lemonade
        Gumdrops, 286–87
    Peppermint Tea Cream, 63
    Sweet Tea with Lemon
        Lollipops, 131
    Tea Syrup, 69
    See also Chai tea; Earl Grey tea
Texture, 29
Thermometers, 23, 113
Throat Soothers, 148
Tools, 12, 22–25
Turtle Caramels, 210–11

V

Vanilla
    bean powder, 57, 293
    Cherry Honey Vanilla
        Lollipops, 145
    Easy Vanilla Bean
        Ice Cream, 100
    Honey Vanilla Lollipops, 144
    Raspberry + Vanilla
        Gumdrops, 279
    Roasted Blueberries with
        Vanilla and Orange, 46
    sugar, 39
    Vanilla Bean
        Caramels, 176–77
    Vanilla Bean Cream, 61
    Vanilla Bean Marshmallows,
        244–47
    Vanilla Bean + Roasted Fruit
        Caramels, 182–83
    Vanilla Bean Whipped
        Cream, 56
    Vanilla Cake Dreams, 234
    Vanilla Cake with
        Sprinkles, 234
    Vanilla Gumdrops, 280–81
    Vanilla Mint Dreams, 229

W

Watermelon + Lime Dreams,
    223
Whipped cream
    Chocolate Magic Dust
        Whipped Cream, 80
    Coffee Whipped Cream, 56
    Earl Grey Tea Whipped
        Cream, 56
    Orange Whipped Cream, 56
    Roasted Fruit Whipped
        Cream, 45
    Vanilla Bean Whipped Cream,
        56
Whisks, 23

White Chocolate + Apricot +
    Coconut Caramels, 183
Wine
    Champagne Hard Candy, 155
    Pinot Gris Lollipops, 133
    Pinot Noir Lollipops, 134
    Rosé Gumdrops, 288–89
    Rosé Lollipops, 135
    Strawberry Bubbly, 41
    Wine Reduction, 71

Published in the United States by Ten Speed Press,
an imprint of the Crown Publishing Group, a division
of Penguin Random House LLC, New York.
www.crownpublishing.com
www.tenspeed.com

Ten Speed Press and the Ten Speed Press colophon
are registered trademarks of Penguin Random House LLC.

Library of Congress Cataloging-in-Publication Data

Names: Curl, Jami, author.
Title: Candy is magic : real ingredients, modern recipes / Jami Curl.
Description: First edition. | Berkeley : Ten Speed Press, 2017. | Includes
    bibliographical references and index.
Identifiers: LCCN 2016047716 (print) | LCCN 2016048680 (ebook) | ISBN
    9780399578397 (hardback) | ISBN 9780399578403 (Ebooks)
Subjects: LCSH: Confectionery. | Candy. | BISAC: COOKING / Courses & Dishes /
    Confectionery. | COOKING / Courses & Dishes / Chocolate. | COOKING /
    Courses & Dishes / Desserts. | LCGFT: Cookbooks.
Classification: LCC TX791 .C87 2017 (print) | LCC TX791 (ebook) | DDC
    641.85/3--dc23
LC record available at https://lccn.loc.gov/2016047716
Hardcover ISBN: 978-0-399-57839-7
eBook ISBN: 978-0-399-57840-3

Printed in China

Design by Ashley Lima
Additional design by Christin Spagnoli on pp iv, 14, 17, 30, 82,
138, 146, 160-165, 214, 247, endpapers, and front cover.

10 9 8 7 6 5 4 3 2 1

First Edition